American Rock

ISBN 0-634-02763-8

7777 W. BLUEMOUND RD. P.O. BOX 13819 MILWAUKEE, WI 53213

For all works contained herein:
Unauthorized copying, arranging, adapting, recording or public performance is an infringement of copyright.
Infringers are liable under the law.

Visit Hal Leonard Online at
www.halleonard.com

American Rock

CONTENTS

4	Call Me the Breeze	LYNYRD SKYNYRD
16	Can't You See	MARSHALL TUCKER
30	Carry on Wayward Son	KANSAS
38	Come Out and Play	THE OFFSPRING
42	Crazy on You	HEART
51	Grind	ALICE IN CHAINS
57	Heartache Tonight	THE EAGLES
67	Higher Ground	RED HOT CHILI PEPPERS
76	Hold My Hand	HOOTIE & THE BLOWFISH
83	I Want You to Want Me	CHEAP TRICK
91	If You Leave Me Now	CHICAGO
96	Jailhouse Rock	ELVIS PRESLEY
99	Learning to Fly	TOM PETTY
104	No Particular Place to Go	CHUCK BERRY
111	Oh, Pretty Woman	VAN HALEN
118	Ramblin' Man	THE ALLMAN BROTHERS BAND
128	Ridin' the Storm Out	REO SPEEDWAGON
140	Rock and Roll All Nite	KISS
147	School's Out	ALICE COOPER
155	Surfin' U.S.A.	THE BEACH BOYS
161	Susie-Q	CREDENCE CLEARWATER REVIVAL
167	Sweet Child O' Mine	GUNS N' ROSES
176	Walk This Way	AEROSMITH
185	We're Ready	BOSTON
194	You Give Love a Bad Name	BON JOVI
199	GUITAR NOTATION LEGEND	

Call Me the Breeze

Words and Music by John Cale

* Chord symbols reflect basic tonality.

Copyright © 1971 by Johnny Bienstock Music
Copyright Renewed
International Copyright Secured   All Rights Reserved
Used by Permission

Verse

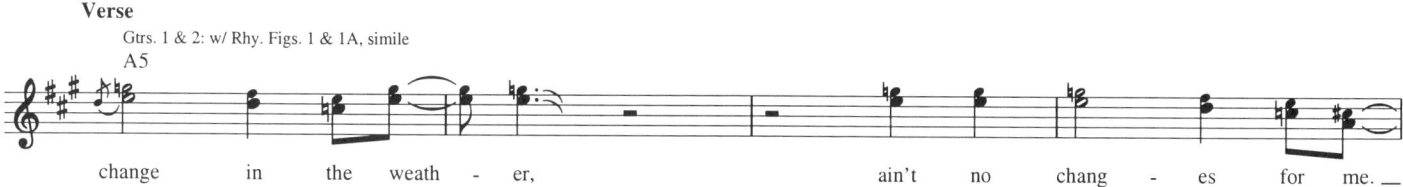

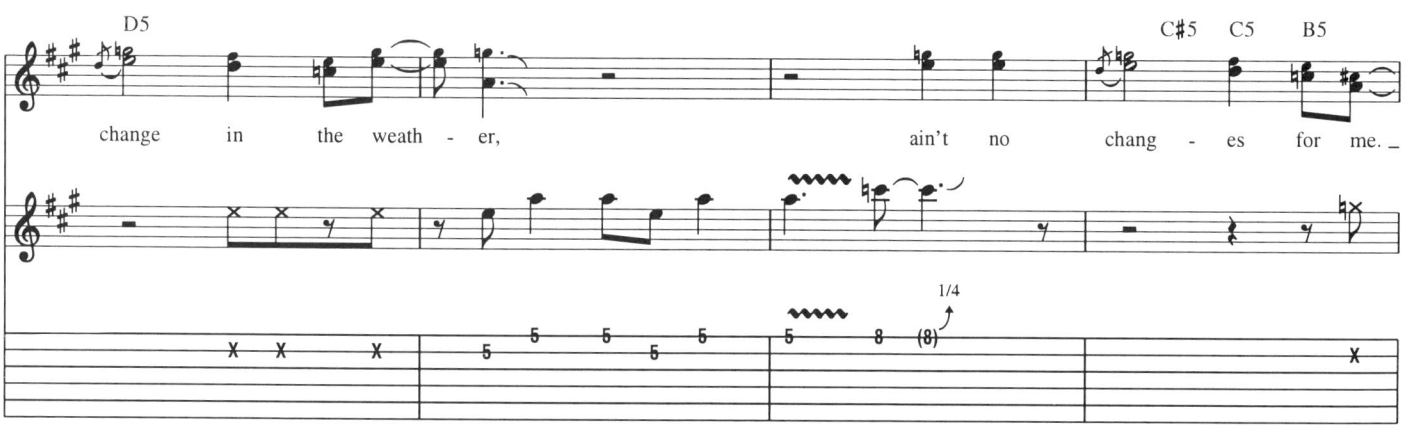

7

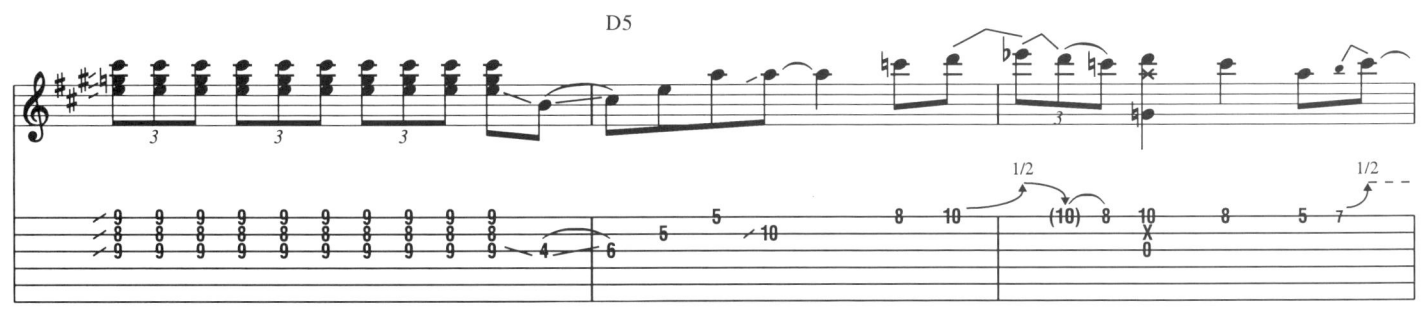
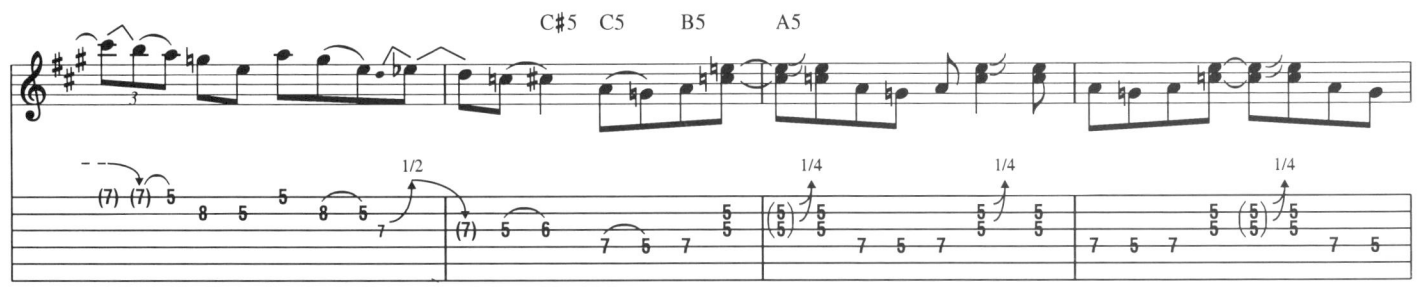

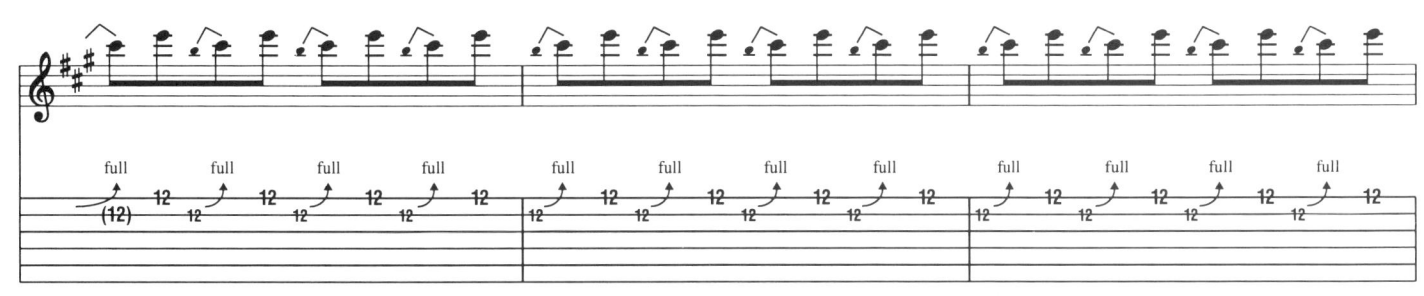

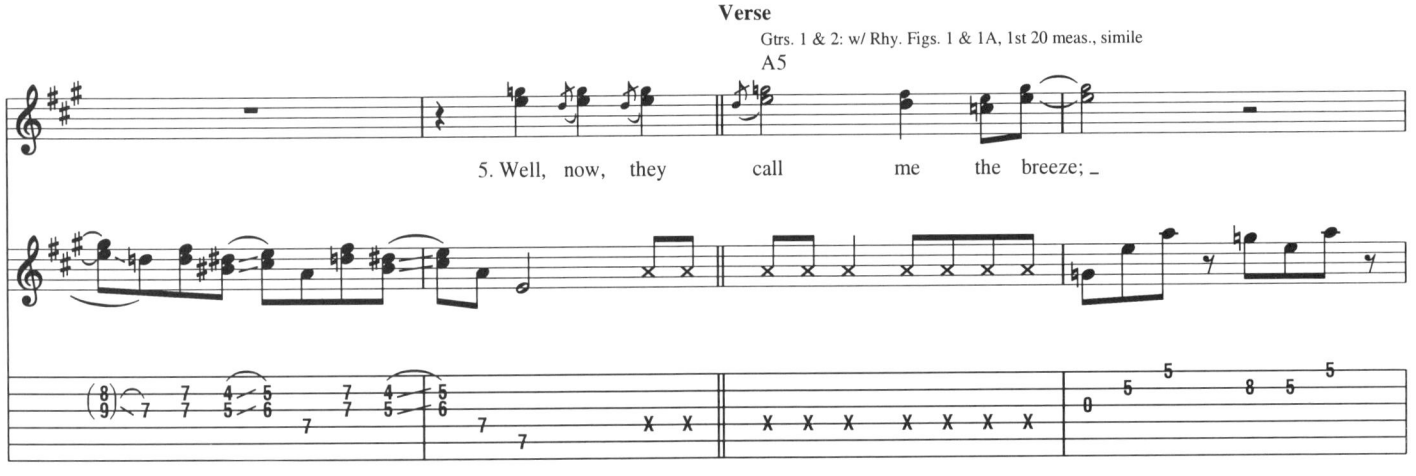
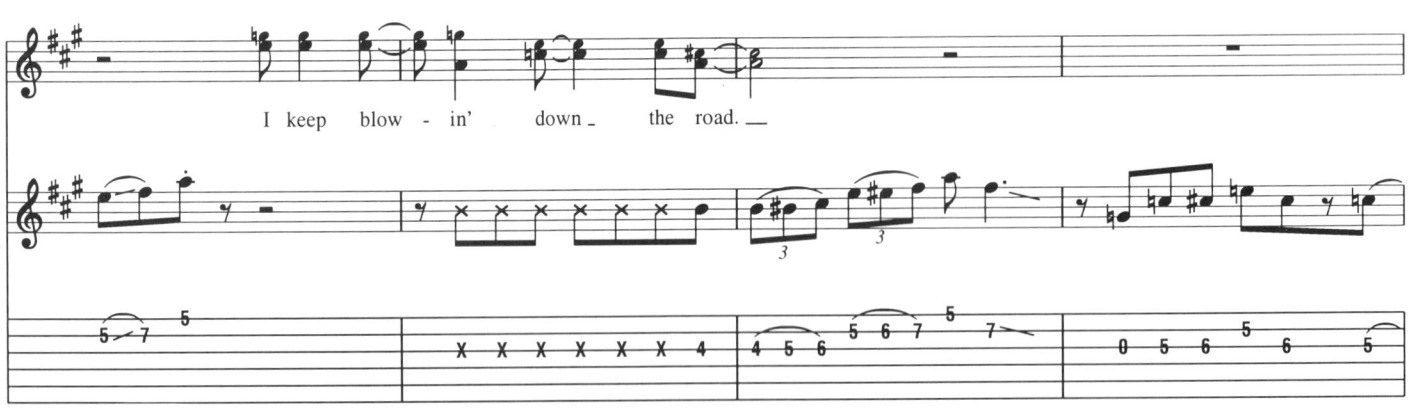

14

Can't You See

Words and Music by Toy Caldwell

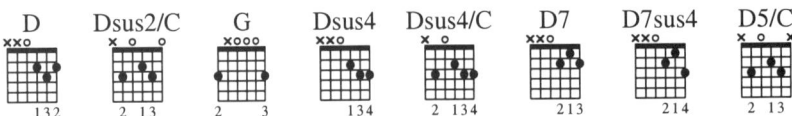

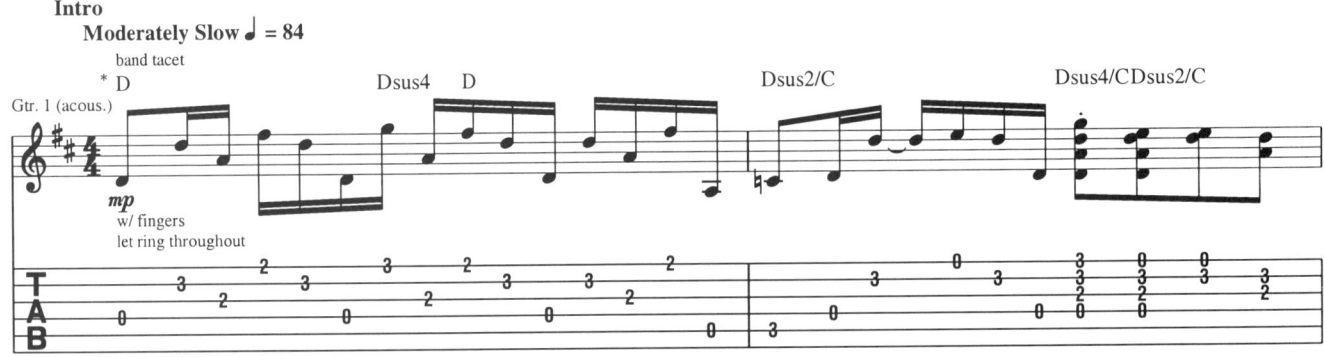

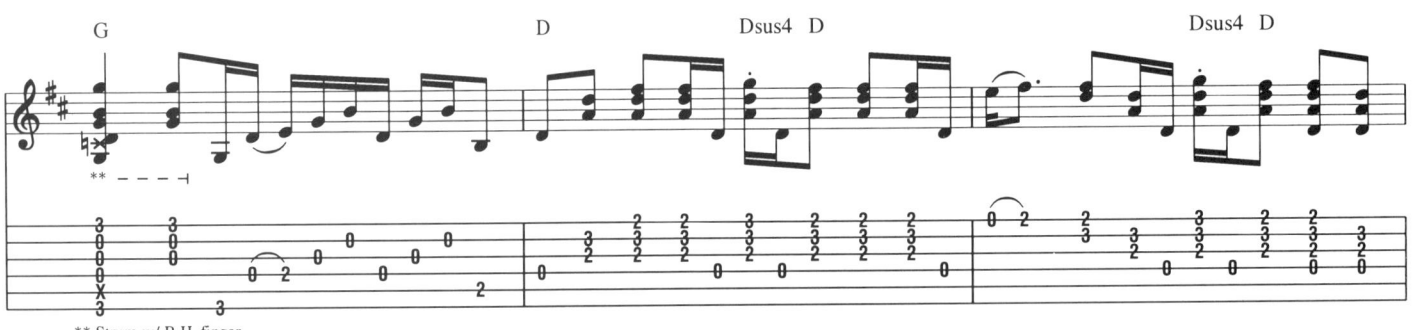

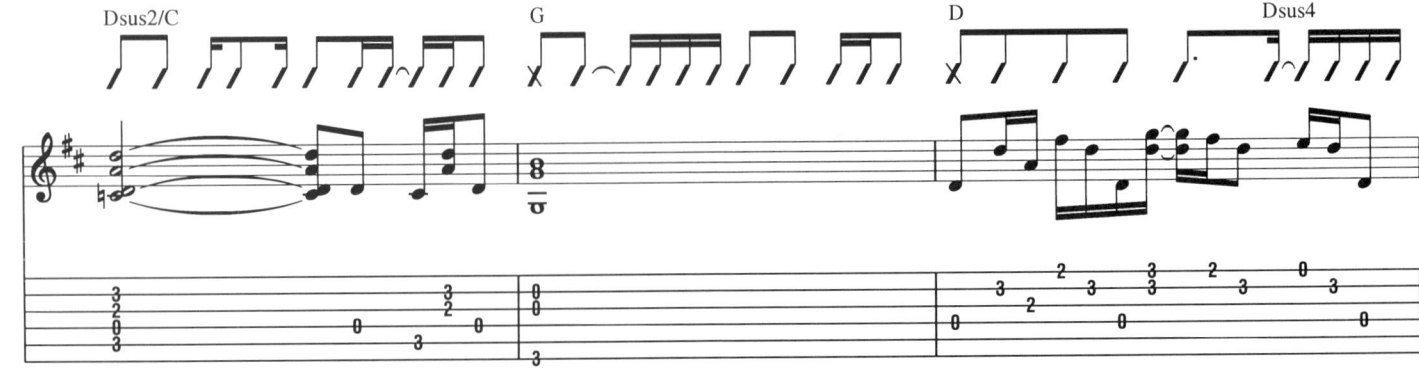

Copyright © 1973, 1975 Spirit One Music, A Division of Spirit Music Group, Inc.
International Copyright Secured   All Rights Reserved

Guitar Solo

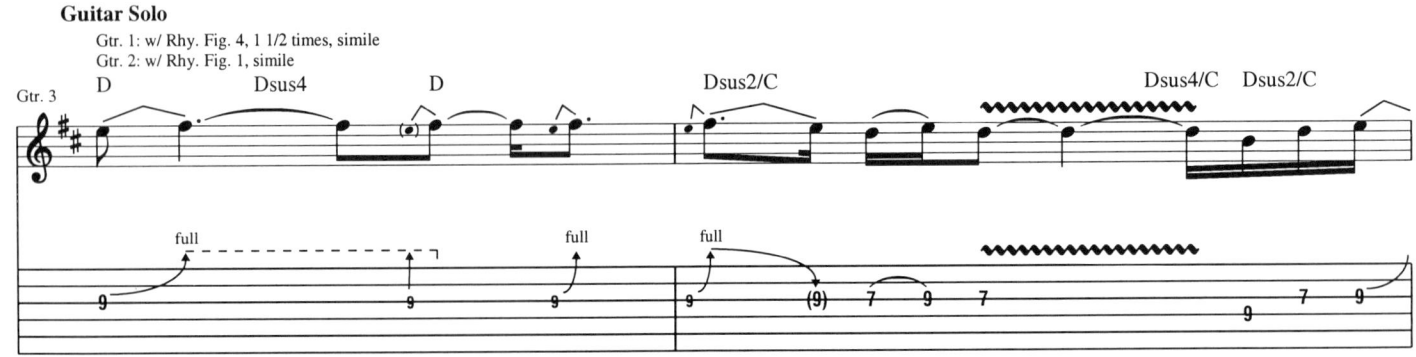

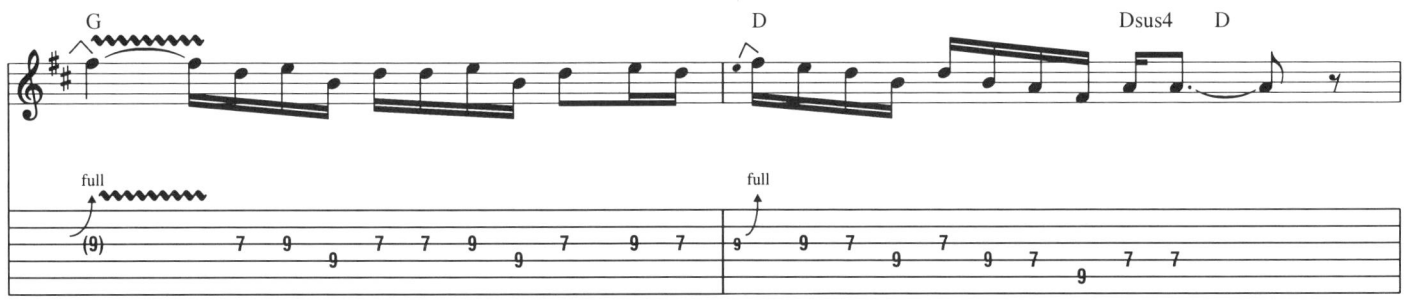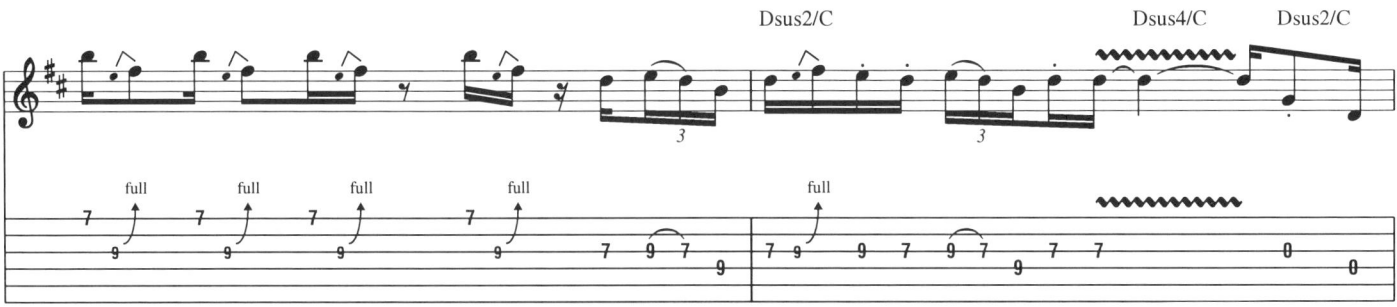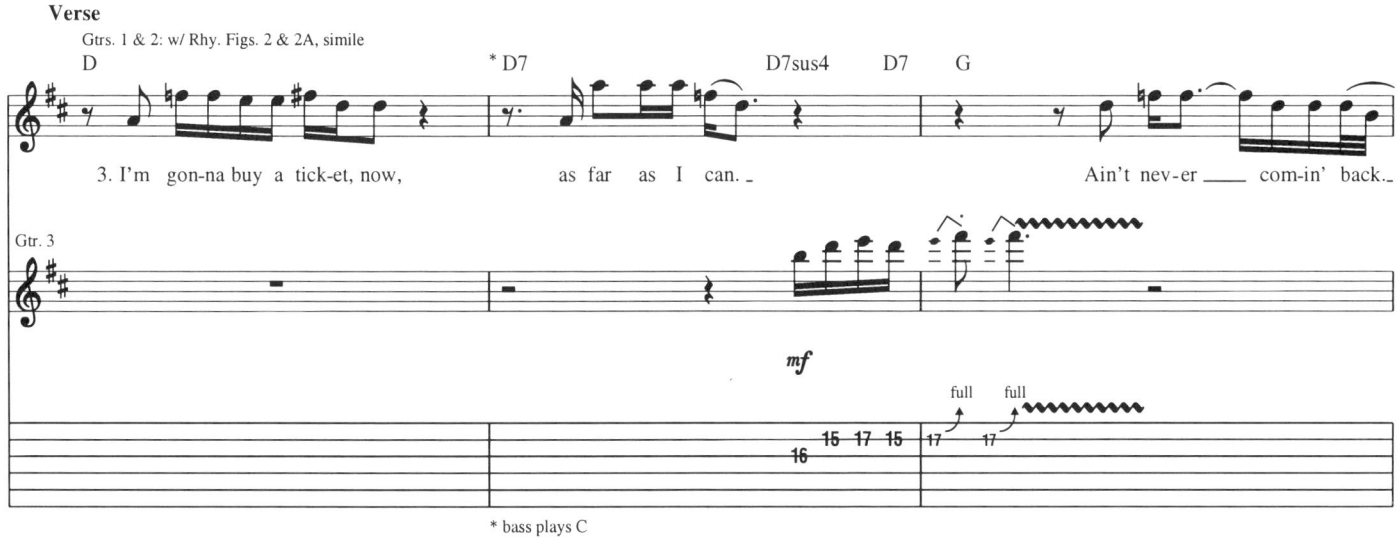

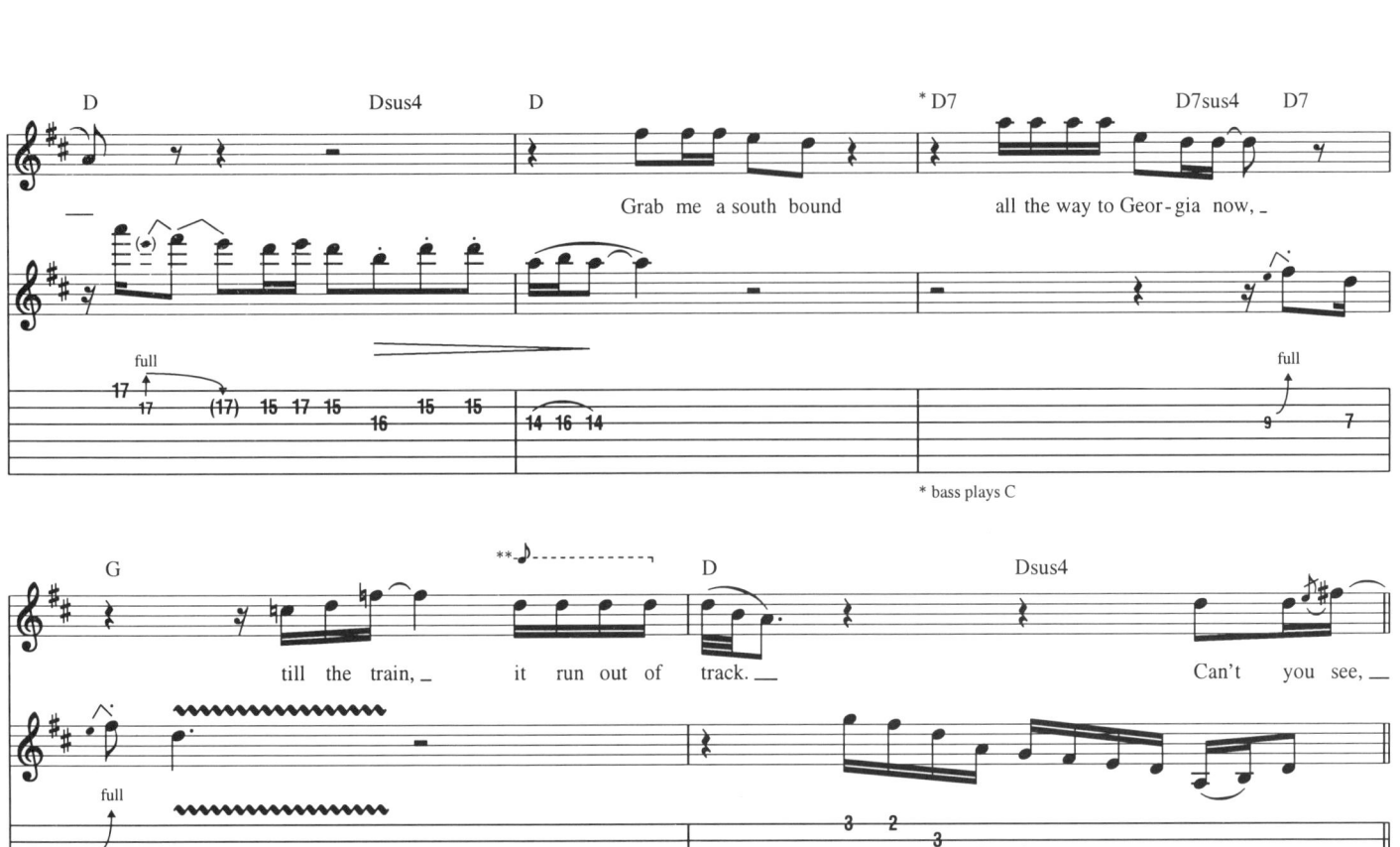
* bass plays C

**Sung behind the beat.

*Played ahead of the beat.

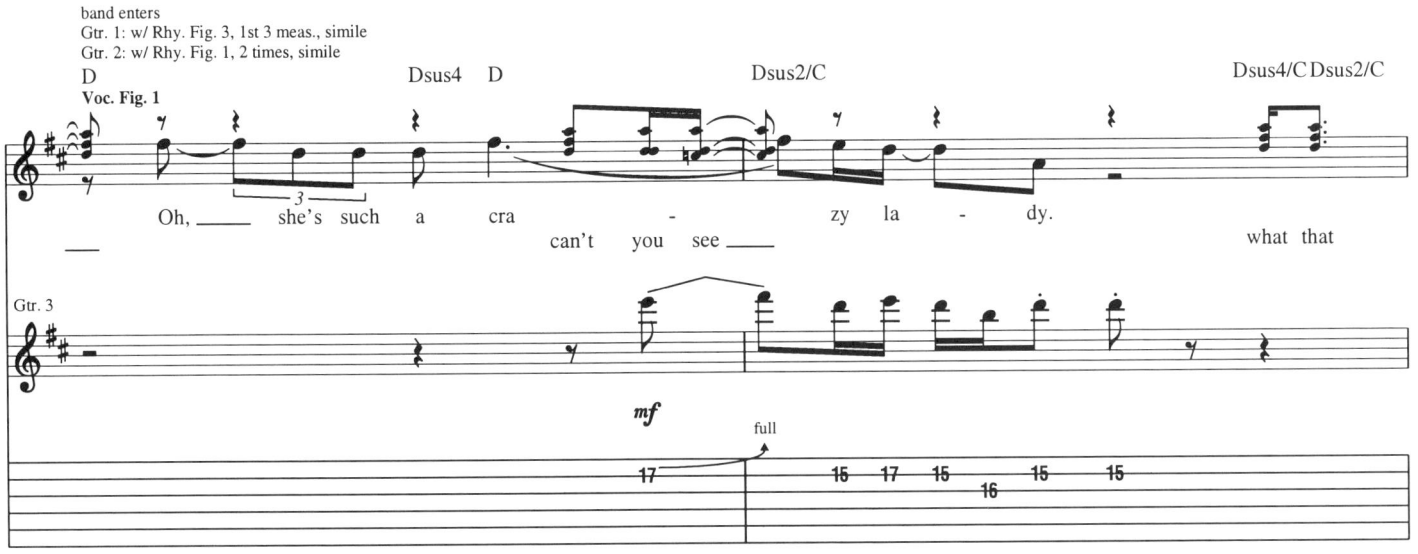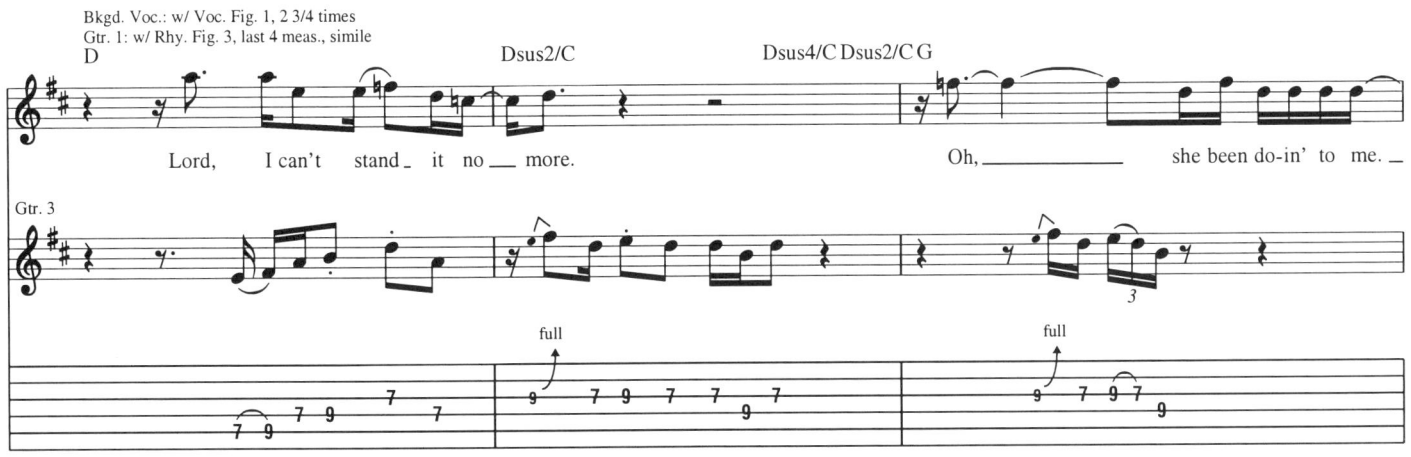

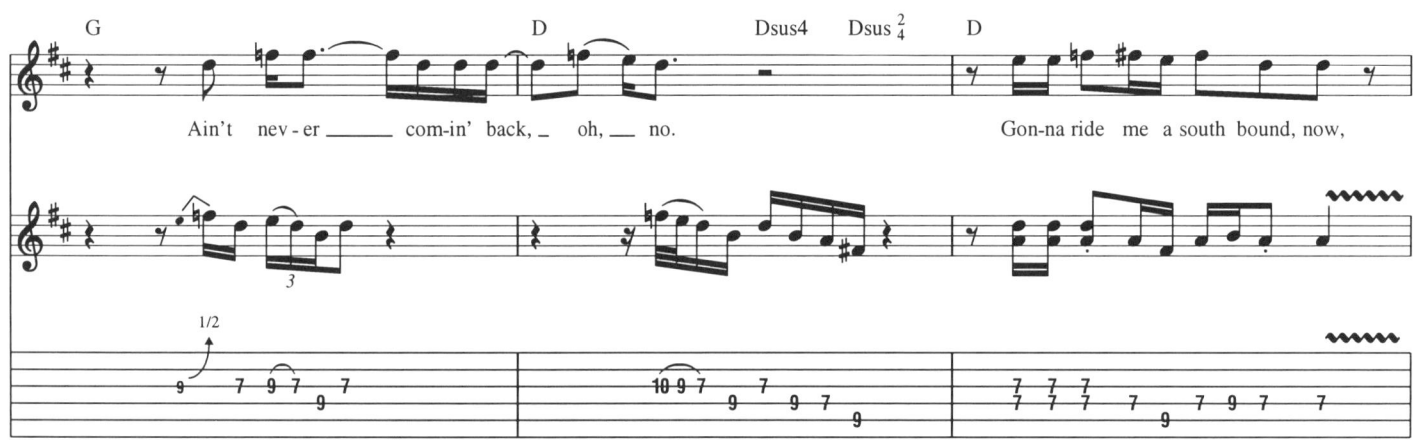

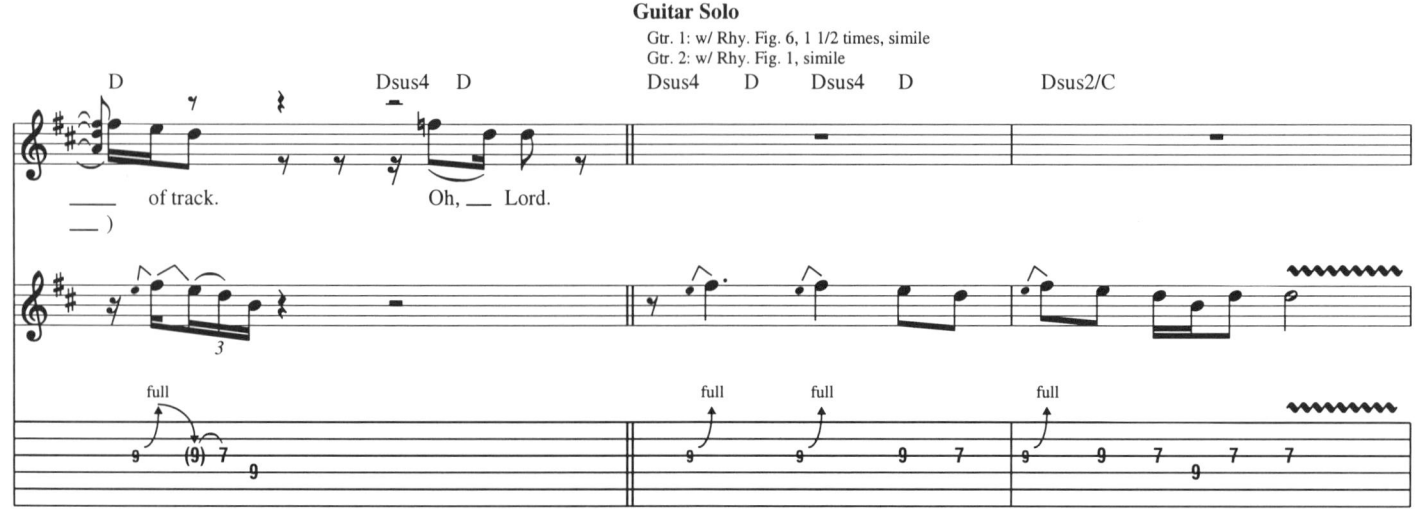

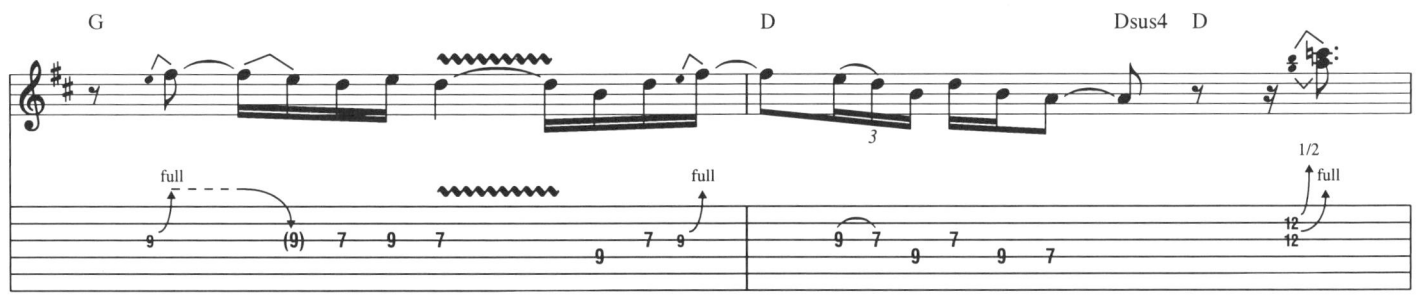
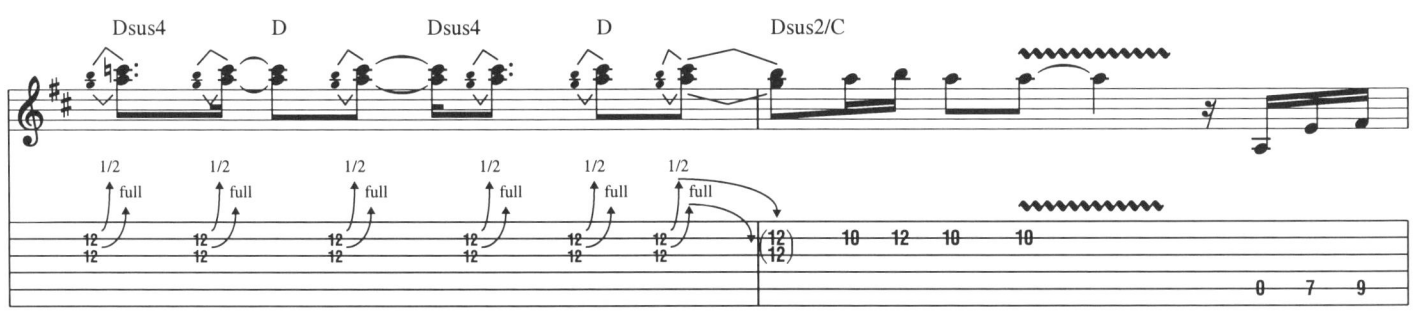
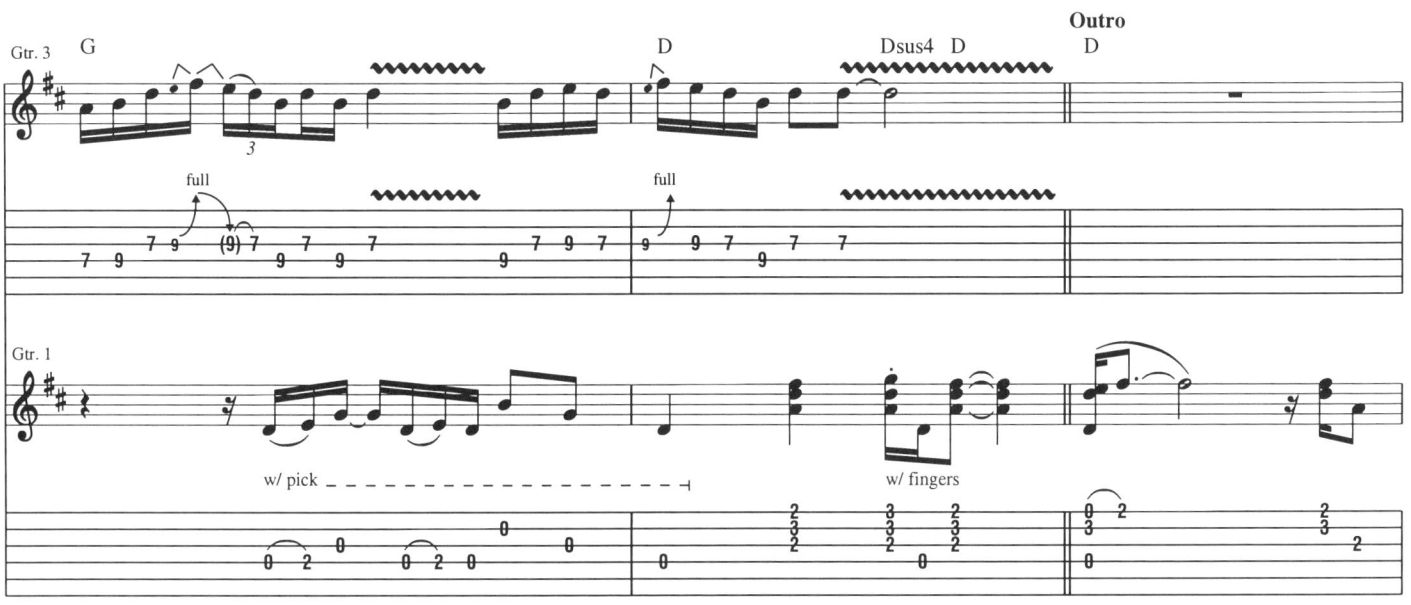

*bass pedals D till end

29

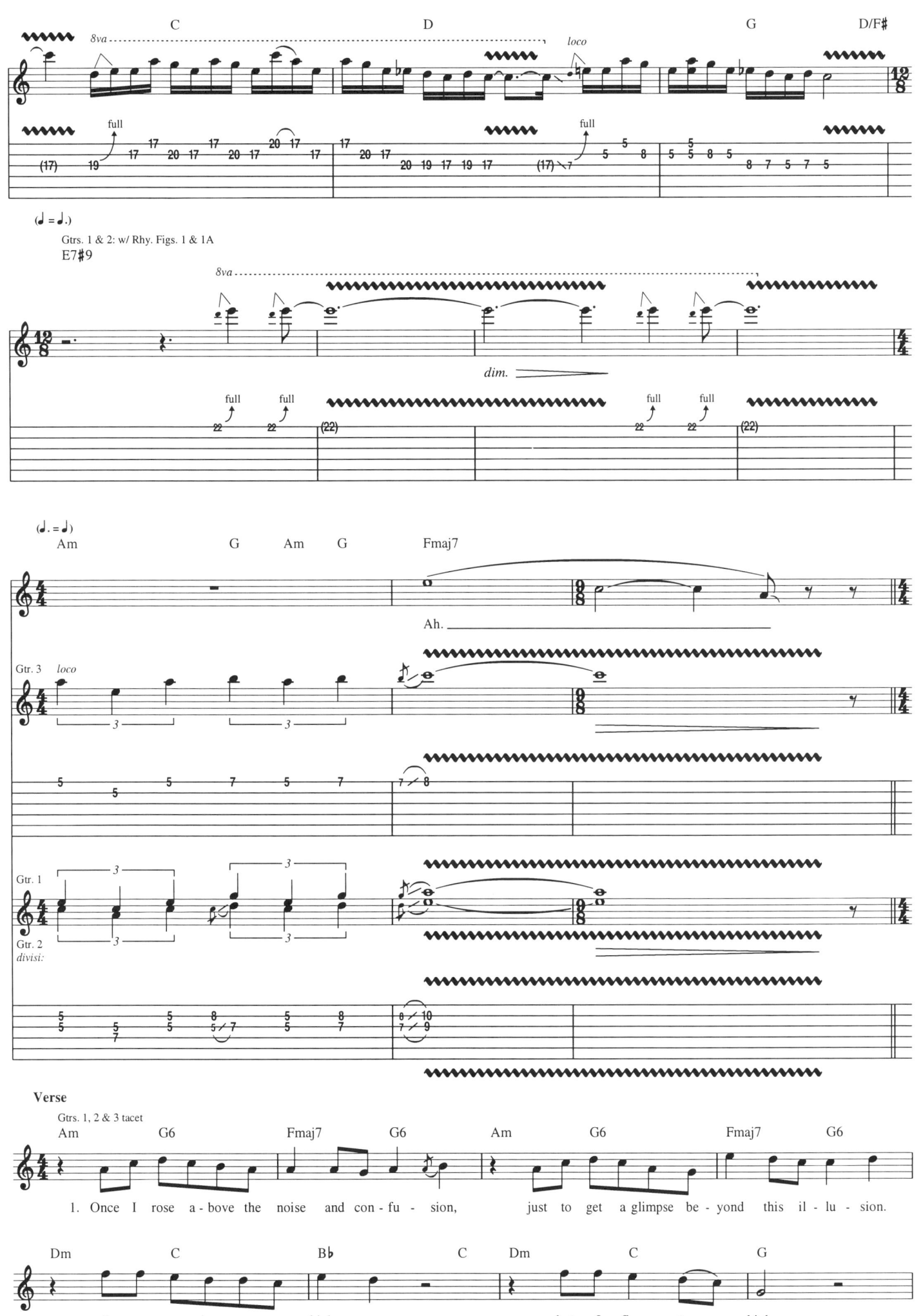

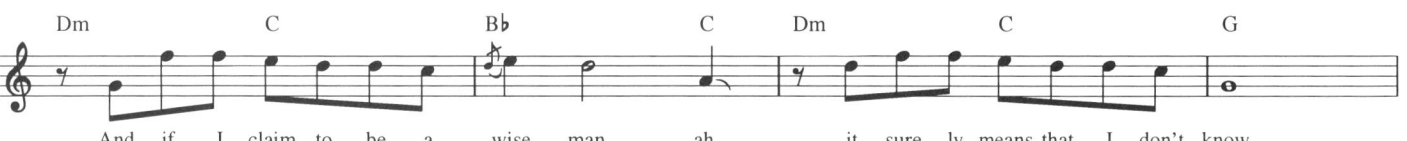
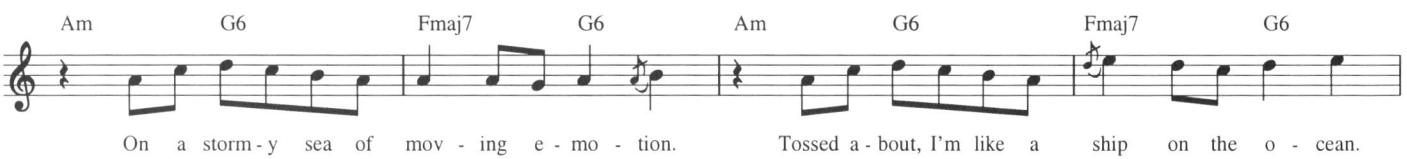
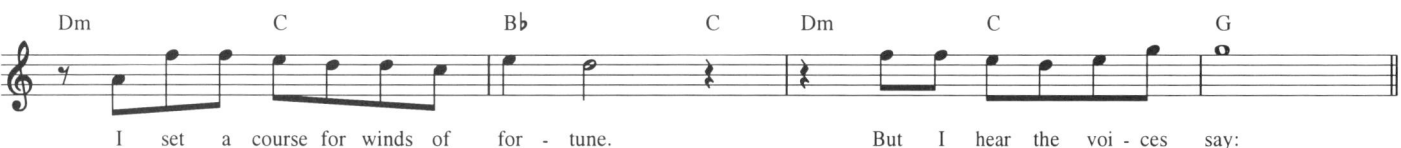

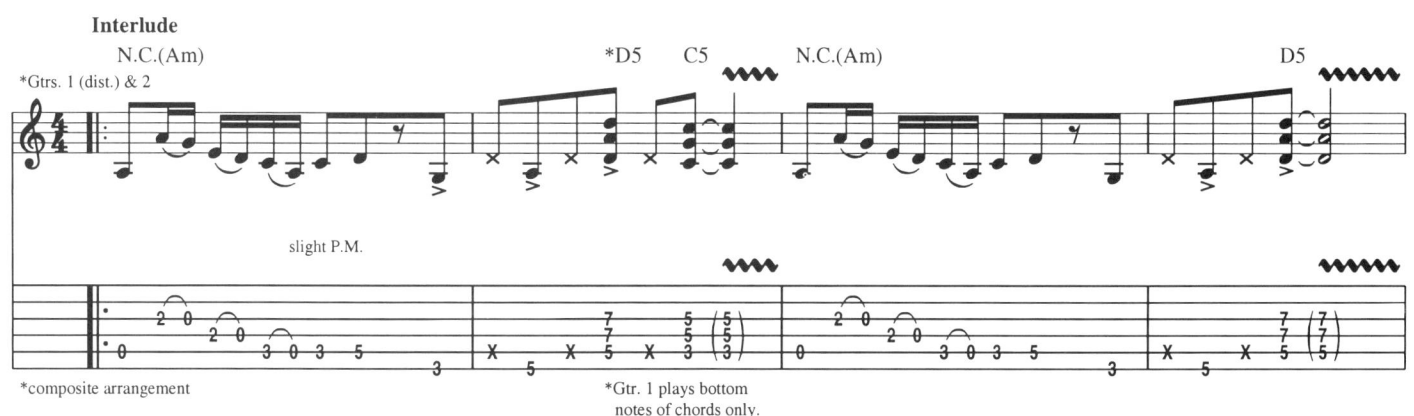

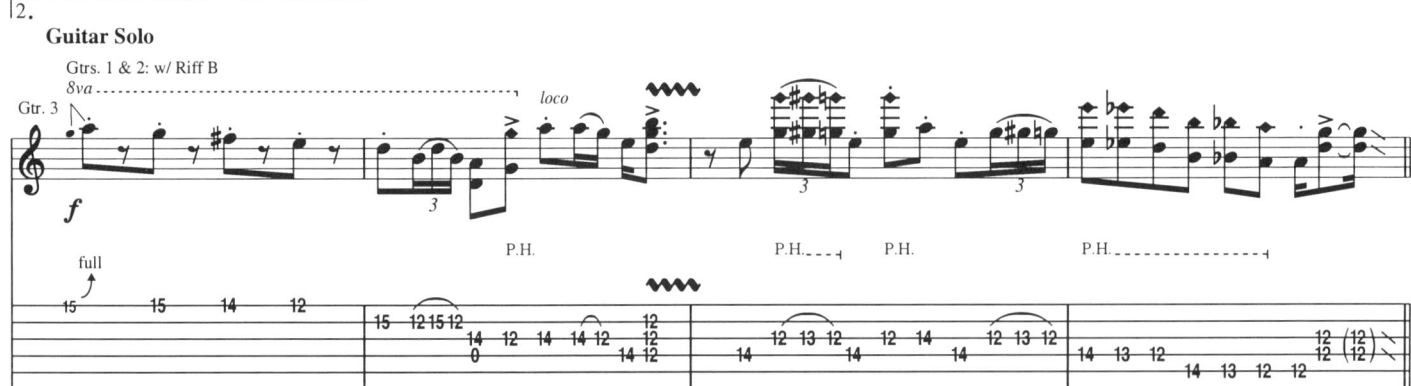

*Gtr. 1 to the left of slash in TAB.

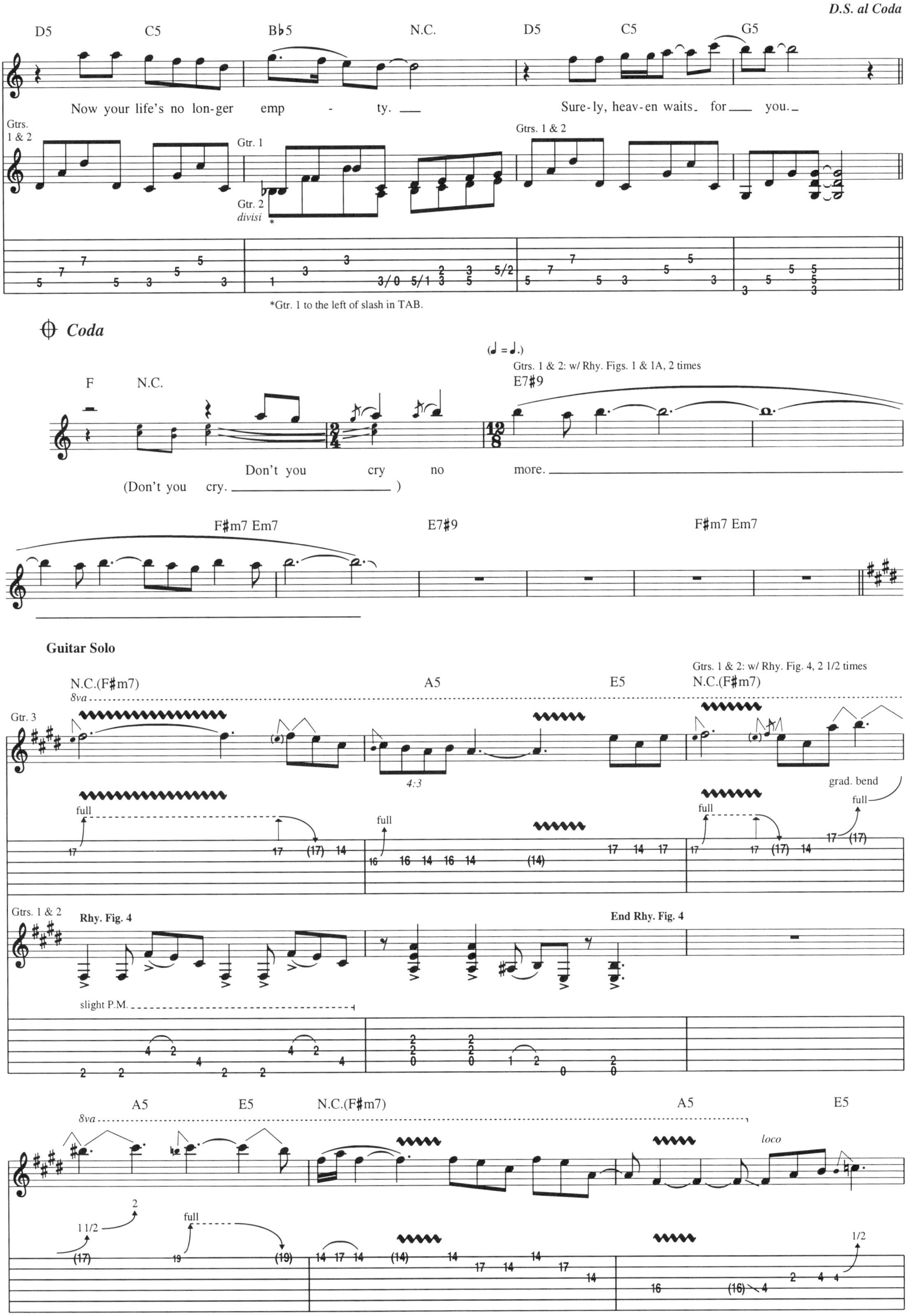

Coda

Don't you cry no more.
(Don't you cry.)

Guitar Solo

37

Come Out and Play

Words and Music by Dexter Holland

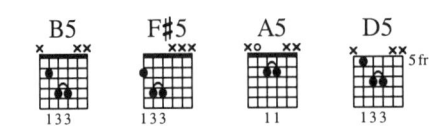

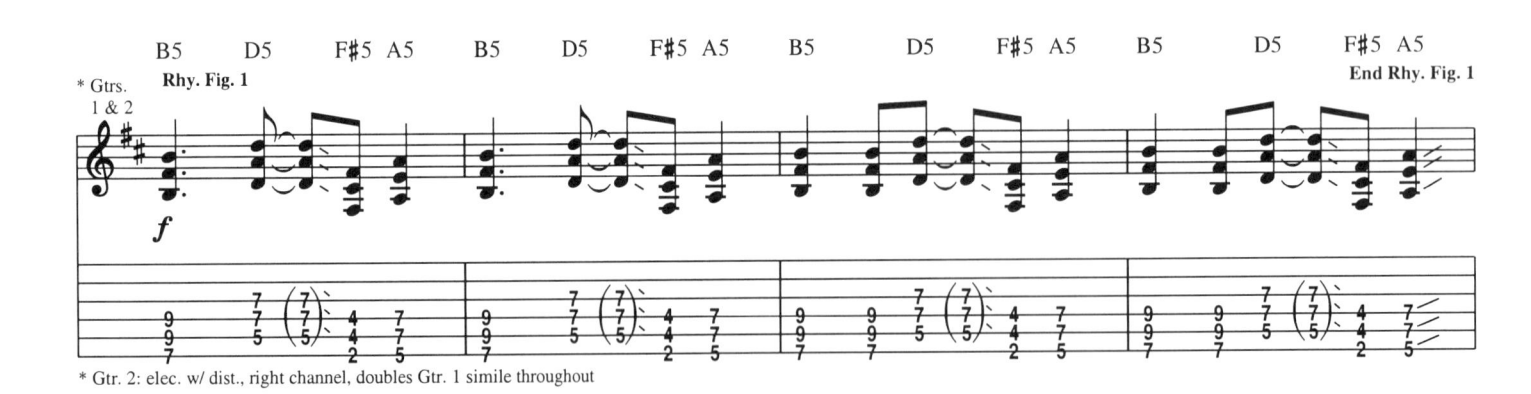

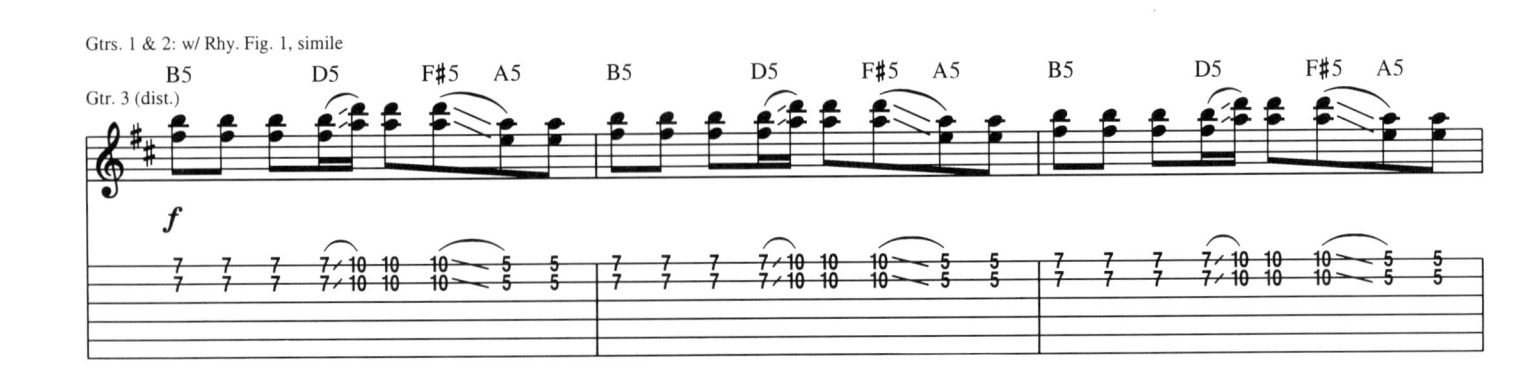

Intro
Moderately Fast Rock ♩ = 158

You got-ta keep 'em sep-a-ra-ted.

*left channel
*Gtr. 2: elec. w/ dist., right channel, doubles Gtr. 1 simile throughout

Copyright © 1994 Gamete Music (BMI)
Administered by Wixen Music Publishing, Inc.
International Copyright Secured All Rights Reserved

Gtrs. 1 & 2: w/ Rhy. Fill 1, 2nd & 3rd times
B5 D5 F♯5 A5 B5 F♯5 A5 B5 F♯5 D5
Rhy. Fig. 2
Gtrs. 1 & 2
P.M.
Gtr. 3
w/clean tone
1.
2.
B5 F♯5 A5 B5 F♯5 D5 B5
End Rhy. Fig. 2
P.M.
Verse
Gtr. 3 tacet
B5 F♯5 A5 B5 D5 F♯5 A5 B5 F♯5 A5
1. Like the lat - est fash - ion, like a spread - ing dis - ease.
2. By the time you hear the si - ren it's al - read - y too late.
Gtrs. 1 & 2
simile on repeats
P.M.
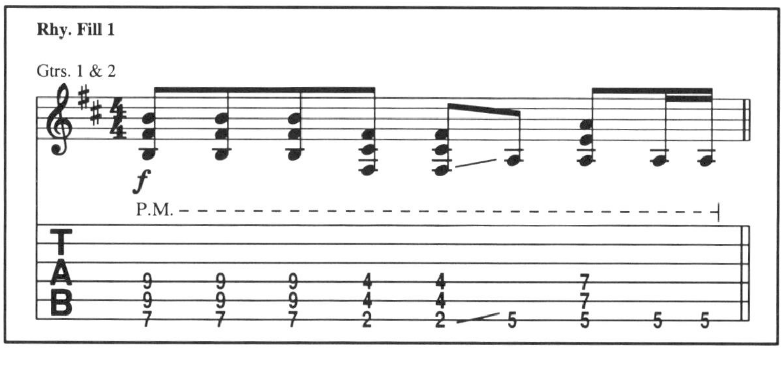
Rhy. Fill 1
Gtrs. 1 & 2
P.M.
T
A
B

B5 D5 F#5 A5 B5 F#5 A5 B5 D5 F#5 A5
The kids are strap-pin' on their way to the class - room,
One goes to the morgue and the oth - er to jail.
P.M.
B5 F#5 A5 B5 D5 F#5 A5
Pre-Chorus
E5 G5 G G5
One get - ting weap-ons with the great - est of ease. 1. The gangs stake out their own
One guy's wast - ed and the oth - er's a waste. 2., 3. It goes down the same as the
P.M.
F#5 B5 D5 E5 G5 F#5 B5 D5
cam - pus lo - cale. And if they catch you slip - pin' then it's all o - ver pal. If
thou - sand be - fore. No one's get - ting smart - er, no one's learn - ing the score. Your
B5 F#5 A5 B5 D5 F#5 A5 F#
one guy's col - ors and the oth - er's don't mix, they're gon - na bash it up, bash it up, bash it up, bash it up.
nev - er end - ing spree of death and vi - o - lence and hate is gon - na tie your own rope, tie your own rope, tie your own.
P.M.

Chorus
B5 D5 F#5 A5 B5 D5 F#5 A5 B5 D5 F#5 A5 B5
1. Hey, man you talk-in' back to me?
2. Hey, man you dis-re-spect-ing me?
Take him out. You got-ta keep 'em sep-a-ra-ted.
Gtrs. 1 & 2
D5 F#5 A5 B5 D5 F#5 A5 E5 C5 B5
Hey, (they) don't pay no mind. If you're un-der eigh-teen you won't be do-ing an-y time.
(3rd time) To Coda 2
To Coda 1
D.S. al Coda 1
D5 F#5 A5 F#5 A5 B5 D5 F#5 A5 B5
Hey, come out and play.
Coda 1
Interlude
Gtrs. 1 & 2: w/ Rhy. Fig. 2, simile
Gtr. 3
B5 F#5 A5 B5 F#5 D5 B5 F#5 A5
w/clean tone
2nd time, D.S.S. al Coda 2
B5 F#5 D5
Coda 2
Gtrs. 1 & 2
B5 D5 F#5 A5 B5

Crazy on You

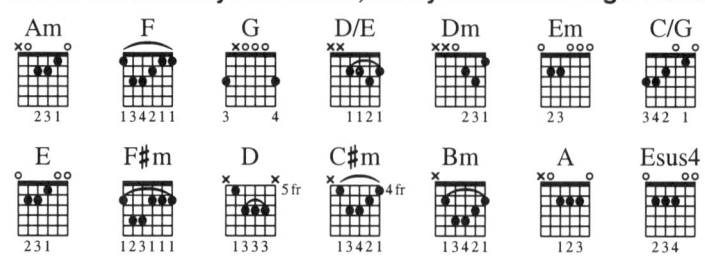

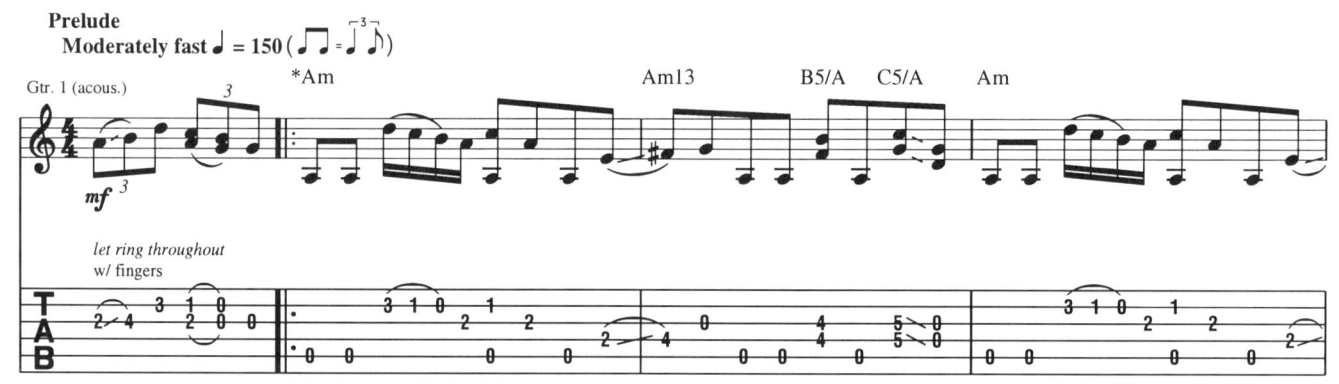

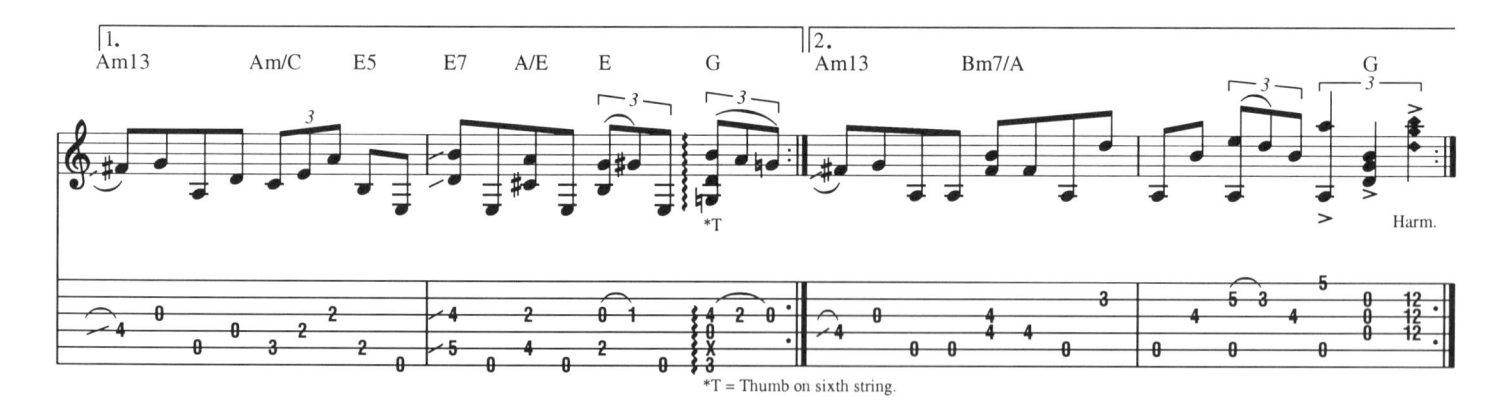

Words and Music by Ann Wilson, Nancy Wilson and Roger Fisher

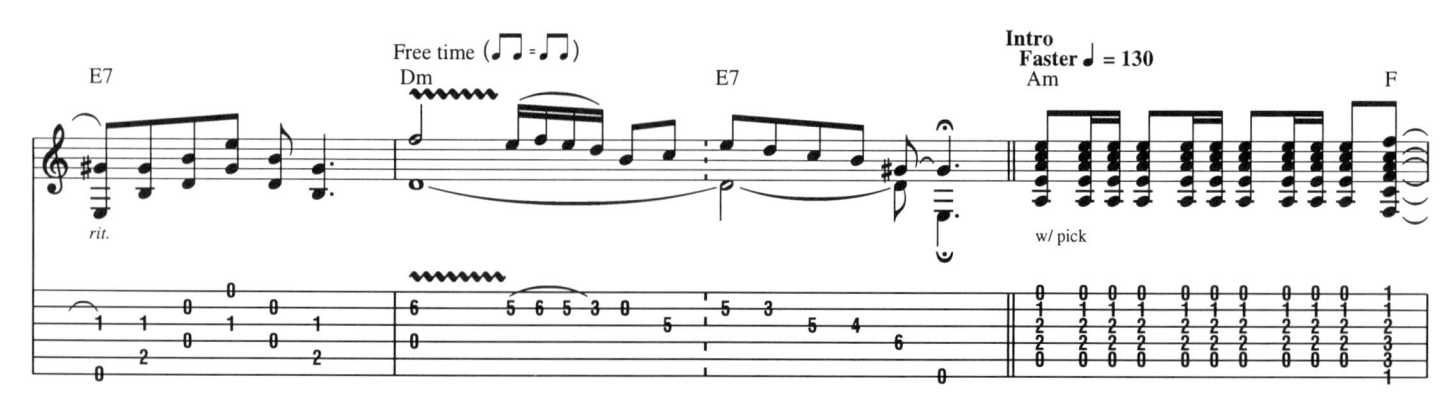

Am
F
G
(cont. in slash)
Am
Rhy. Fig. 1
F
G
Am
F
Gtr. 1
Gtr. 2 (elec.)
Riff A
f w/ dist.
G
Am
G
F
Verse
1st time, Gtr. 2 tacet
2nd & 3rd times, Gtr. 2: w/ Fill 1 (2 times)
G
End Rhy. Fig. 1
Am
(cont. in notation)
1. We may still have time, we might
love is the eve - ning breeze
was a wil - low last night
End Riff A
Rhy. Fig. 2
Gtr. 1
Fill 1
Gtr. 2
mp

still get by. Ev-'ry time I think a - bout it I wan-na cry. With
touch-ing your skin, the gen-tle, sweet sing-ing of leaves in the wind. The
in a dream, I bent down o - ver a clear run-ning stream. I

bombs and the dev-il, lit-tle kids keep com-in'. No
whis-per that calls af-ter you in the night and
sang you this song that I heard up a - bove and you

way to breathe eas - y, no time to be young. I
kiss - es your ear in the ear - ly light.
kept me a - live with your

Pre-Chorus

But I tell my - self that I was do-in' al - right. There's
And you don't need to won-der; your do-in' fine.

Dm
E
noth - in' left to do to - night but go
My love, the pleas - ure's mine. Let me go
cra -
8va
let ring
Chorus
1st time, Gtr. 1: w/ Rhy. Fig. 1
1st time, Gtr. 2: w/ Riff A
2nd time, Gtr. 1: w/ Rhy. Fig. 1 (1st 6 meas.)
2nd time, Gtr. 2: w/ Riff A (1st 6 meas.)
Am F G Am F G
- zy on you, cra - zy on you. Let me go
Am G F G
cra - zy, cra - zy on you, oh. 2. My
Bridge
F G Am F♯m
3fr
Rhy. Fill 1
Gtr. 1
End Rhy. Fill 1
Rhy. Fig. 3
While the man's world is
Voc. Fig. 1
(Oo.
Gtr. 2
Fill 2
End Fill 2
mp
w/ clean tone

cry - ing in pain, what - cha gon-na do ____ when ev - 'ry - bod - y's in - sane? ____

Oo. ____

So a-fraid of won - ders, so a - fraid of you, what-cha gon - na do? ____

Oo. ____ Oo. ____

Chorus

-zy on you, cra - zy on you.

Let me go cra - zy, crazy on you, oo. 3. I

D.S. al Coda

Coda
Chorus
Gtr. 1: w/ Rhy. Fig. 1 (1st 6 meas.)
Gtr. 2: w/ Riff A (1st 6 meas.)
E Am F G Am F
sweet flow-ing love.
Cra - zy,
Yeah.
cra - zy, on
G Am G F Am
Gtr. 1: w/ Rhy. Fill 1 (1st meas.)
Gtr. 2: w/ Fill 2 (1st meas.)
you. Let me go cra - zy, cra - zy on you, oo. Cra -
Gtr. 1: w/ *Rhy. Fig. 1 (1st 6 meas.)
Gtr. 2: w/ *Riff A (1st 6 meas.)
F G Am F
- zy on you, cra - zy on you.
Gtr. 4
f w/ dist.
Gtr. 5
f w/ dist.
*Beat 1 is tied from the previous meas., not struck.
Gtr. 1: w/ Rhy. Fill 1 (1st meas.)
Gtr. 2: w/ Fill 2 (1st meas.)
G Am G F Am
Let me go cra - zy, cra - zy on you, yeah.

Gtr. 1: w/ *Rhy. Fig. 1 (1st 6 meas.)
Gtr. 2: w/ *Riff A (1st 6 meas.)
F
G
Am
F
G
(Oo.
Oo.
8va
* Beat 1 is tied from the previous meas., not struck.
Gtr. 1: w/ Rhy. Fill 1
Gtr. 2: w/ Fill 2
Am
G
F
Am
Oo.
8va
grad. bend
8va
grad. bend
Interlude
Bkgd. Voc.: w/ Voc. Fig. 1
Gtr. 1: w/ Rhy. Fig. 3
Gtrs. 4 & 5 tacet
Gtr. 2
F♯m
D
C♯m
D
w/ clean tone
Gtr. 6 (elec.)
mp
w/ clean tone
(cont. in slash)

C♯m
Gtr. 6
D
C♯m
Gtr. 2
1
1
Bm
Gtr. 3: w/ Riff B
A
1 hold bend
1 hold bend
Gtrs. 2 & 6 tacet
E
Gtr. 1
Bkgd. Voc.: w/ Voc. Fig. 2
F♯m11/E
Emaj7
Aadd9/E
Asus 2/4 /E
Outro-Chorus
Gtr. 1: w/ Rhy. Fig. 1 (1st 6 meas.)
Gtr. 2: w/ Riff A (1st 6 meas.)
Am
F
G
Am
F
G
Cra - zy on you, cra - zy on you. Let me go
Gtr. 1: w/ *Rhy. Fill 1
Gtr. 2: w/ *Fill 2
Am
G
F
Am
cra - zy, cra - zy on you, oh.
* Last meas. w/ fermata

Grind

Written by Jerry Cantrell

Verse

1. In the darkest hole you'd be well advised not to plan my fun'ral 'fore the body dies, yeah. yeah.
2. Sure to play a part so you love the game, and in truth your lies become one and same,

Come the mornin' light, it's a see-through show. What you may have heard and what you think you know, yeah.
I could set you free, rather hear the sound of your body breakin' as I take you down, yeah.

Fill 1

Chorus

Let the sun never blind your eyes. Let me sleep so my teeth won't grind.

Hear a sound from a voice inside.

Gtr. 1 tabbed to the left.   pitch: F#

53

from a voice in - side.

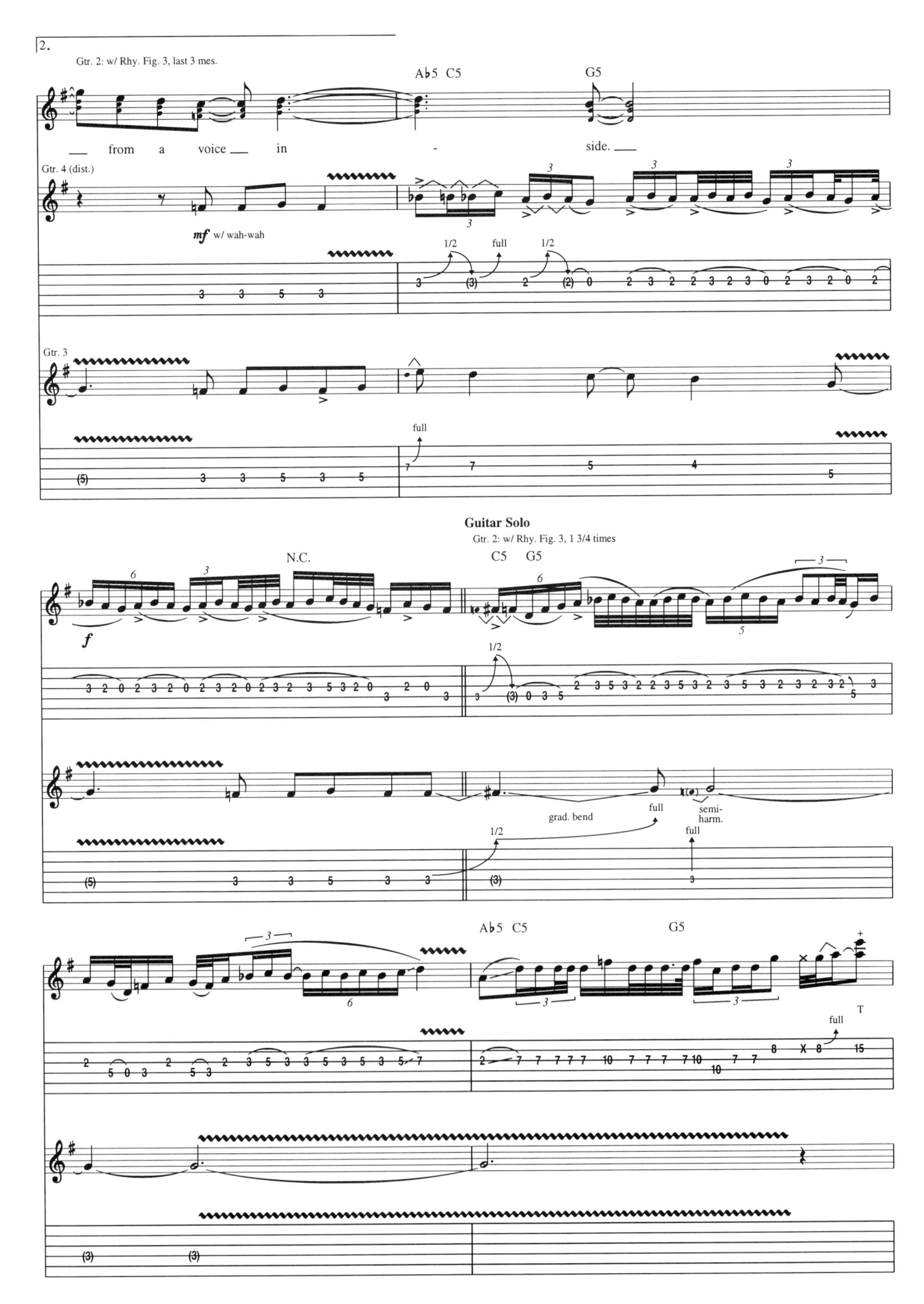

Guitar Solo

Verse

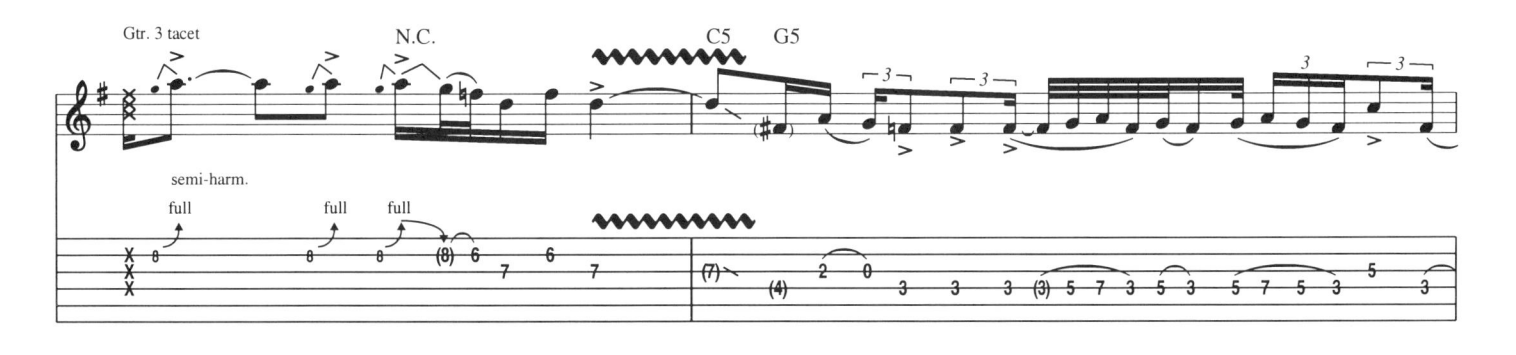

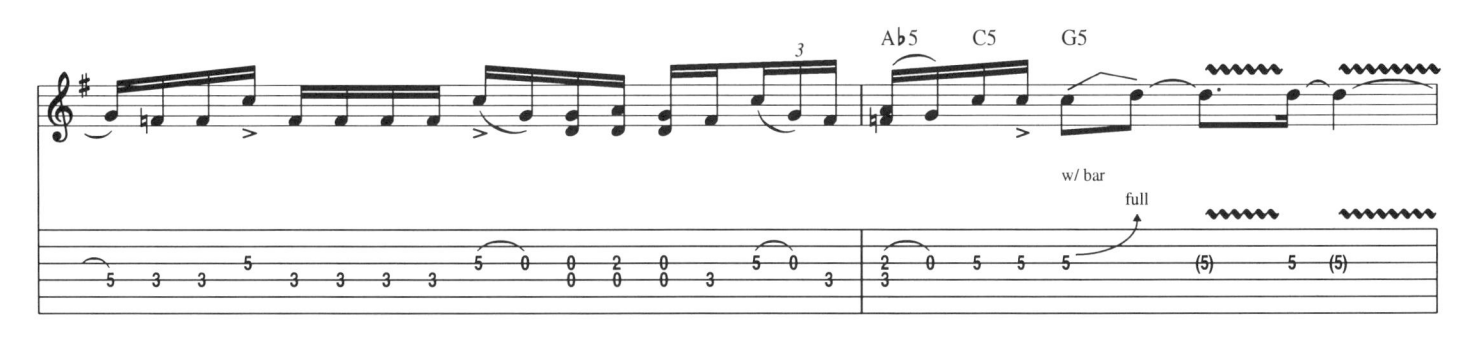

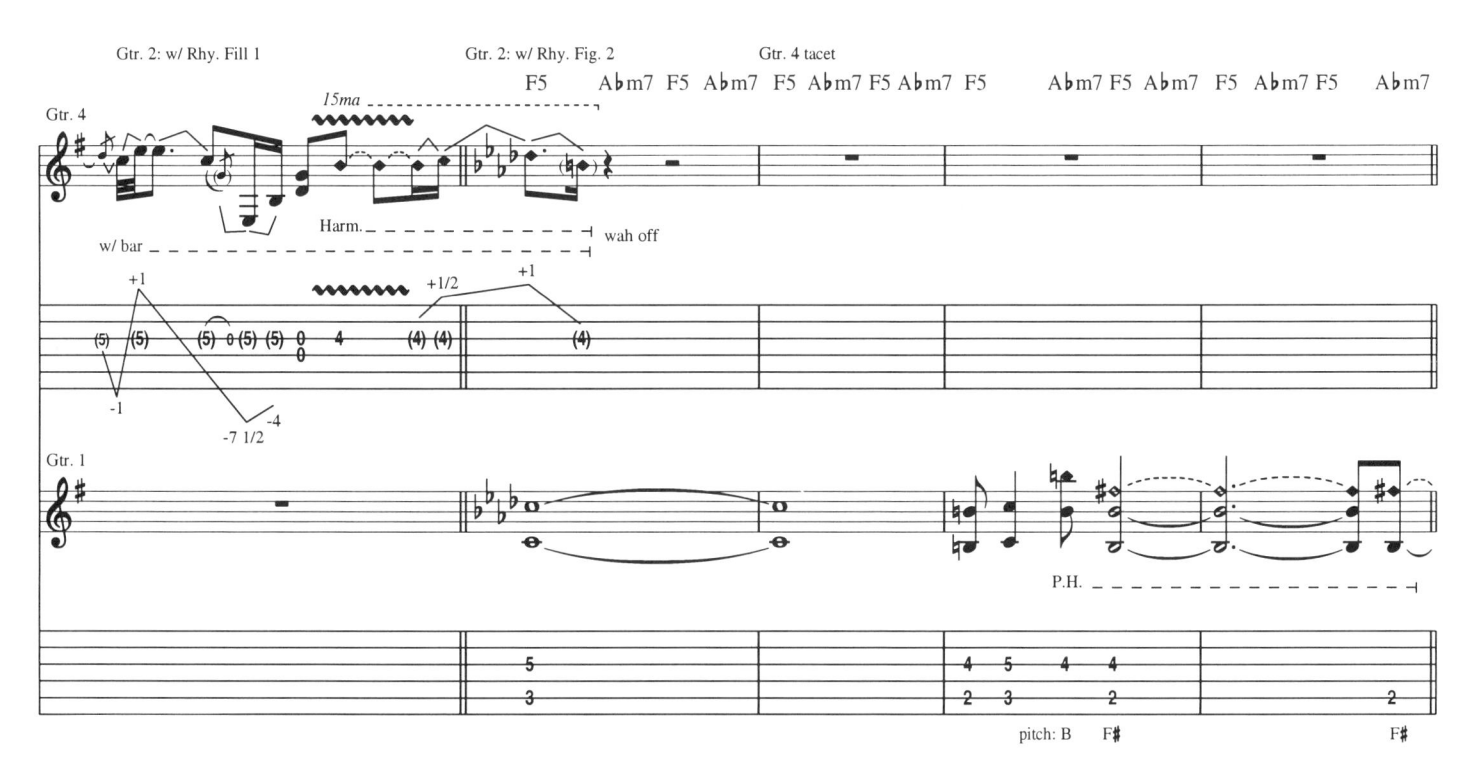

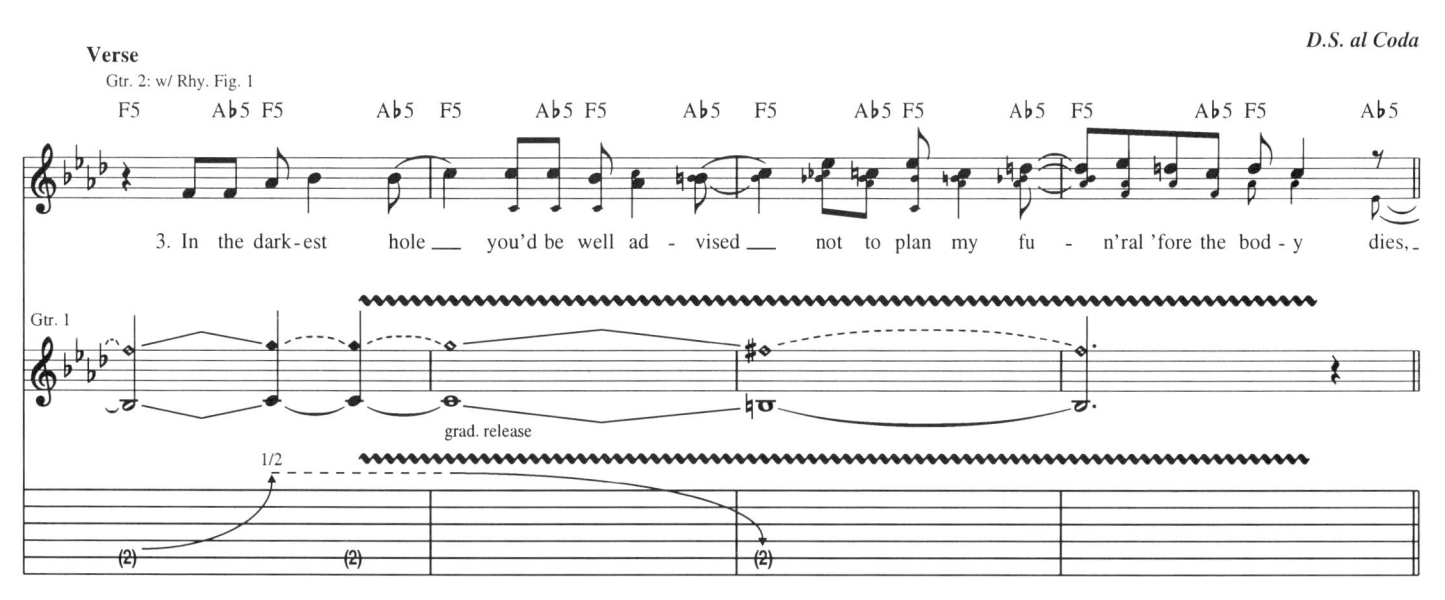

3. In the darkest hole _ you'd be well advised _ not to plan my funeral 'fore the body dies, _

D.S. al Coda

Coda
Gtr. 2: w/ Rhy. Fig. 3, last 3 meas.
Ab5 C5 G5
N.C.
from a voice in - side.
Gtr. 3
full
Gtr. 2: w/ Rhy. Fig. 3, 1 3/4 times
Gtr. 3: w/ Riff A, 1 3/4 times
C5 G5
Ab5 C5 G5
N.C.
Let the sun never blind your eyes. Let me sleep so my teeth won't grind.
Gtr. 4
full
C5 G5
Ab5 C5 G5
Gtrs. 2 & 3: w/ Rhy. Fills 1 & 1A
N.C.
Hear a sound from a voice in - side.
full
1/2
Outro
Gtr. 2: w/ Rhy. Fig. 2
Gtrs. 3 & 4 tacet
F5 Abm7 F5 Abm7 F5 Abm7 F5 Abm7 F5 Abm7 F5 Abm7 F5 Abm7 F5 Abm7
Gtr. 4
Gtr. 1
Gtr. 3
divisi
w/ wah-wah
grad. bend
grad. bend
w/ echo repeats
1/2
1/2

Heartache Tonight

Words and Music by John David Souther, Don Henley, Glenn Frey and Bob Seger

58

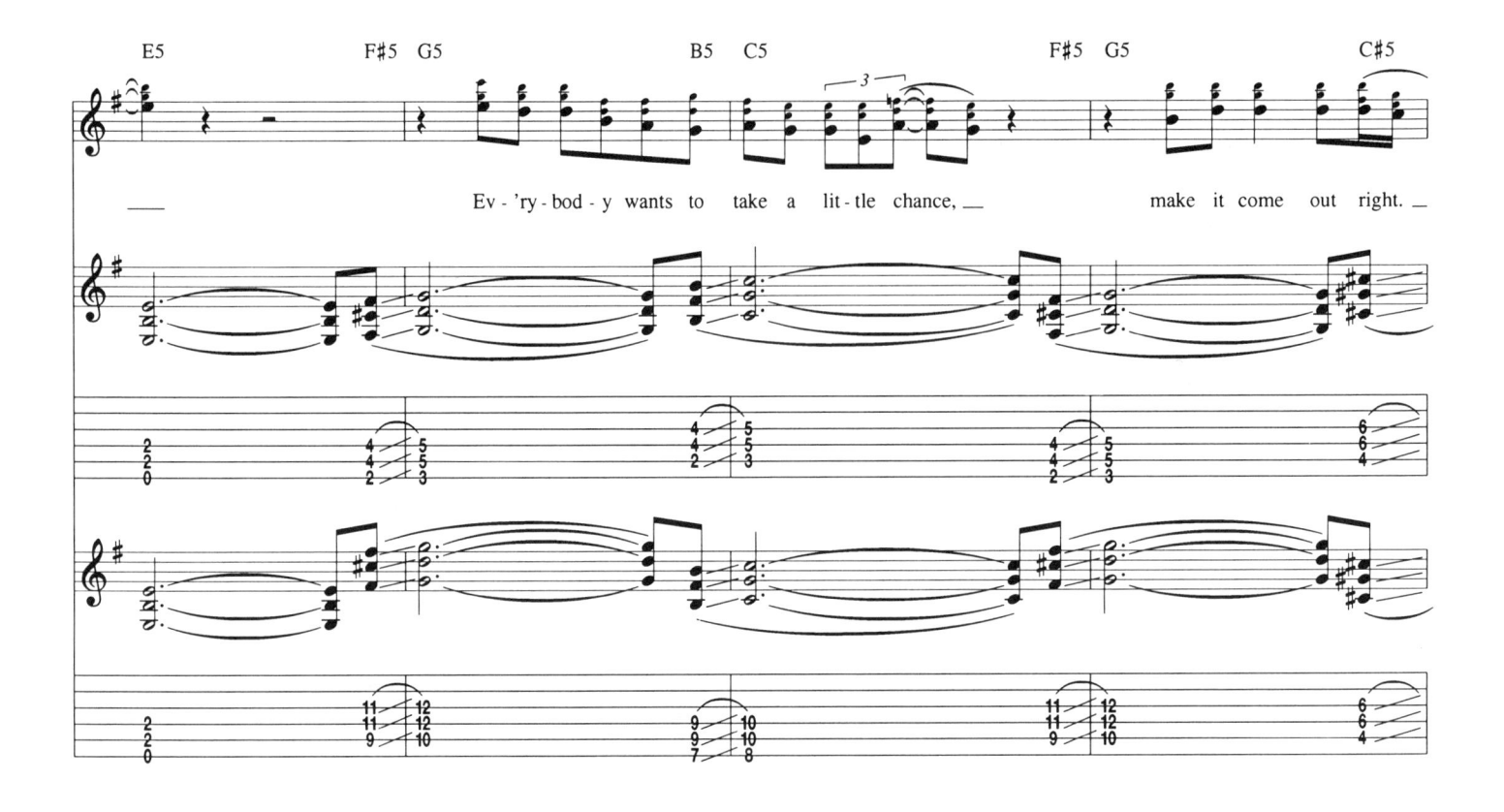

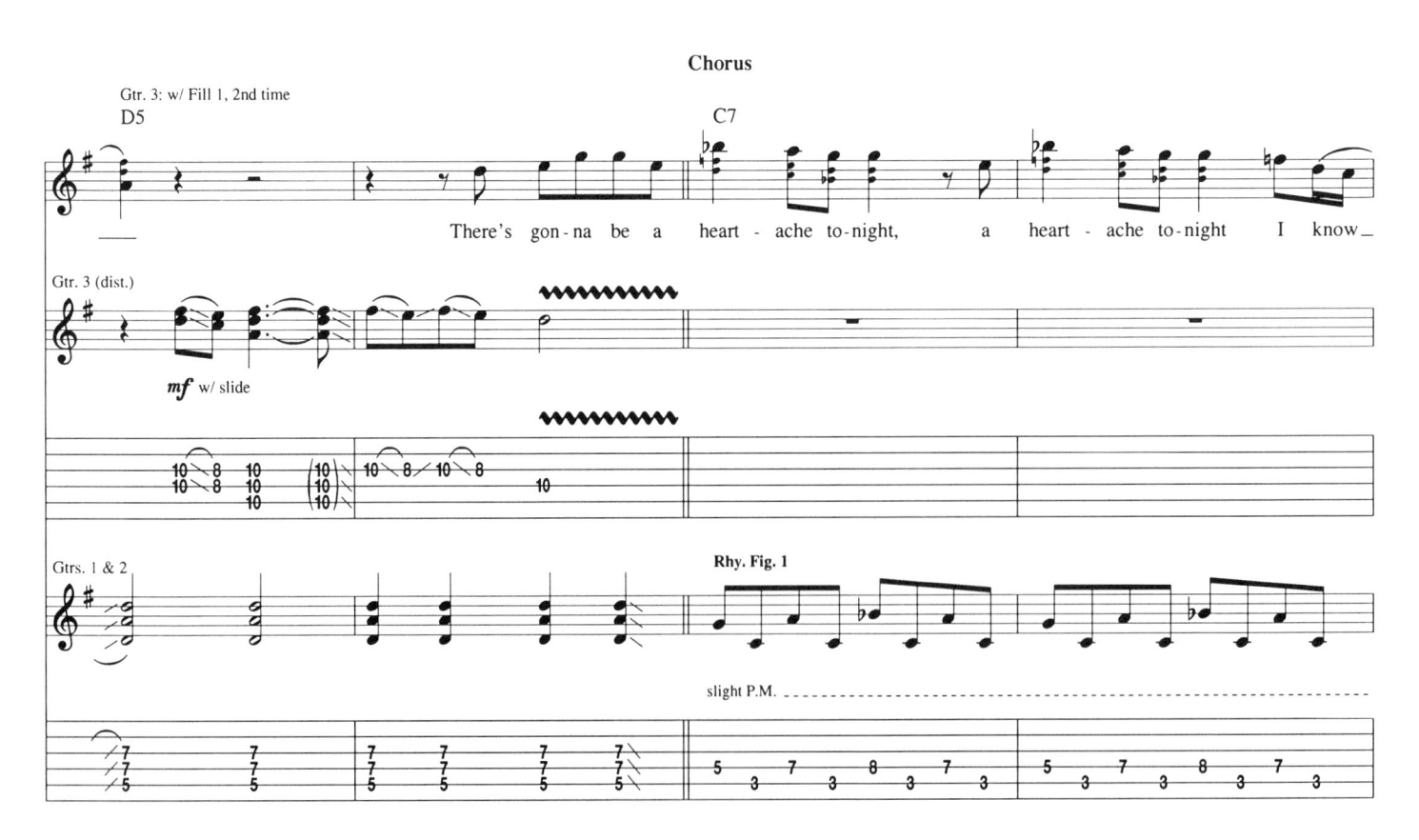

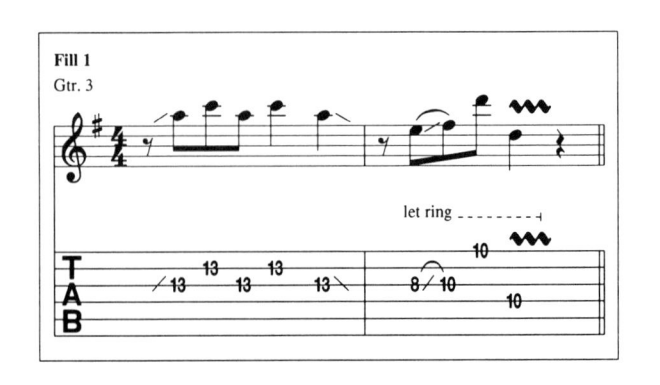

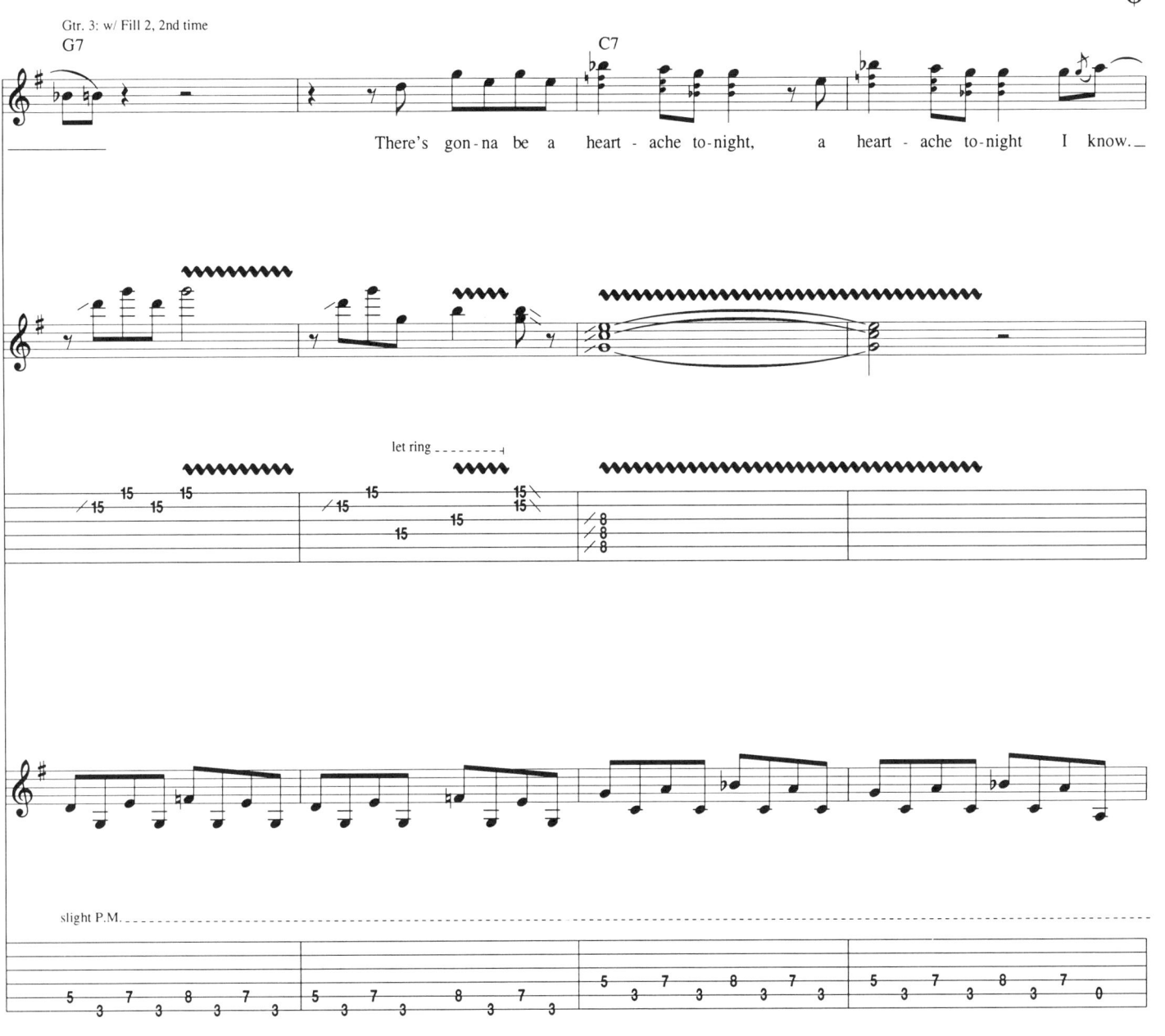

There's gon-na be a heart-ache to-night, a heart-ache to-night I know.

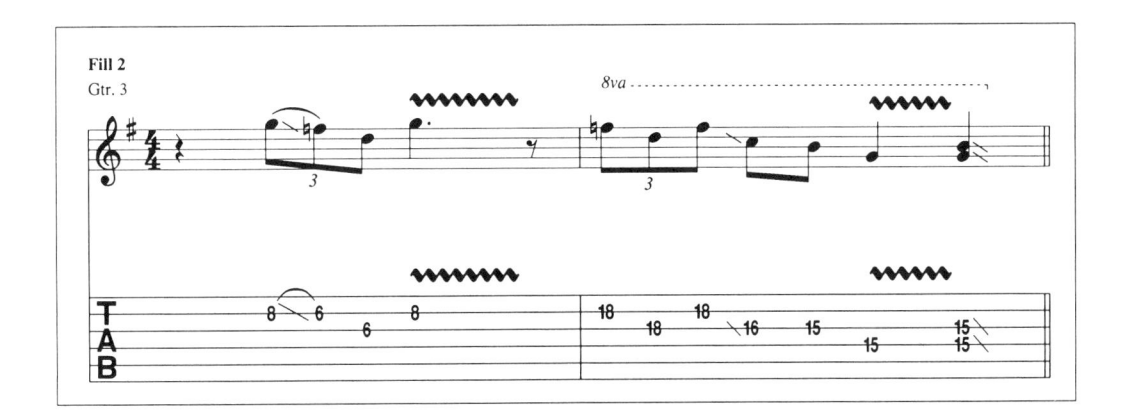

Verse
Gtr. 3 tacet
A7
D7
G
Em
Lord, I know.
2. Some peo-ple like to stay out late.
Gtr. 3
let ring
let ring
Gtr. 1
End Rhy. Fig. 1
slight P.M.
Gtr. 2
Rhy. Fig. 2
slight P.M.
G
Em
G
C
Some folks can't hold out that long.
But no - bod - y wants to go home now;
Gtr. 1
Gtr. 2

there's too much go-in' on. ___ This night is gon-na

last for-ev-er; last all, last all sum-mer long. ___ Some-time be-fore the

61

C G D
sun comes up, the ra-di-o is gon-na play that song. There's gon-na be a
Gtr. 3
let ring
Gtr. 1
Chorus
Gtrs. 1 & 2: w/ Rhy. Fig. 1, simile
C7 G7
heart-ache to-night, a heart-ache to-night I know. There's gon-na be a
Gtr. 3
C7 A7 D7
heart-ache to-night, a heart-ache to-night I know. Lord, I know. There's gon-na be a

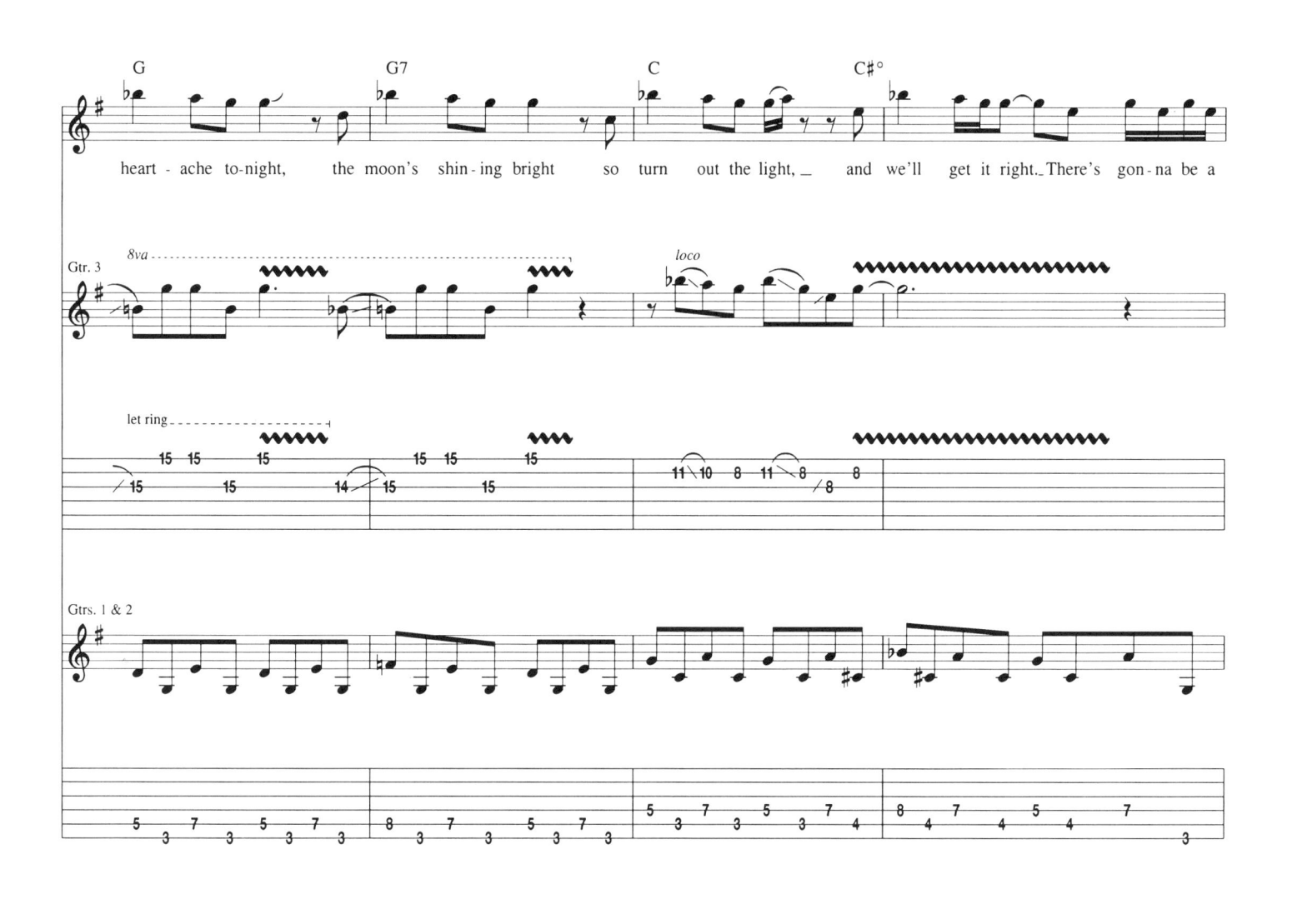

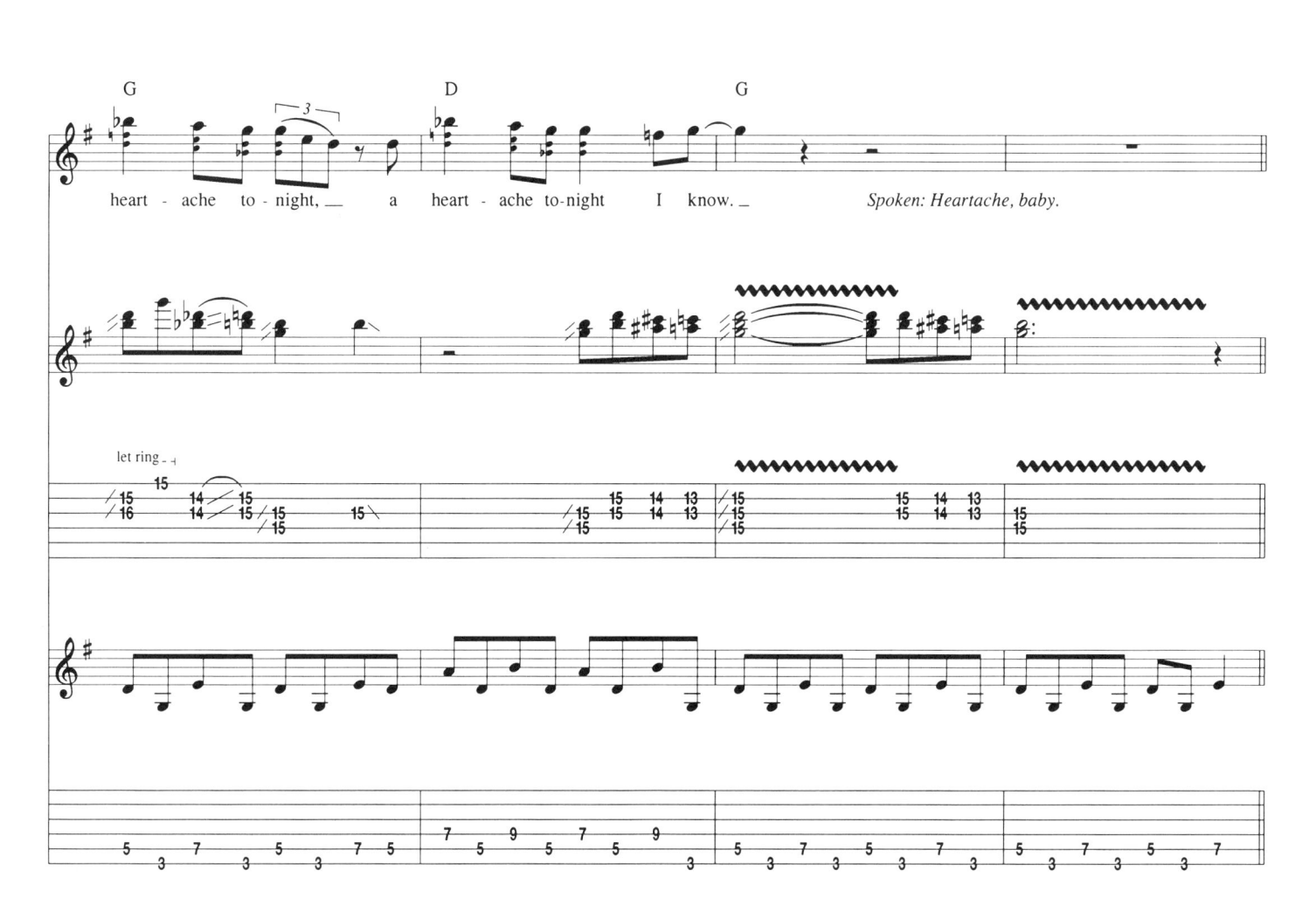

heart-ache to-night, the moon's shin-ing bright so turn out the light, ___ and we'll get it right. There's gon-na be a

heart-ache to-night, ___ a heart-ache to-night I know. ___ *Spoken: Heartache, baby.*

Guitar Solo
Bb F C G Bb F C G
grad. slide
Rhy. Fig. 3
D.S. al Coda
Bb F C G Bb F C G
8va
loco
End Rhy. Fig. 3
Coda
A7 D7 G
Let's go.
We can beat a-round the bush-es we can
Gtr. 3
let ring
let ring
8va
Gtrs. 1 & 2

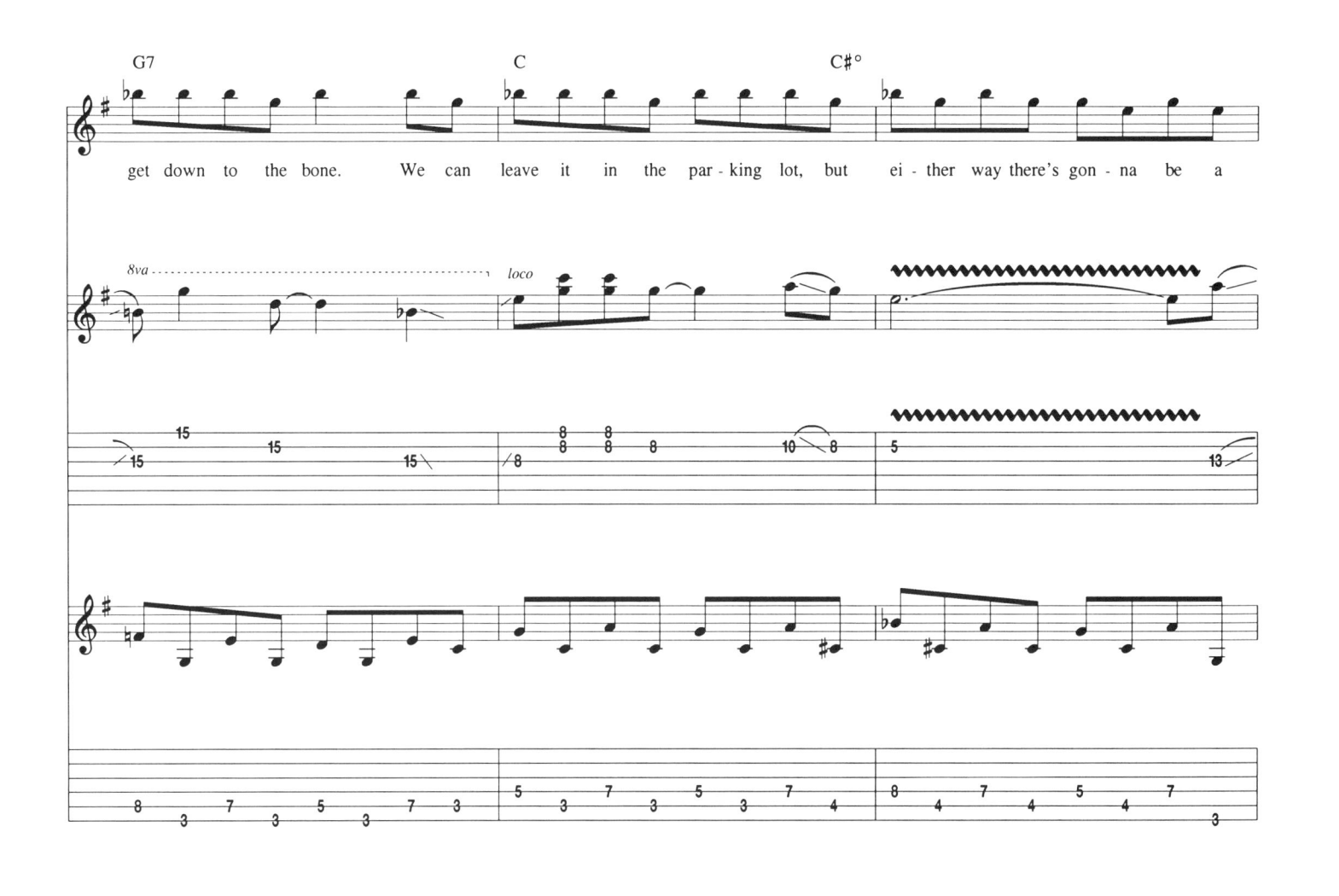

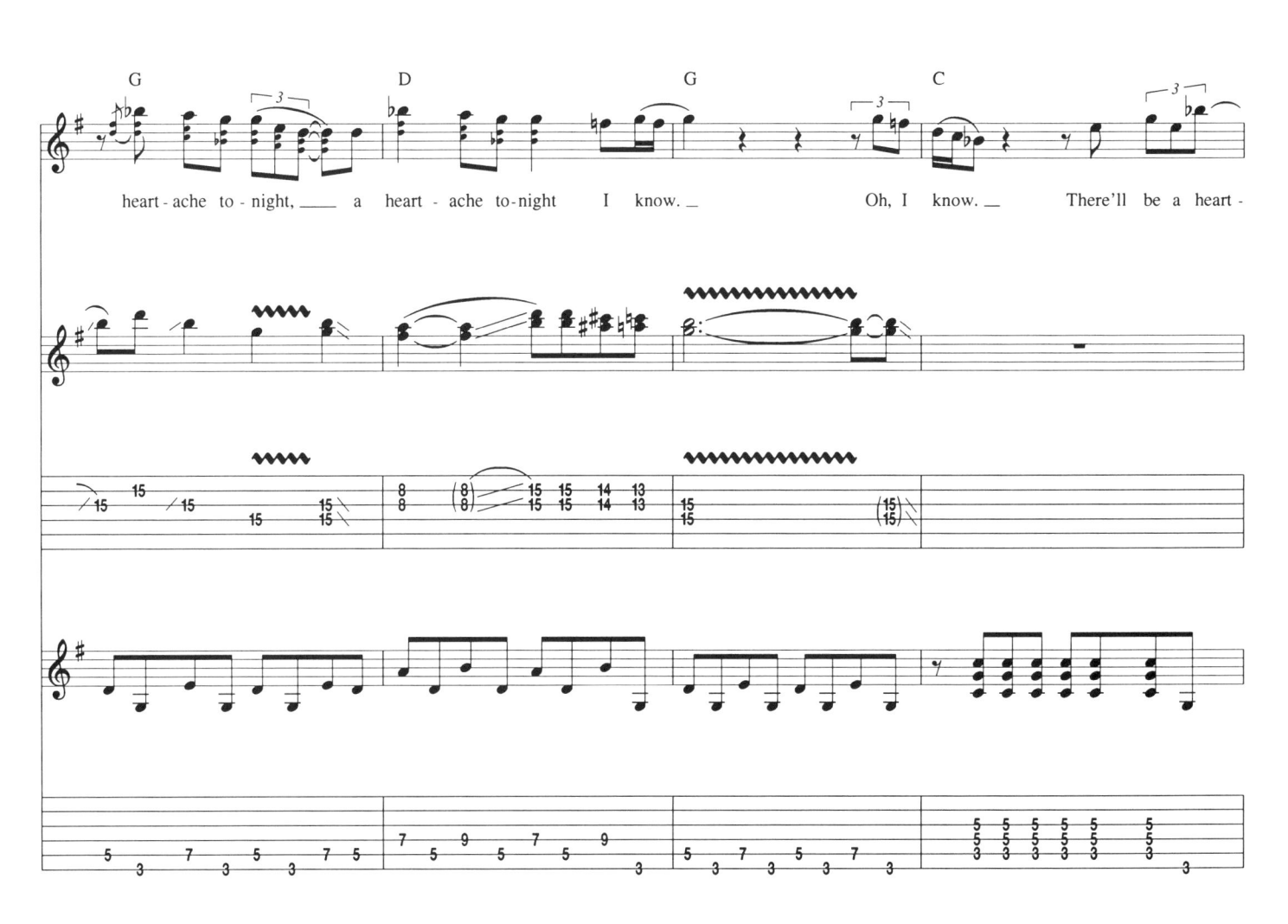

get down to the bone. We can leave it in the par-king lot, but ei-ther way there's gon-na be a heart-ache to-night,_ a heart-ache to-night I know._ Oh, I know._ There'll be a heart-

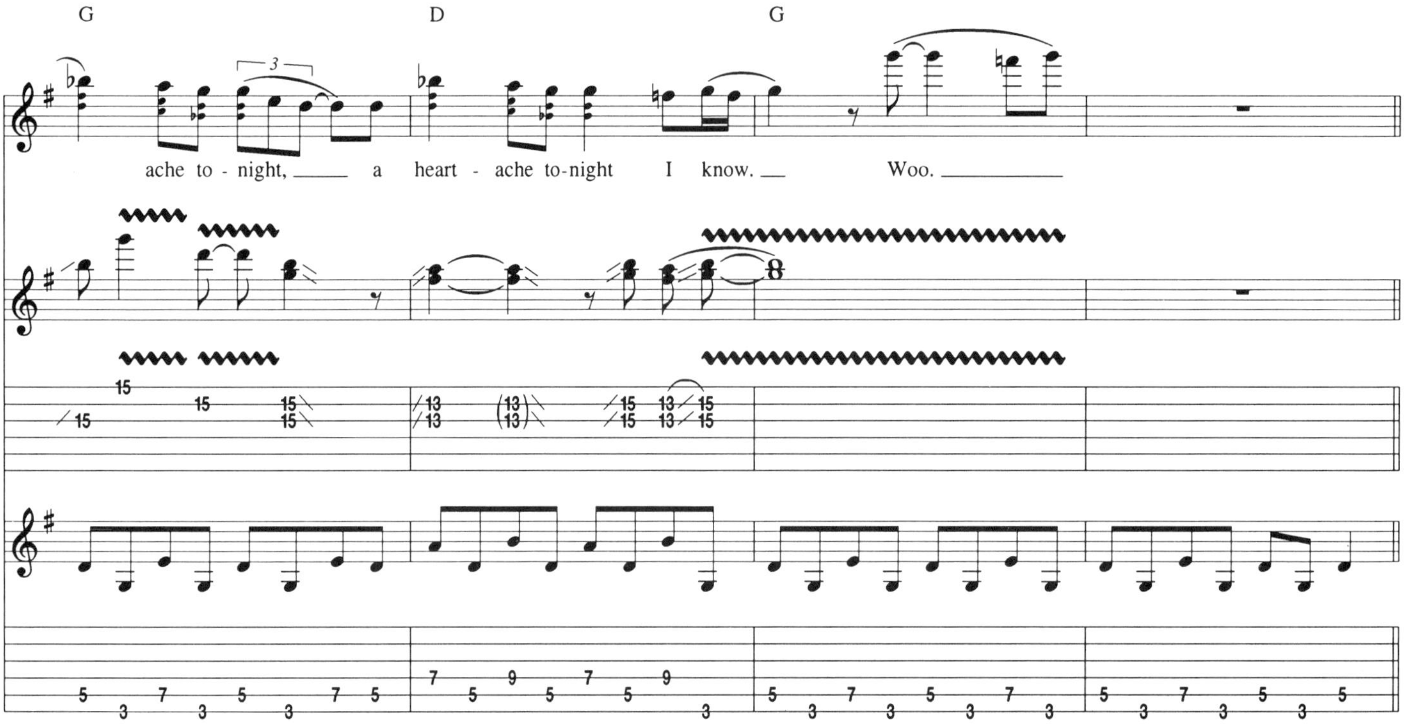

Outro-Guitar Solo

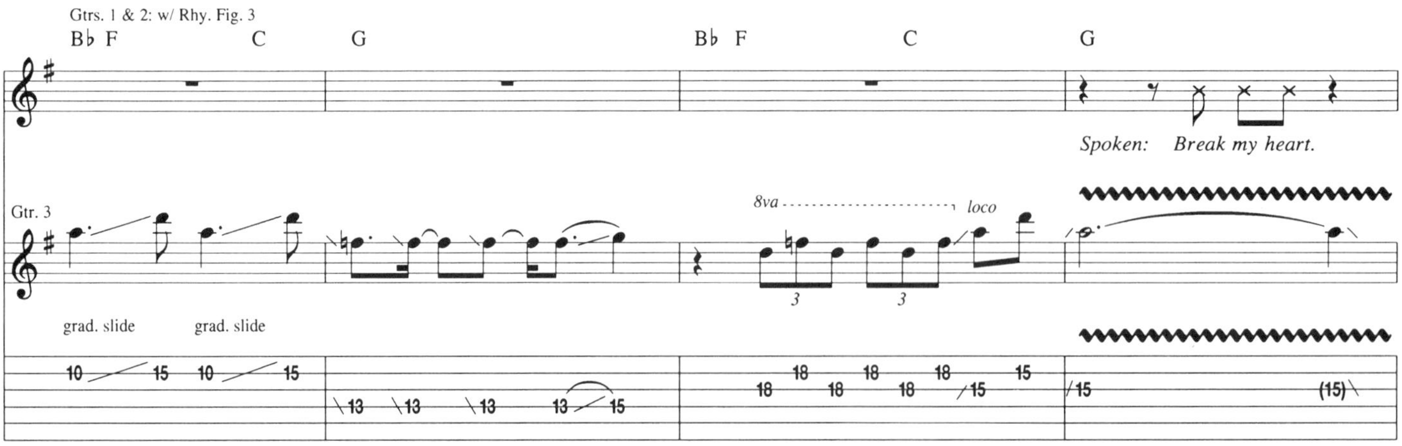

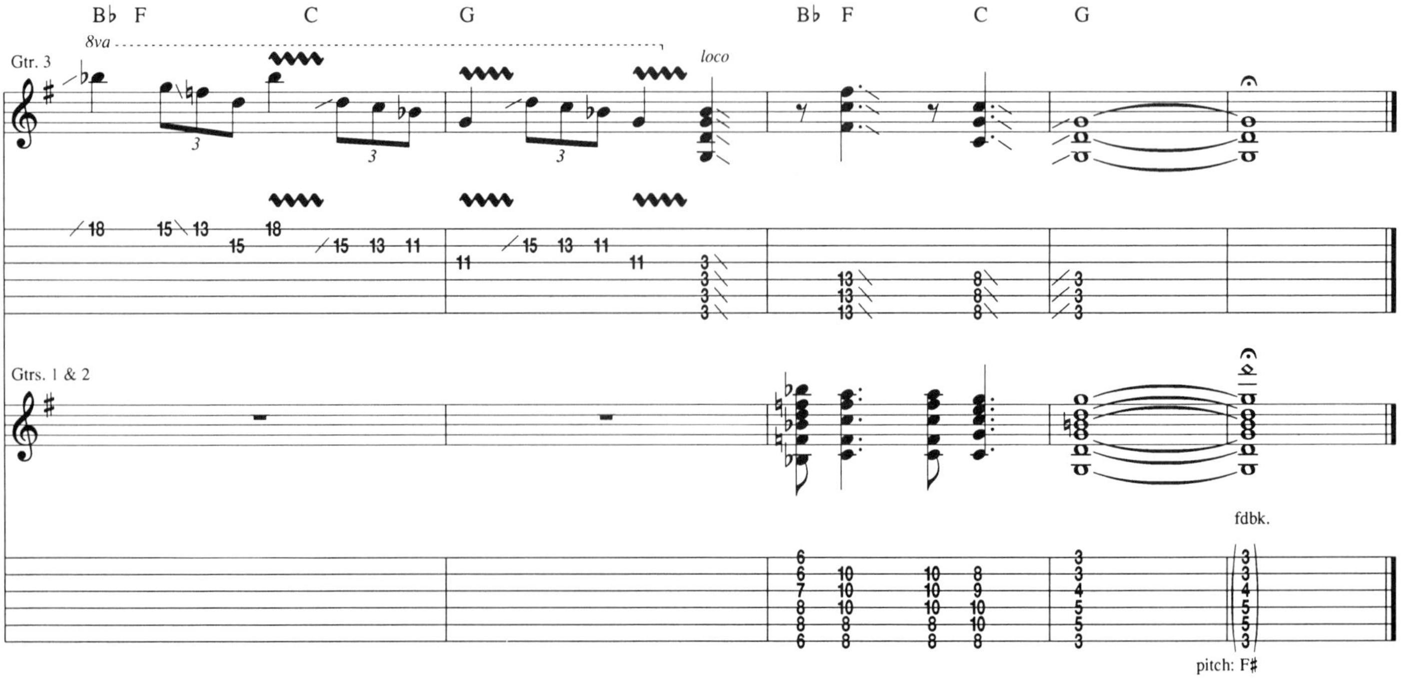

Higher Ground

Words and Music by Stevie Wonder

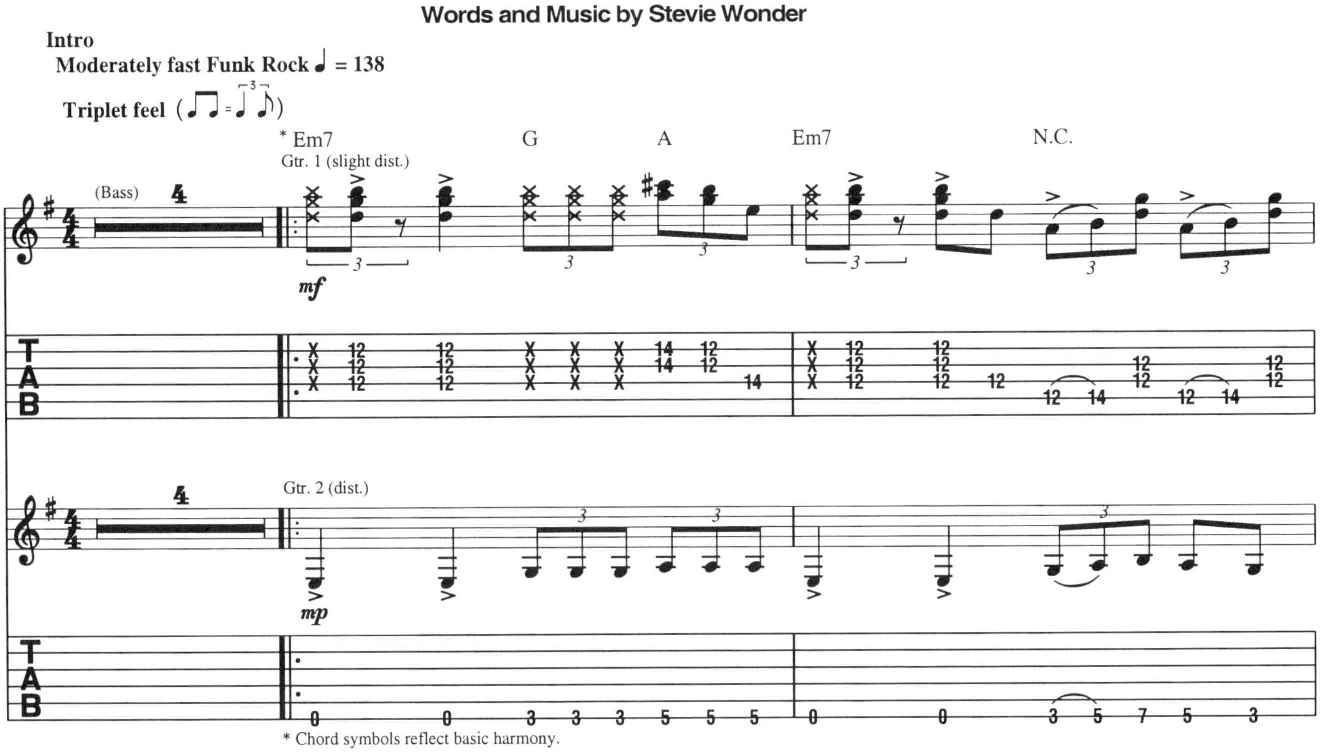

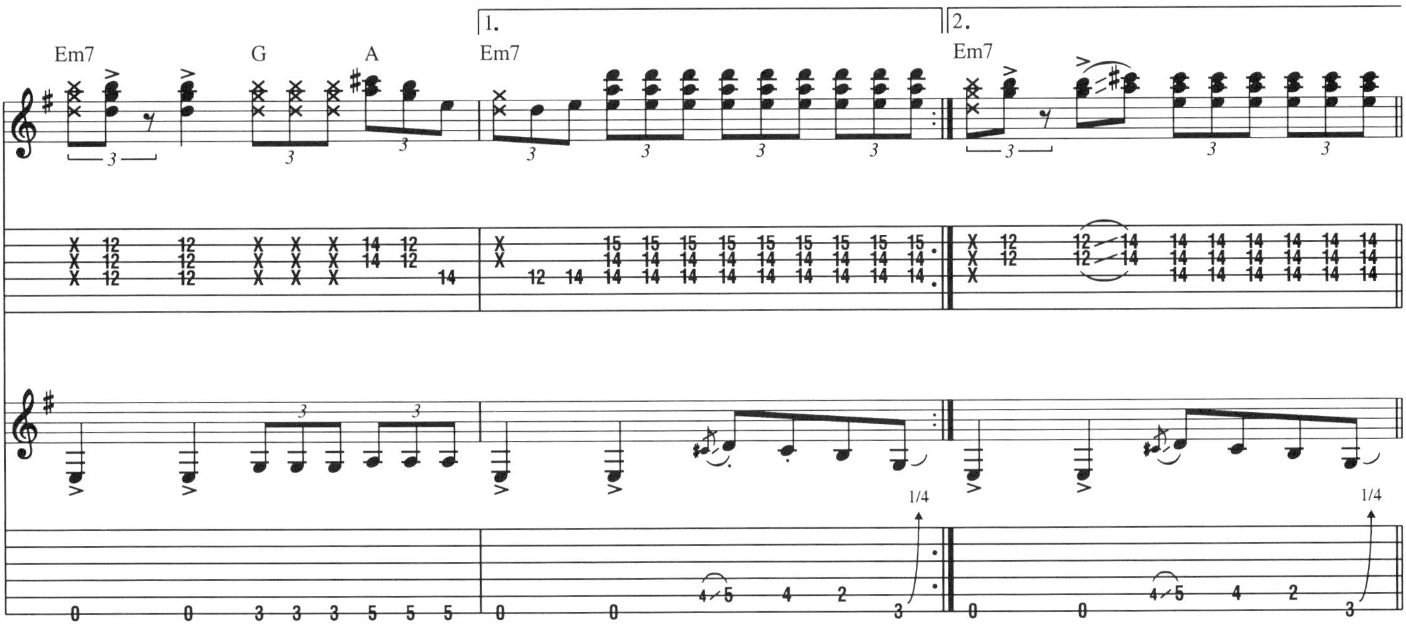

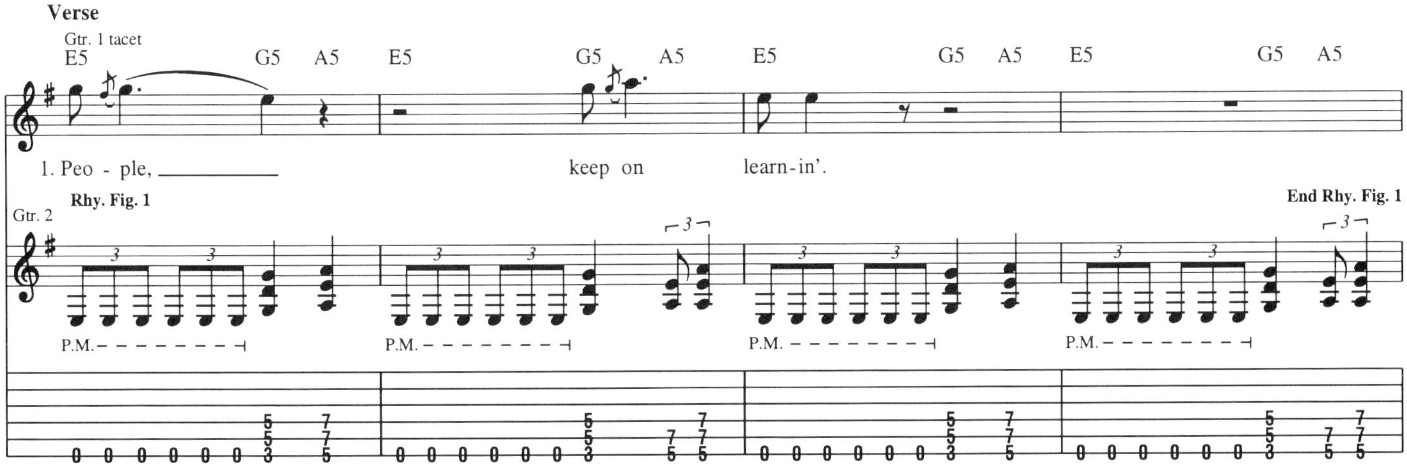

Gtr. 2: w/ Rhy. Fig. 1
E5 G5 A5 E5 G5 A5 E5 G5 A5 E5 G5 A5
Sol - diers, keep on war - rin'. Uh,
F#m7 A B F#m7 A B A
world, keep on turn - in',
Rhy. Fig. 2
Gtr. 1
End Rhy. Fig. 2
Gtr. 2
Rhy. Fig. 2A
D N.C. Em7 G A
'cause it won't be too long.

Em7 G A Em7 G A Em7 G A
2. Uh,
End Rhy. Fig. 2A
Verse
Gtr. 2: w/ Rhy. Fig. 1 (2 times)
Gtr. 1: w/ Rhy. Fill 1 (4 times)
E5 G5 A5 E5 G5 A5 E5 G5 A5 E5 G5 A5
pow - ers a keep on ly - in', while your
E5 G5 A5 E5 G5 A5 E5 G5 A5 E5 G5 A5
peo - ple a keep on dy - in'. Uh,
Gtrs. 1 & 2: w/ Rhy. Figs. 2 & 2A
Gtr. 1: w/ Rhy. Fill 2
F♯m7 A B F♯m7 A B A D N.C.
world, keep on turn - in', 'cause it won't a be too
Rhy. Fill 1
Gtr. 1
Rhy. Fill 2
Gtr. 1

long.

Chorus

I'm so darn glad he let me try it a-gain, 'cause my last time on earth I lived a whole world of sin. I'm so glad that I know more

*Gang vocals, next 9 meas.

2nd time, To Coda
Em7
F#5
B7#5
than I knew then. Gon - na keep on try - in' till I reach the high - est
P.M.
* T
let ring
w/ bar
* T = Thumb on 6th str.
Em7 G A Em7 G A Em7 G A Em7 G A
ground. 3. Uh,
rake
Riff A
End Riff A
Verse
Gtr. 2: w/ Rhy. Fig. 1 (2 times)
E5 G5 A5 E5 G5 A5 E5 G5 A5 E5 G5 A5
teach - ers, a keep on teach - in'. Uh,

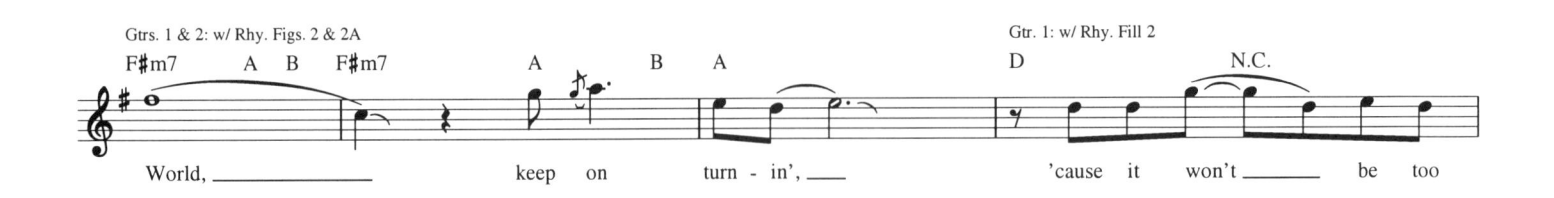

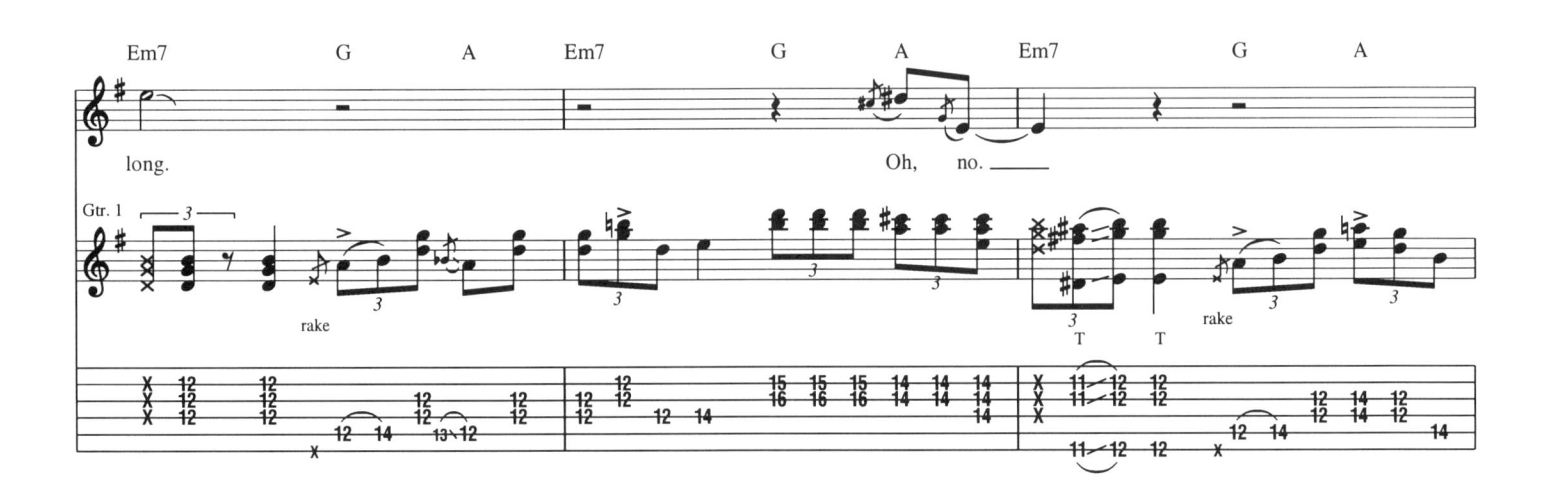

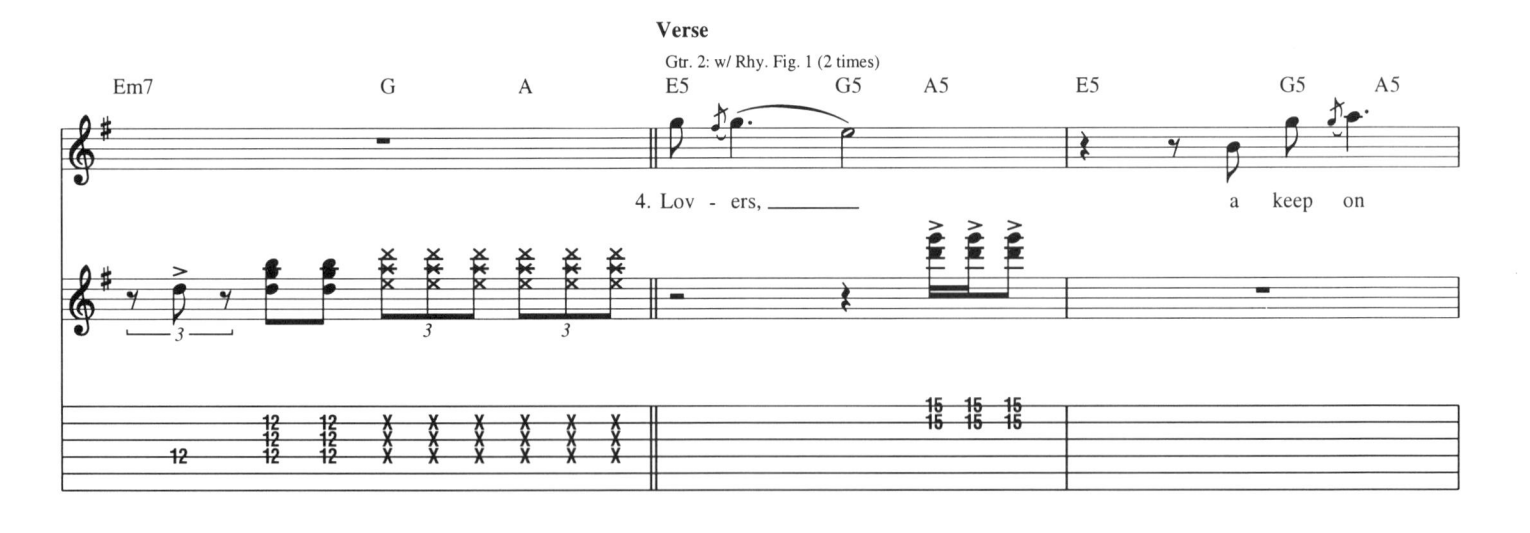

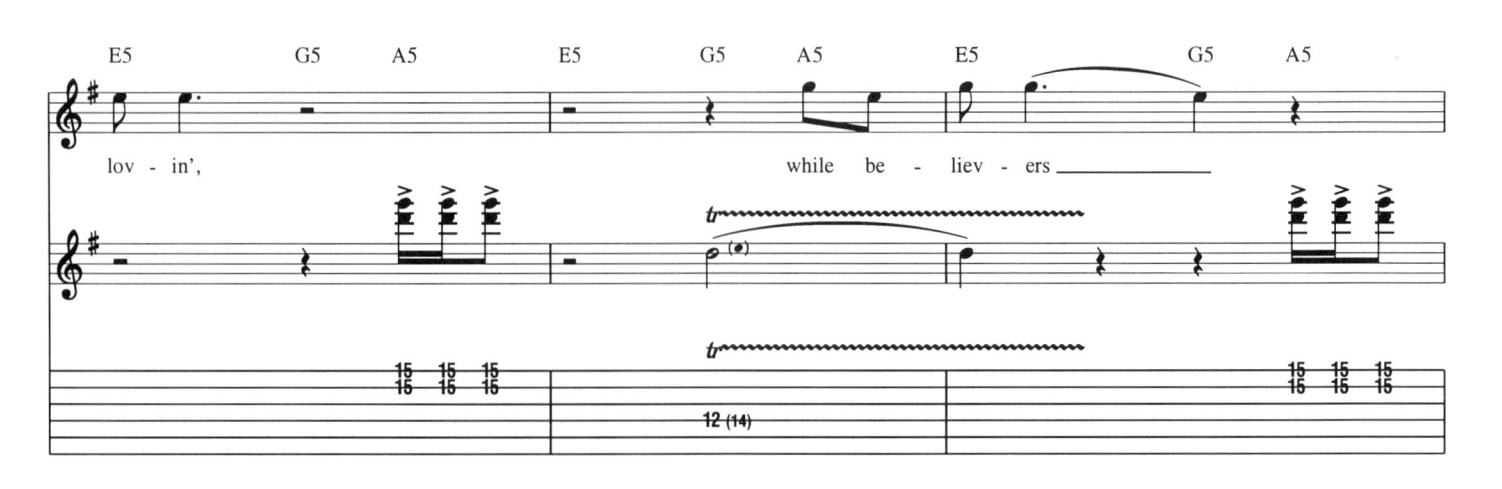

preach - ers, a keep on preach - in'.

World, keep on turn - in', 'cause it won't be too

long. Oh, no.

4. Lov - ers, a keep on

lov - in', while be - liev - ers

73

Em7
G
A
Em7
I reach the high - est ground.
'Cause me 'n' Stev-ie, see, we're gon-na be a sail-in' on
rake
rake
Riff B
1/4
Gtr. 2: w/ Riff B (2 times)
G
A
Em7
G
A
Till I reach the high - est ground.
the get funk-y sound.
Bust - in' out, an' I'll
End Riff B

75

Hold My Hand

Words and Music by Darius Carlos Rucker, Everett Dean Felber, Mark William Bryan and James George Sonefeld

Intro
Moderately Slow ♩ = 82
band tacet

Verse
bass enters

1. With a little love and some tenderness, we'll walk upon the water, we'll rise above the mess. With a little peace and some harmony, we'll

Fill 1
Gtr. 2 (elec.)
mf w/ slight dist.

© 1994 EMI APRIL MUSIC INC. and MONICA'S RELUCTANCE TO LOB
All Rights Controlled and Administered by EMI APRIL MUSIC INC.
All Rights Reserved   International Copyright Secured   Used by Permission

77

Gtr. 1: w/ Rhy. Fig. 2, 2 times
Gtr. 2: w/ Fill 1
Bsus2
E
Bsus2
E
up and let me see you smile. We'll
up, and then I screamed a - loud. I don't wan-na
Gtr. 2: w/ Fill 2
Bsus2
E
Bsus2
E
take a walk to - geth - er, walk the road a - while." 'Cause,
be part of your prob - lems, don't wan-na be part of your crowd, no.
Gtr. 1
let ring
Pre-Chorus
Gtrs. 1 & 2: w/ Rhy. Fig. 3, 2 times
F#
E
B
I got a hand for you.
('Cause, I got a hand for you.)
*Lead harmony 2nd time.
F#
E
B
Won't you let me run with you.
(I wan - na run with you.)
Chorus
B VII
E VII
F# IX
F#sus4
F# IX
F#sus4
Rhy. Fig. 4A
End Rhy. Fig. 4A
Gtr. 3
(clean elec.)
mp
1. Want you to hold my hand.
2. Want you to hold my hand.
(Hold my hand.)
Gtr. 1 & 2
Rhy. Fig. 4
End Rhy. Fig. 4

Gtr. 3: w/ Rhy. Fig. 4A, 2 times
B E F# F#sus4 F# F#sus4
I'll take you to a place where you
I'll take you to the prom - ised
(Hold my hand)
Rhy. Fig. 5
End Rhy. Fig. 5
Gtrs. 1 & 2: w/ Rhy. Fig. 4
B E F# F#sus4 F# F#sus4
can be an - y - thing you wan - na be, be-cause
land. May-be we can change the world but
(Hold my hand.)
E
Gtr. 3
1.
I wan - na love you the best that, the best that I can.
I wan - na love you the
Gtrs. 1 & 2
Gtr. 1: w/ Rhy. Fig. 2, 3 times
Gtr. 2: w/ Fill 1
Gtr. 3 tacet
Bsus2 E Bsus2 E
Gtr. 2: w/ Fill 2
Bsus2 E

2.
Guitar Solo
Gtr. 1: w/ Rhy. Fig. 2, 4 times
Gtr. 3 tacet
Bsus2
E
3. See, I was wast- best that, the best that I can.
Yeah.
Gtr. 1
Gtr. 2
let ring
Gtrs. 1 & 3: w/ Rhy. Fig. 3, 2 times
F♯
B
Oh.
full
hold bend

F♯ E B
Let me run, won't you let me run with you.
hold bend
full
Chorus
*Gtrs. 1 & 2: w/ Rhy. Fig. 4
Gtr. 3: w/ Rhy. Fig. 4A, 3 times
Gtrs. 1 & 2: w/ Rhy. Fig. 5
B E F♯ B E F♯
Want you to hold my hand.
(Hold my hand.) (Hold my hand.
* Gtr. 2 holds notes from end of solo for two beats, then resumes with Rhy. Fig. 4
Gtrs. 1 & 2: w/ Rhy. Fig. 4
F♯7 B E F♯
I'll take you to a place where you can be anything you wanna be, because
) (Hold my hand.)
E IX
Gtr. 3
I, oh, no, no, no, no, no.
Gtrs. 1 & 2

Gtrs. 1 & 2: w/ Rhy. Fig. 4
Gtr. 3: w/ Rhy. Fig. 4A, 3 times
B E F♯
Want you to hold my hand.
(Hold my hand.)
Gtrs. 1 & 2: w/ Rhy. Fig. 5
B E F♯
(Hold my hand.
F♯7
I'll take you to the prom - ised land.
)
Gtrs. 1 & 2: w/ Rhy. Fig. 4
B E F♯
(Hold my hand.)
May-be we can't change the world, but
E^IX
Gtr. 3
I wan - na love you the best that, the best that I can.
Gtrs. 1 & 2
Gtr. 1: w/ Rhy. Fig. 2, 2 times, simile
Gtr. 2: w/ Fill 1
Gtr. 3: tacet
Bsus2 E Bsus2 E
Oh.
Best that I can.
Bsus2 E E Bsus2 E E
open
Gtr. 3
Gtrs. 1 & 2

I Want You To Want Me (Live)

Words and Music by Rick Nielsen

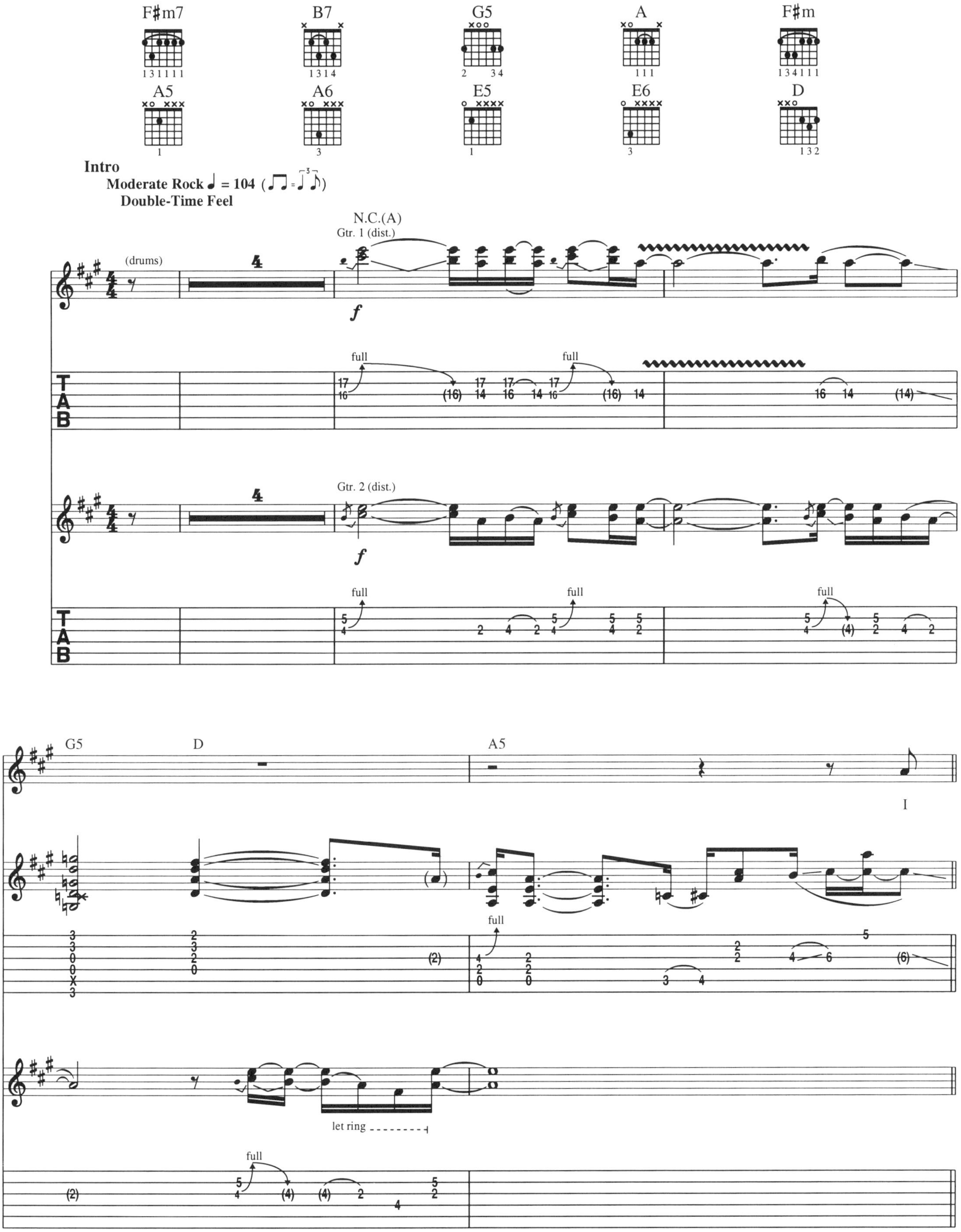

84

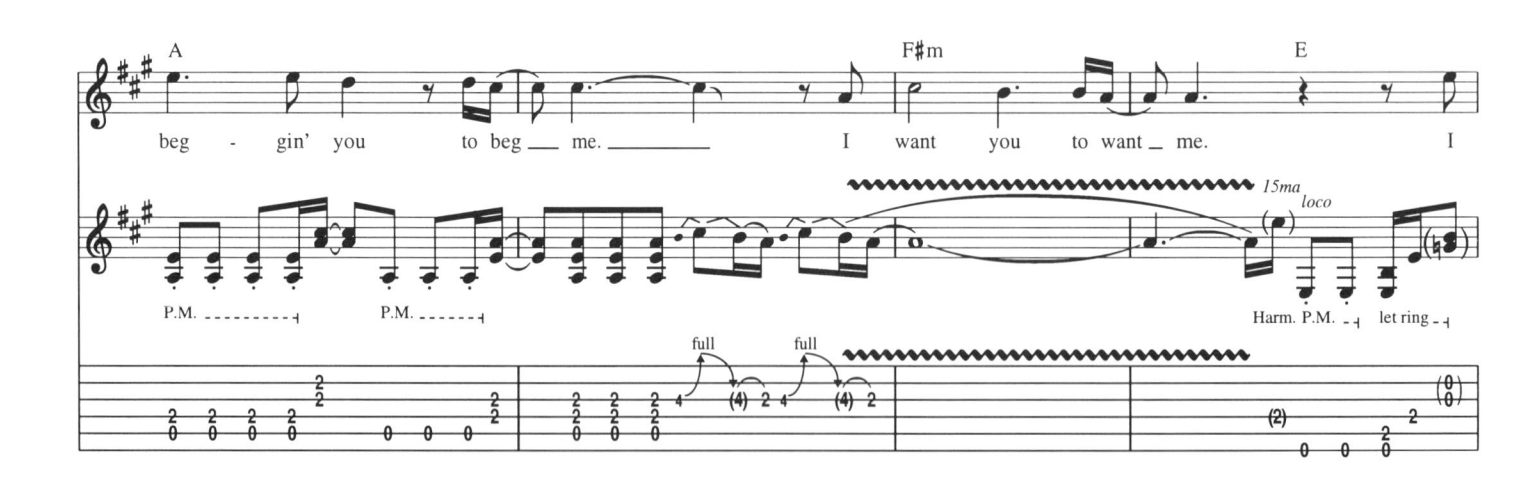

shine up the old brown shoes, put on a brand-new shirt. I'll get home ear-ly from work if you say that you love me.

Pre-Chorus

Did-n't I, did-n't I, did-n't I see you cry-in'? Oh, did-n't I, did-n't I, did-n't I see you cry-in'?

Feel-in' all a-lone with-out a friend, you know you feel like dy-in'. Oh,

Chorus
Gtr. 2 tacet
F♯ F♯m D A
6 2fr
P.M.
End Rhy. Fig. 1A
End Rhy. Fig. 1
did-n't I, did-n't I, did-n't I see you cry - in'? I want you to want
me. I need you to need me. I'd love you to love
me. I'm beg - gin' you to beg me. I'll
shine up the old brown shoes, put on a brand - new shirt. I'll
A/G♯ F♯m E D D/C♯ A A/G♯ F♯m7 B5 G5 G6 G5 A5
full
let ring
1/2

F#m7 B7 G G5 F#m F#5 G5 G#5
⑥ 3fr
Gtr. 2
(cont. in notation)
get home ear-ly from work if you say that you love me.
*Gtrs. 1 & 2
let ring
P.M. P.M.
*Composite arrangement
Pre-Chorus
Gtr. 1: w/ Rhy. Fig. 1, 1st 3 meas., simile
Gtr. 2: w/ Rhy. Fig. 1A, 2 times, simile
A5 A6 A5 A6 A5 E5 E6 E5 E6 F#m D
Did-n't I, did-n't I, did-n't I see you cry - in'? Oh, did-n't I, did-n't I, did-n't I see you cry -
Gtr. 1: w/ Rhy. Fill 1
Gtr. 1: w/ Rhy. Fig. 1, last 3 meas., simile
A5 A6 A5 A6 A5
- in'? Feel - in' all a - lone with - out a friend, you know you feel like dy -
E5 E6 E5 E6 F#m D
- in'. Oh, did - n't I, did - n't I, did - n't I see you cry -
Guitar Solo
Gtr. 2: w/ Rhy. Fig. 1A, simile
A5 A6 A5 A6 A5 E5 E6 E5 E6
- in'? Oh.
Gtr. 1
1/4 1/2 1/2 1/2 1/2 1/2 1/2 1/2
Rhy. Fill 1
Gtr. 1
full
T A B

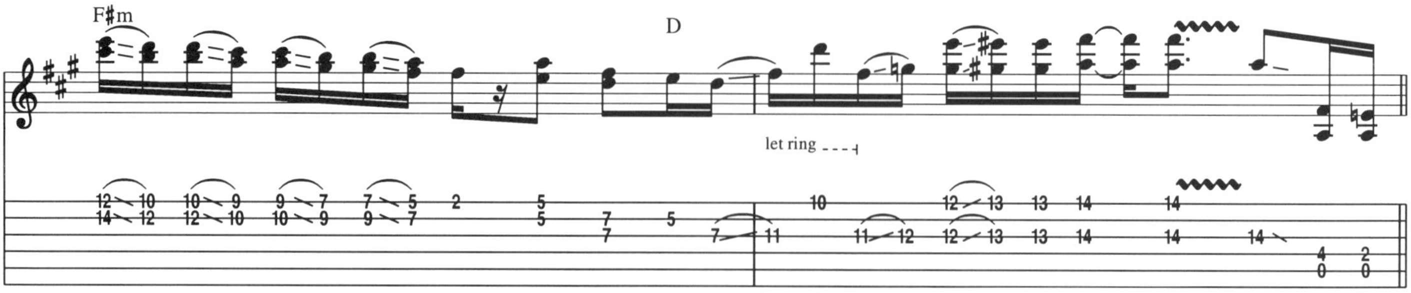

Pre-Chorus

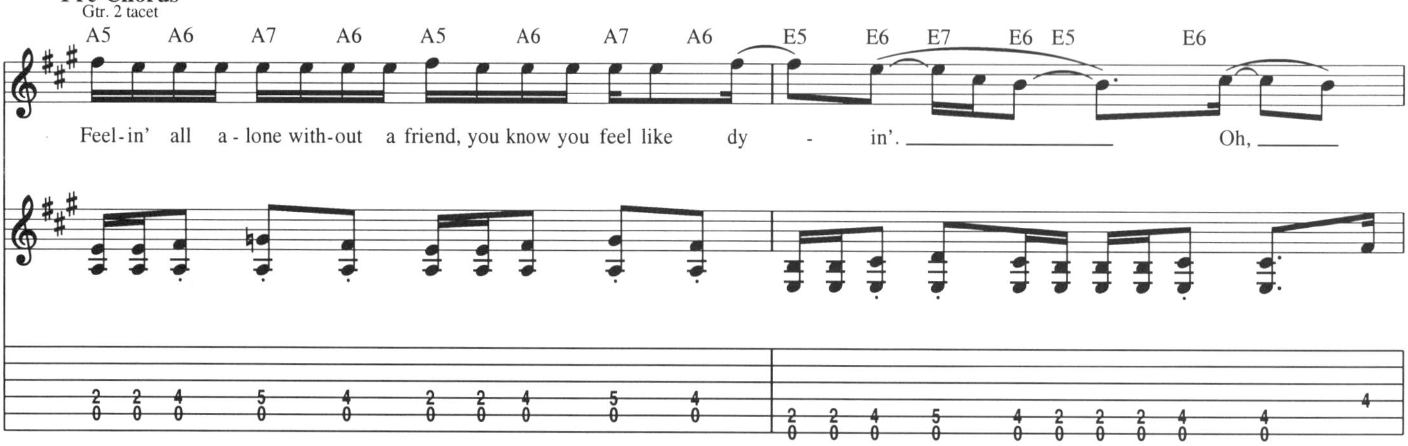

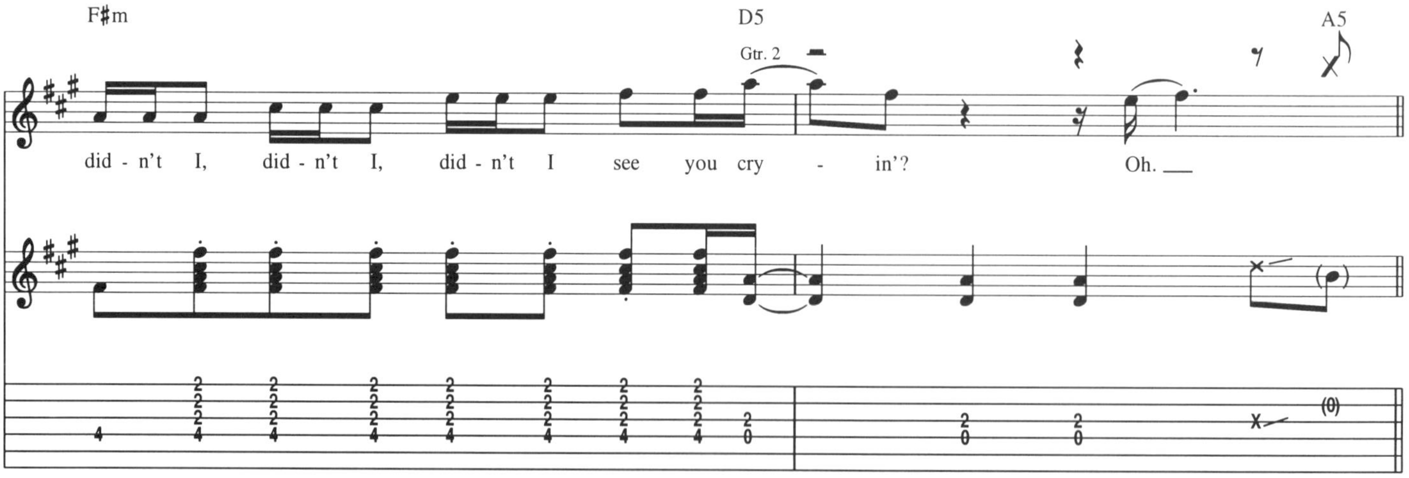

Guitar Solo

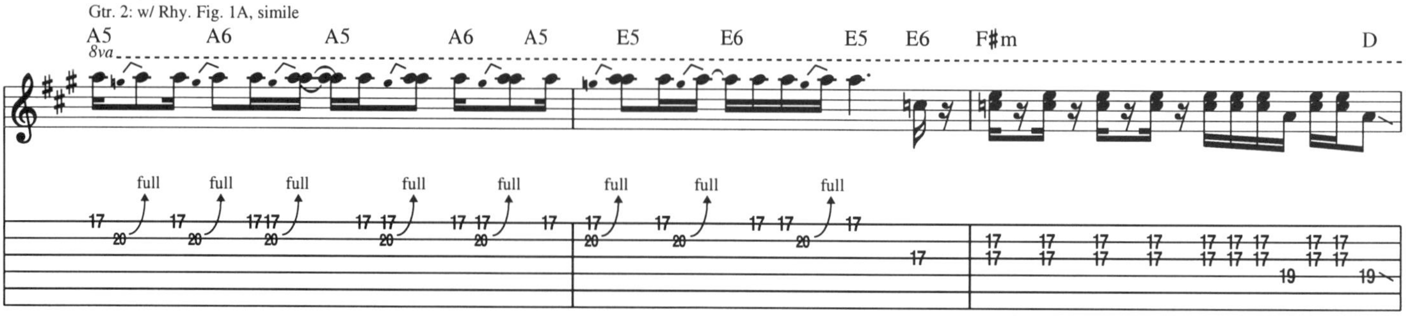

Chorus
Gtr. 2 tacet
A
A/G♯
I want you to want me. I
8va
loco
P.M.
full
*Chords implied by bass (next 8 bars).
F♯m
E
D
D/C♯
need you to need me. I'd love you to love me. I'm
begin' you to beg me. I
Breakdown
End Double-Time Feel
N.C.(A)
want you to want me. I
want you to want me. I want you to want
1/2

me. I want you to want me.

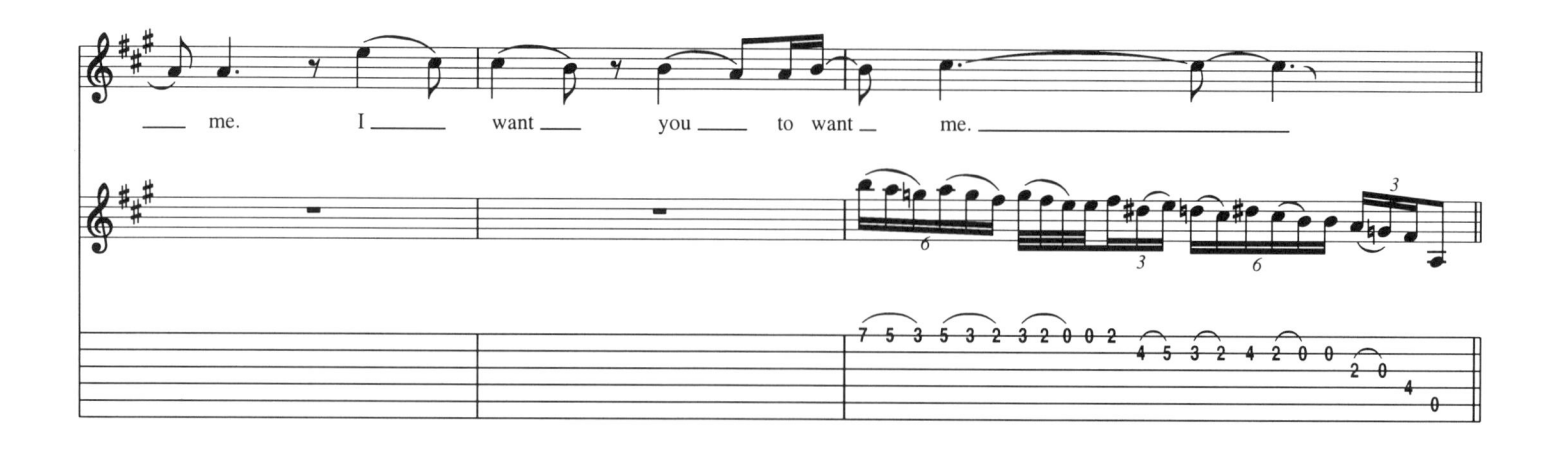

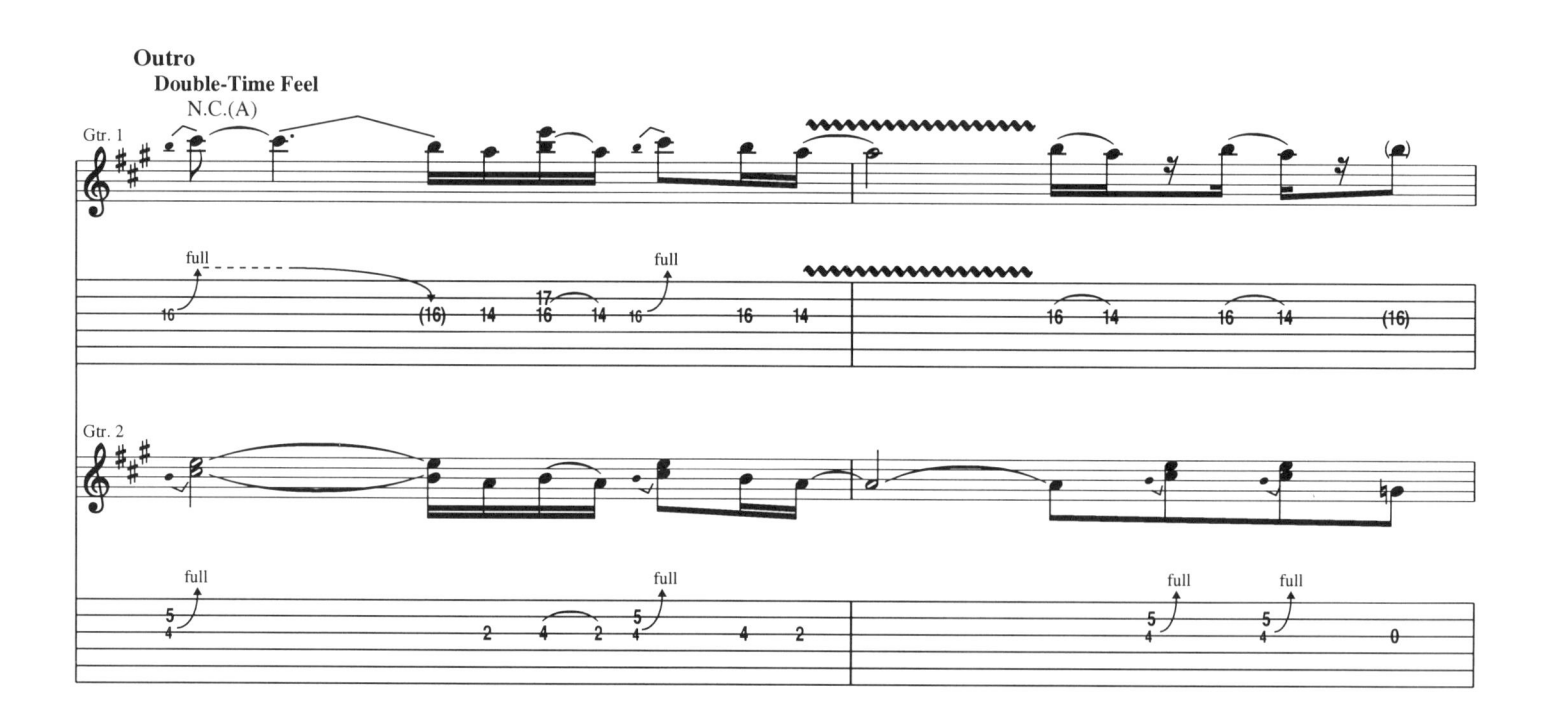

Outro
Double-Time Feel

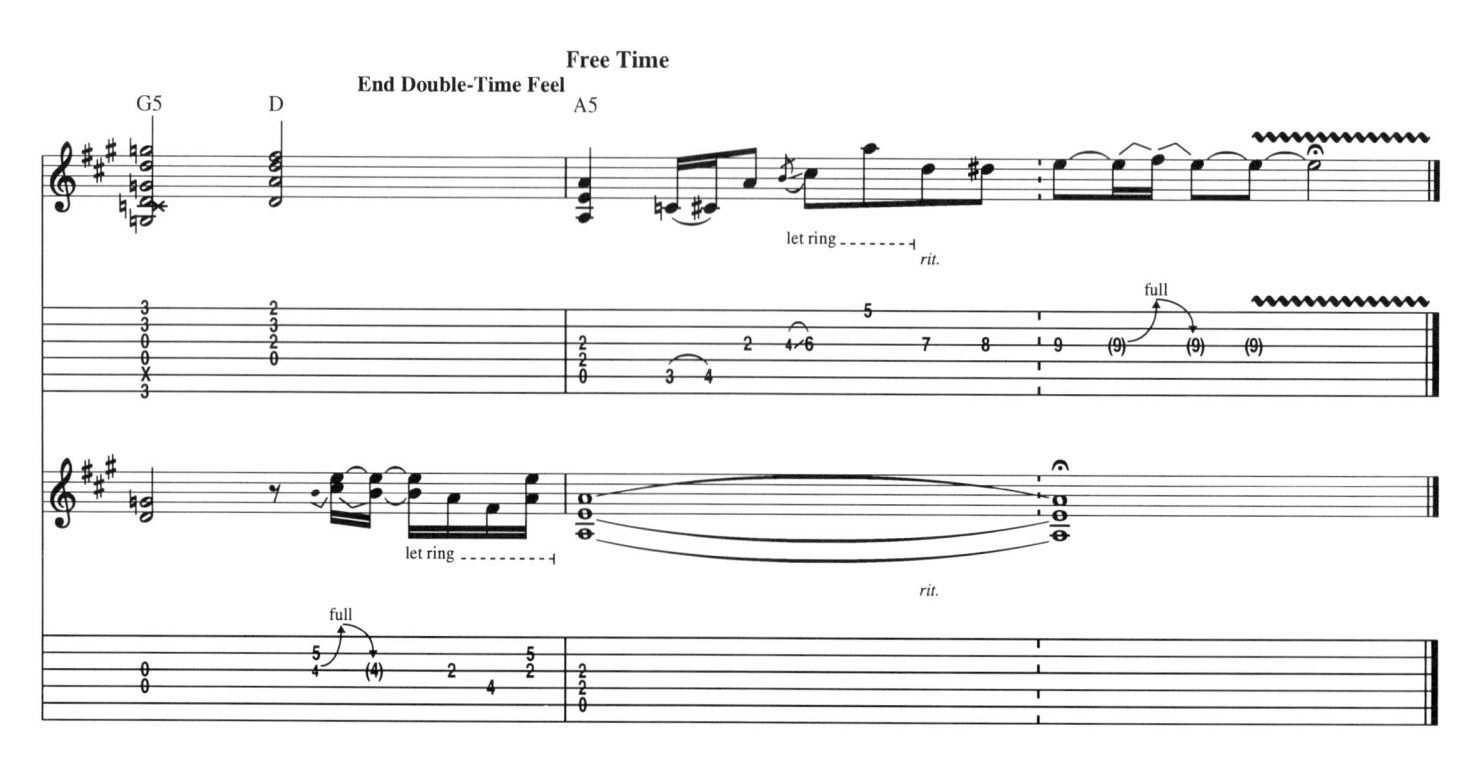

Free Time
End Double-Time Feel

If You Leave Me Now

Words and Music by Peter Cetera

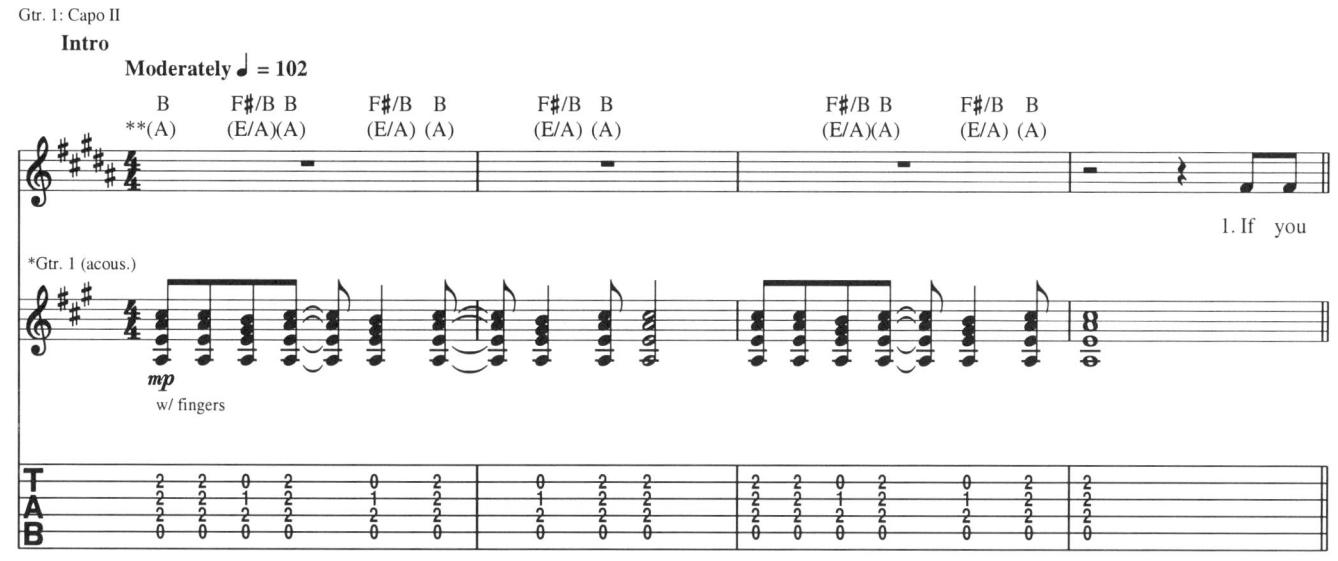

Gtr. 1: Capo II

Intro — Moderately ♩ = 102

Gtr. 1 (acous.) — mp, w/ fingers

* Two gtrs. arr. for one.
** Symbols in parentheses represent chord names respective to capoed guitar. Symbols above reflect actual sounding chord. Capoed fret is "0" in TAB.

Verse — *Rhy. Fig. 1, let ring throughout* ... *End Rhy. Fig. 1*

Copyright © 1976 by BMG Songs, Inc. and Big Elk Music
International Copyright Secured   All Rights Reserved

92

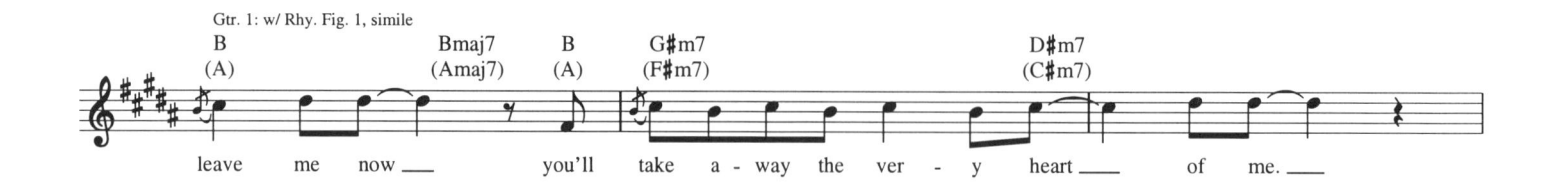

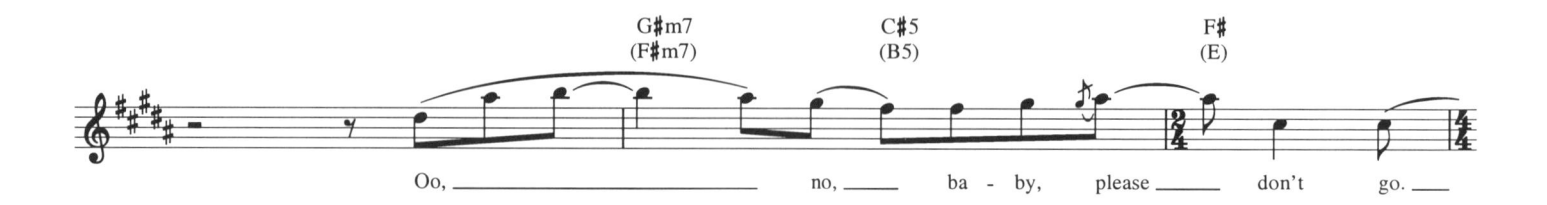

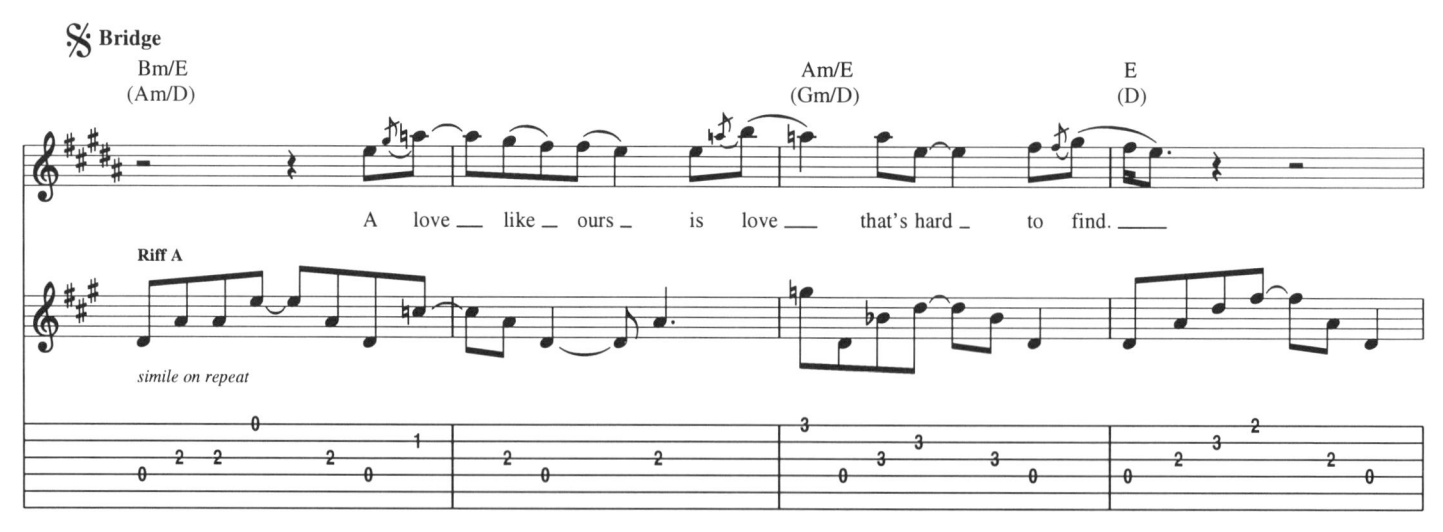

Gtr. 1: w/ Riff A, simile
Bm/E (Am/D)
Am/E (Gm/D)
E (D)
We've come too far to leave it all be - hind.
G♯m7 (F♯m7)
E (D)
F♯ (E)
B (A)
How could we end it all this way? When to - mor -
D♯m7 (C♯m7)
G♯m7 (F♯m7)
Gtr. 2 tacet
C♯m7 (Bm7)
- row comes and we both re - gret the things we said to - day.
Gtr. 2 (acous.)
mf
Gtr. 1
To Coda
Guitar Solo
Bm/E (Am/D)
Bmaj7 (Amaj7)
G♯m7 (F♯m7)
Gtr. 3 (12-str. acous.)
mf
Gtr. 2
w/ pick & fingers
Gtr. 1

* Played behind the beat.

D.S. al Coda

2. If you leave_ me now_ you'll take a-way the big-gest part_

Gtr. 4: w/ Fill 1
Gtr. 2 tacet
G#m7 (F#m7)
C#5 (B5)
F# (E)
of me.
Oo,
1., 3. no, ba - by, please don't go.
2. Oo, girl, just got to have you by
4. Oo, my, my, I just got to have your lov -
Gtr. 3
Gtr. 1
Play 4 Times and Fade
B (A)
G#m7 (F#m7)
C#5 (B5)
F# (E)
B (A)
F#/B B (E/A)(A)
F#/B B (E/A)(A)
F#/B B (E/A)(A)
my side.
- in', yeah.
Gtr. 3
Gtr. 1
Fill 1
Gtr. 4 (elec.)
mp
w/ clean tone
H.H.
let ring

Jailhouse Rock

Words and Music by Jerry Leiber and Mike Stoller

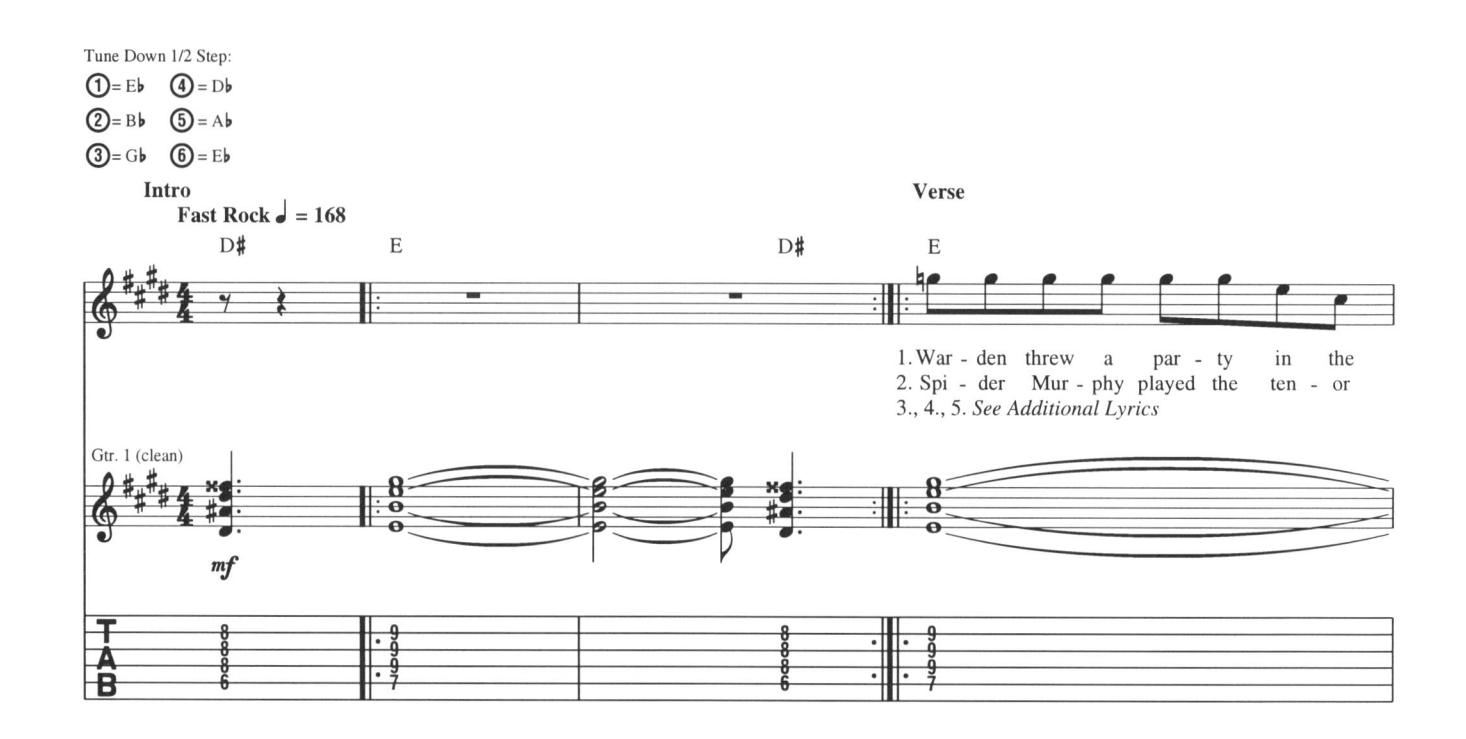

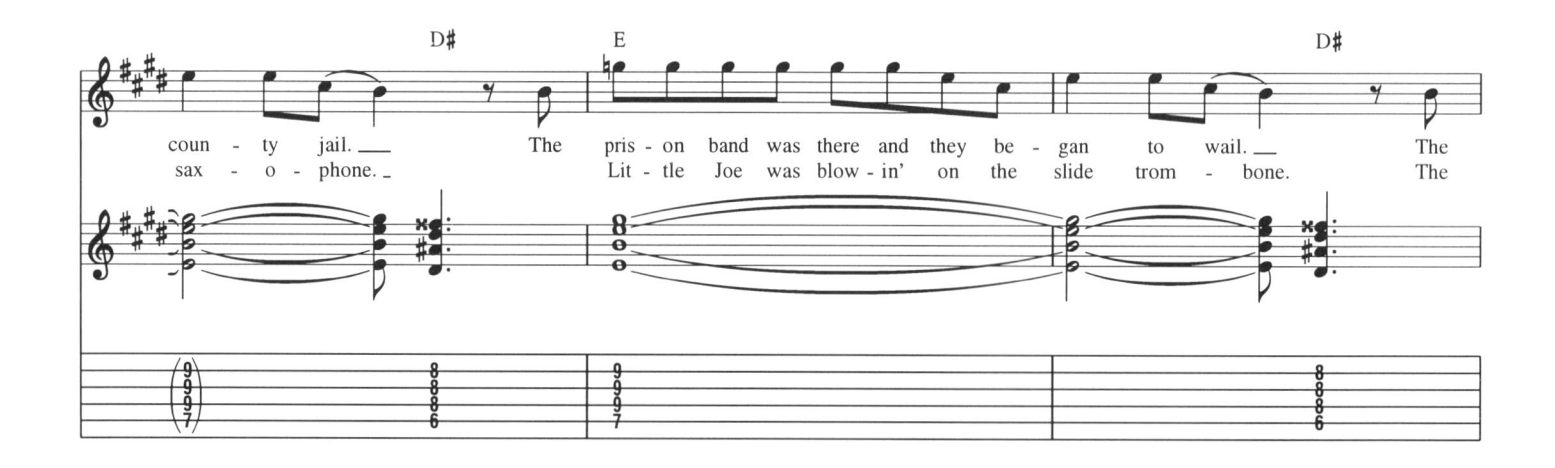

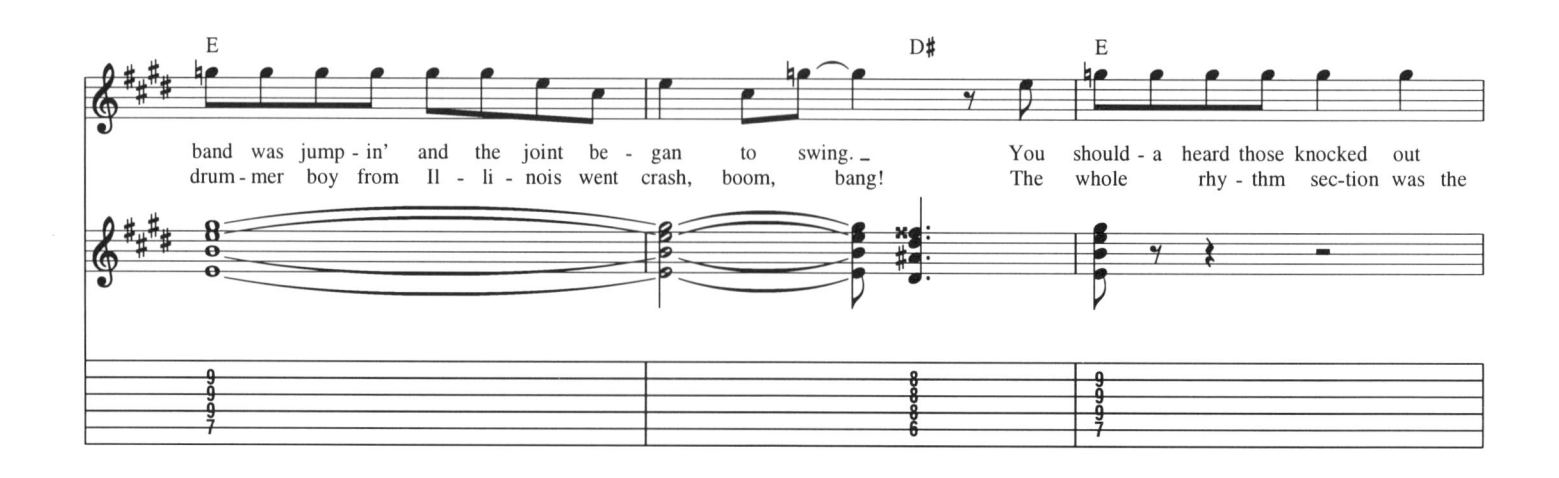

Tune Down 1/2 Step:
① = E♭ ④ = D♭
② = B♭ ⑤ = A♭
③ = G♭ ⑥ = E♭

Intro
Fast Rock ♩ = 168

1. War-den threw a par-ty in the coun-ty jail. The pris-on band was there and they be-gan to wail. The band was jump-in' and the joint be-gan to swing. You should-a heard those knocked out
2. Spi-der Mur-phy played the ten-or sax-o-phone. Lit-tle Joe was blow-in' on the slide trom-bone. The drum-mer boy from Il-li-nois went crash, boom, bang! The whole rhy-thm sec-tion was the
3., 4., 5. *See Additional Lyrics*

© 1957 (Renewed) JERRY LEIBER MUSIC and MIKE STOLLER MUSIC
All Rights Reserved

97

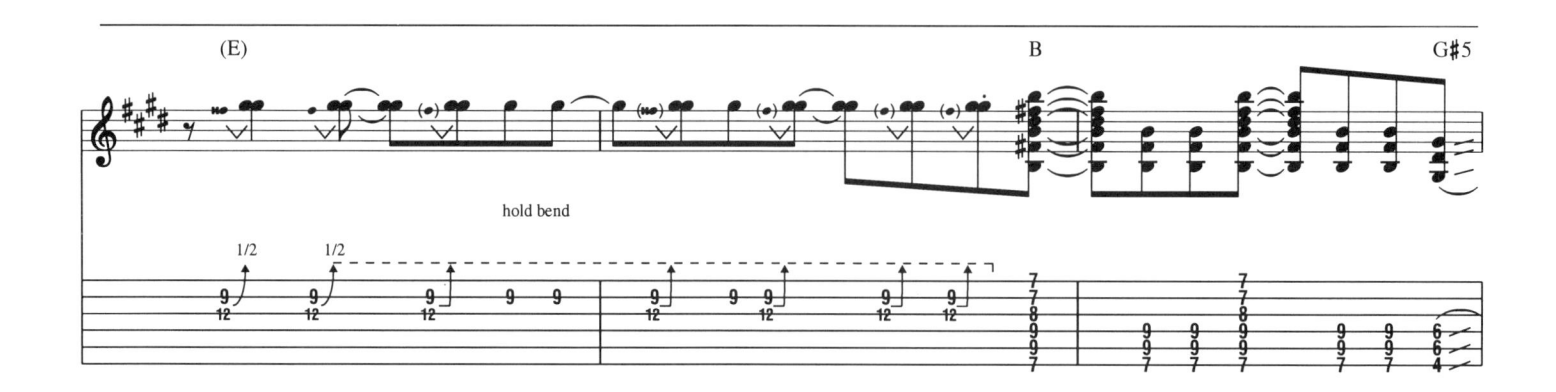

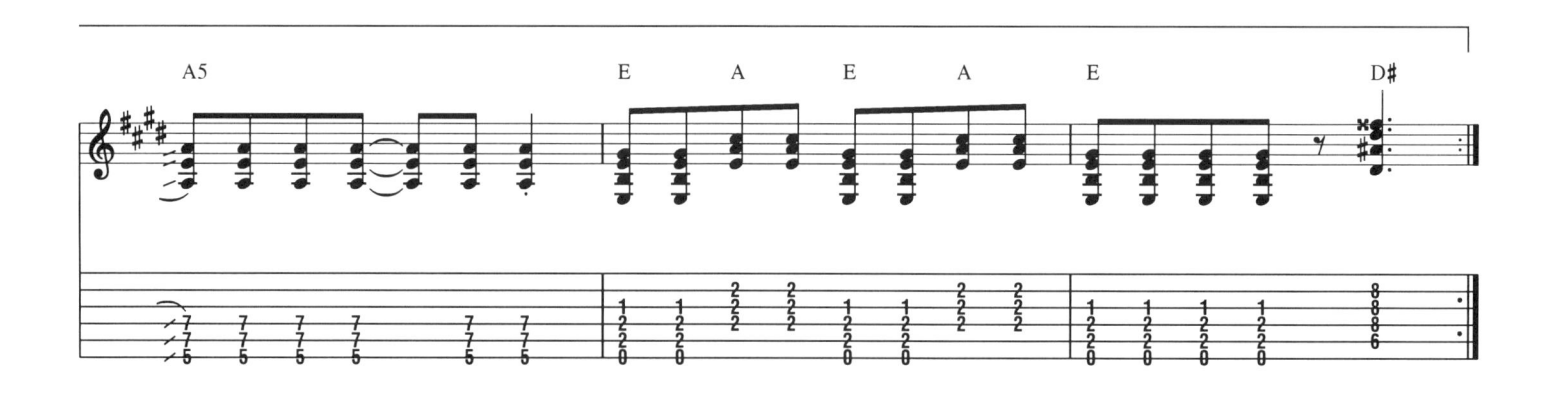

Additional Lyrics

3. Number forty-seven said to number three,
   "You the cutest jailbird I ever did see.
   I sure would be delighted with your company.
   Come on, and do the Jailhouse Rock with me."

4. Sad Sack was sittin' on a block of stone,
   Way over in the corner weepin' all alone.
   The warden said, "Hey, buddy, don't you be no square.
   If you can't find a partner use a wooden chair."

5. Shifty Henry said to Bugs "For heaven's sake,
   No one's lookin', now's our chance to make a break."
   Bugs, he turned to Shifty and he said, "Nix, nix,
   I wanna stick around awhile to get my kicks."

Learning to Fly

Words and Music by Jeff Lynne and Tom Petty

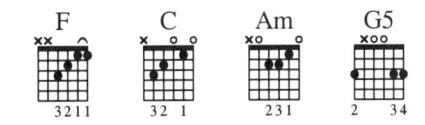

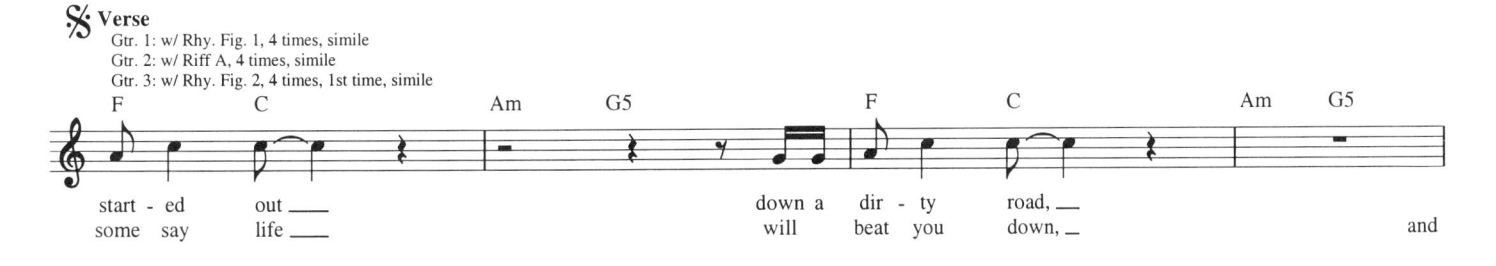

Gtr. 3: w/ Rhy. Fig. 2, 2 times, simile
2nd time, Bkgd. Voc.: w/ Voc. Fill 1, 4 times
F C Am G5 F C Am G5
sun went down as I crossed the hill. And the
start - ed out for God knows where. I
F C Am G5 F C
town lit up, the world got still.
guess I'll know when I get there.
Chorus
Gtr. 1: w/ Rhy. Fig. 1, 2 times, simile
Gtr. 2: w/ Riff A, 2 times, simile
Gtr. 3: w/ Rhy. Fig. 2, 2 times, simile
Am G5 F C Am G5 F C Am G5
I'm learn-ing to fly but I ain't got wings.
a-round the clouds.
Gtr. 4 (elec.) Riff B
mf
w/ clean tone & chorus
let ring
12 13 13 14 12 12 12 13 13 14 12 12
To Coda
F C Am G5 F C Am G5
Com - ing down is the hard - est thing. 2. Well, the
What goes up must come down.
End Riff B
let ring
13 13 14 12 12 12 13 13 14 12
Verse
Gtr. 1: w/ Rhy. Fig. 1, 2 times, simile
Gtr. 2: w/ Riff A, 2 times, simile
Gtr. 3: w/ Rhy. Fig. 2, 2 times, simile
Gtr. 4 tacet
F C Am G5 F C Am G5
good old days may not re - turn and the
Voc. Fill 1
(Oo.)

Gtr. 4: w/ Riff B, simile
F C Am G5 F C Am G5
rocks might melt and the sea may burn. I'm
Chorus
Gtr. 1: w/ Rhy. Fig. 1, 2 times, simile
Gtr. 2: w/ Riff A, 2 times, simile
Gtr. 3: w/ Rhy. Fig. 2, 2 times, simile
F C Am G5 F C Am G5
learn-ing to fly but I ain't got wings.
Voc. Fig. 1
End Voc. Fig. 1
(Learn-ing to fly. Learn-ing to fly.)
Bkgd. Voc.: w/ Voc. Fig. 1, simile
F C Am G5 F C
Com-ing down is the hard - est thing.
Am G5 G5
Rhy. Fig. 3
End Rhy. Fig. 3
*Gtrs. 1 & 3
Riff C
End Riff C
Gtr. 2
Guitar Solo
Gtr. 1: w/ Rhy. Fig. 1, 2 times, simile
Gtr. 2: w/ Riff A, 2 times, simile
Gtr. 3: w/ Rhy. Fig. 2, 2 times, simile
F C Am G5 F C Am G5
Gtr. 5 (elec.)
f
w/ dist. & slide
steady gliss.

D.S. al Coda
F C Am G5 F C Am G
3. Well,
w/o slide
Coda
Interlude
Gtrs. 1 & 3: w/ Rhy. Fig. 3
Gtr. 2: w/ Riff C, simile
Am G F C Am G
Ay!
Rhy. Fig. 4
Gtrs. 1 & 2
End Rhy. Fig. 4
Chorus
Bkgd. Voc.: w/ Voc. Fig. 1, 1st 3 meas.
Gtr. 1: w/ Rhy. Fig. 1, till fade
Gtr. 2: w/ Riff A, till fade
Gtr. 3: w/ Rhy. Fig. 2, till fade
Gtr. 5 tacet
Gtrs. 1 & 2: w/ Rhy. Fig. 4
Gtr. 4: w/ Riff B, till fade
F C Am G F C Am G F C Am G
I'm learn-ing to fly but I ain't got wings.
Gtr. 5
Gtr. 6 (elec.)
mp
w/ clean tone
Riff D
End Riff D
P.M.
Gtr. 6: w/ Riff D, till end
F C Am G F C Am G
Com-ing down is the hard - est thing. I'm

Bkgd. Voc.: w/ Voc. Fig. 1, 1st 3 meas.
F C Am G F C Am G F C
learn-ing to fly a - round the clouds. And what goes up
Gtr. 5
steady gliss.
Am G F C Am G F C Am G F C
must come down. I'm learn-ing to fly.
Bkgd. Voc.: w/ Voc. Fig. 1, till fade
steady gliss.
Am G F C Am G F C Am G
I'm learn-ing to fly.
steady gliss.
Begin Fade
Fade Out
F C Am G F C Am G F C

No Particular Place to Go

Words and Music by Chuck Berry

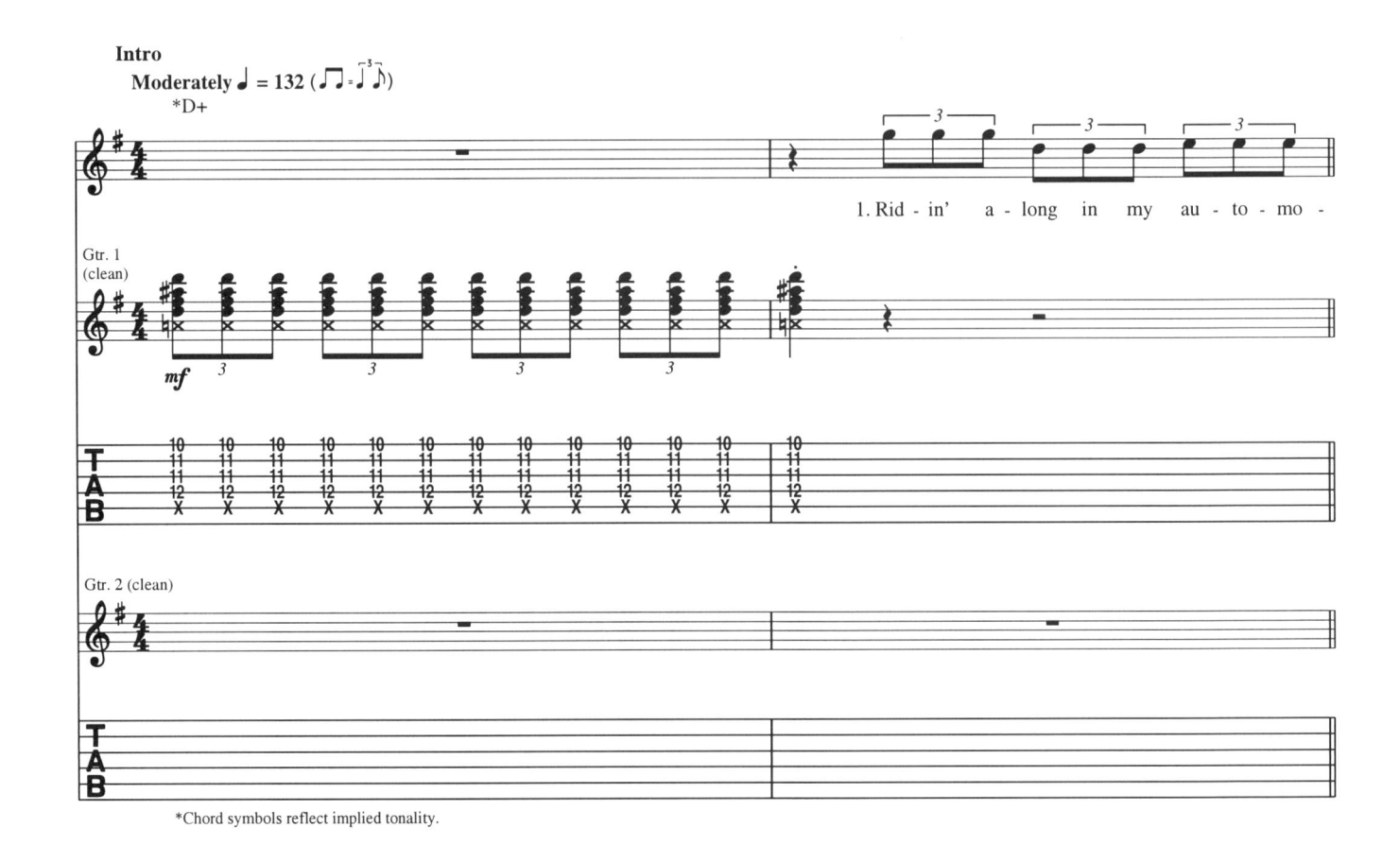

Intro
Moderately ♩ = 132

*D+

1. Rid-in' a-long in my au-to-mo-

*Chord symbols reflect implied tonality.

Verse
G

-bile, my ba-by be-side me at the wheel.
go, so we parked way out on the Ko-ko-mo.

Rhy. Fig. 1

slight P.M. throughout

Copyright © 1964 (Renewed) by Arc Music Corporation (BMI)
International Copyright Secured   All Rights Reserved
Used by Permission

I stole a kiss at the turn of a mile. My curiosity runnin' wild.
The night was young and the moon was gold, so we both decided to take a stroll.

Cruis - in' and play - in' the ra - di - o
Can you i - mag - ine the way I felt?

106

Cud - dl - in' more and driv - in' slow
Cruis - in' and play - in' the ra - di - o

with no par - tic - u - lar place to go.
with no par - tic - u - lar place to

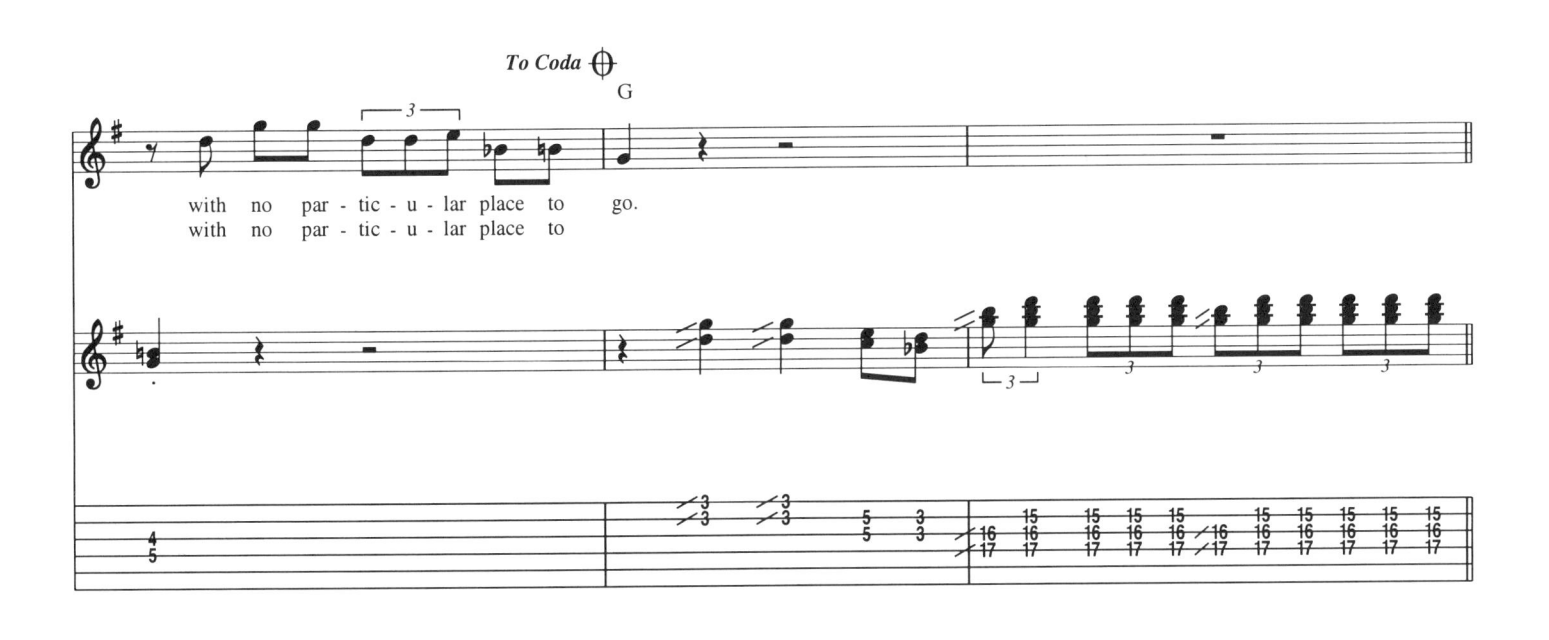

Guitar Solo

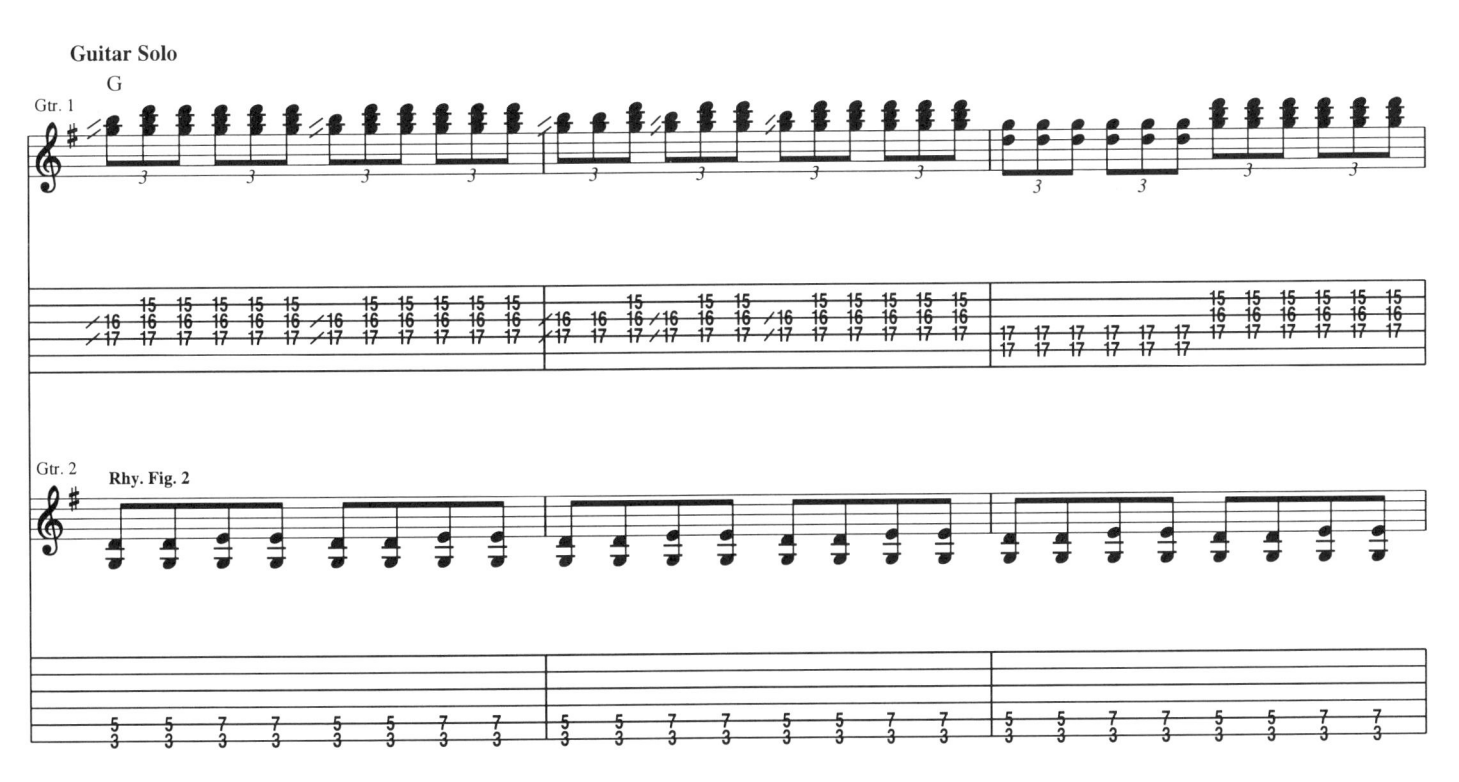

3. No par-tic-u-lar place to

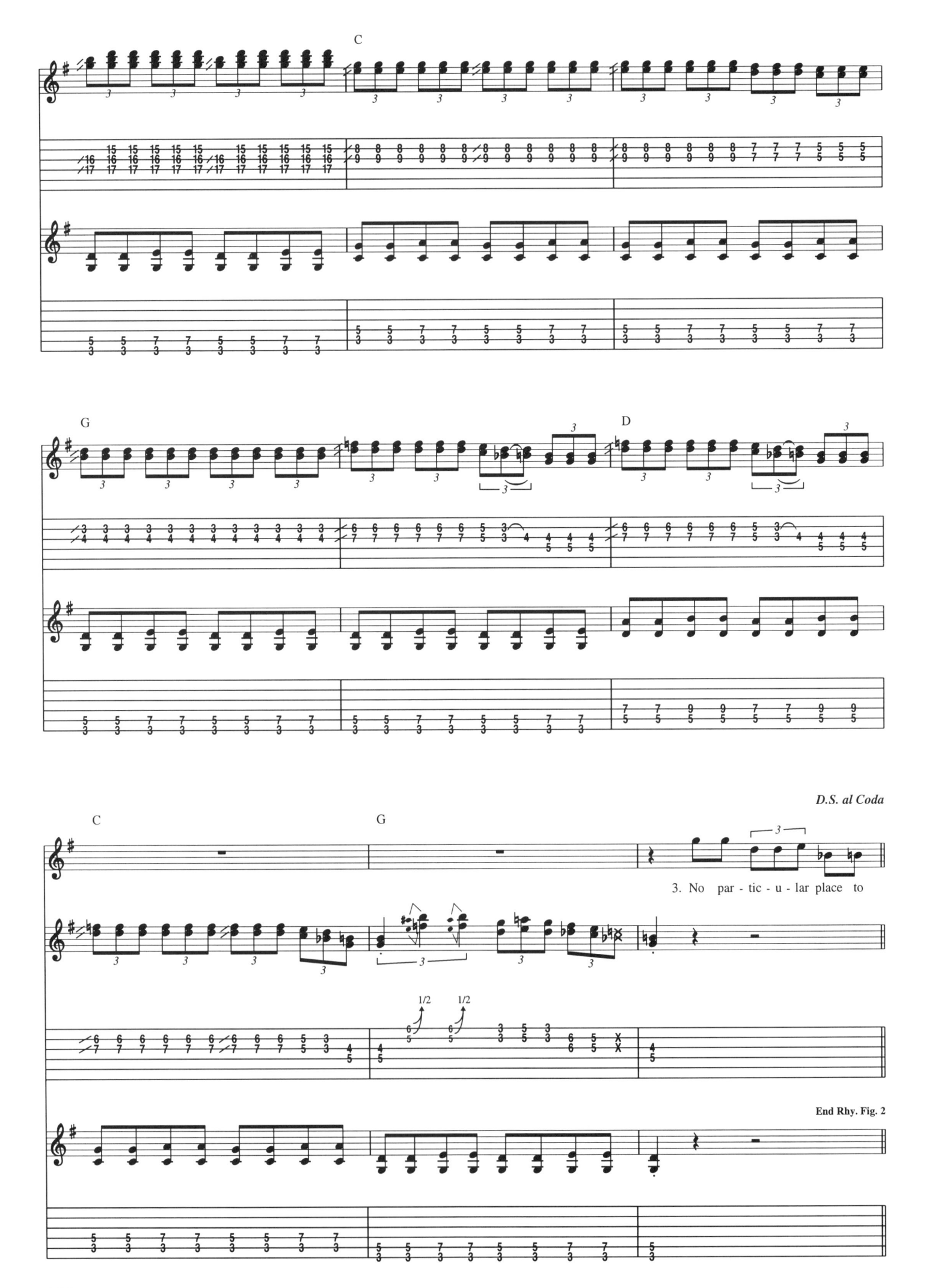

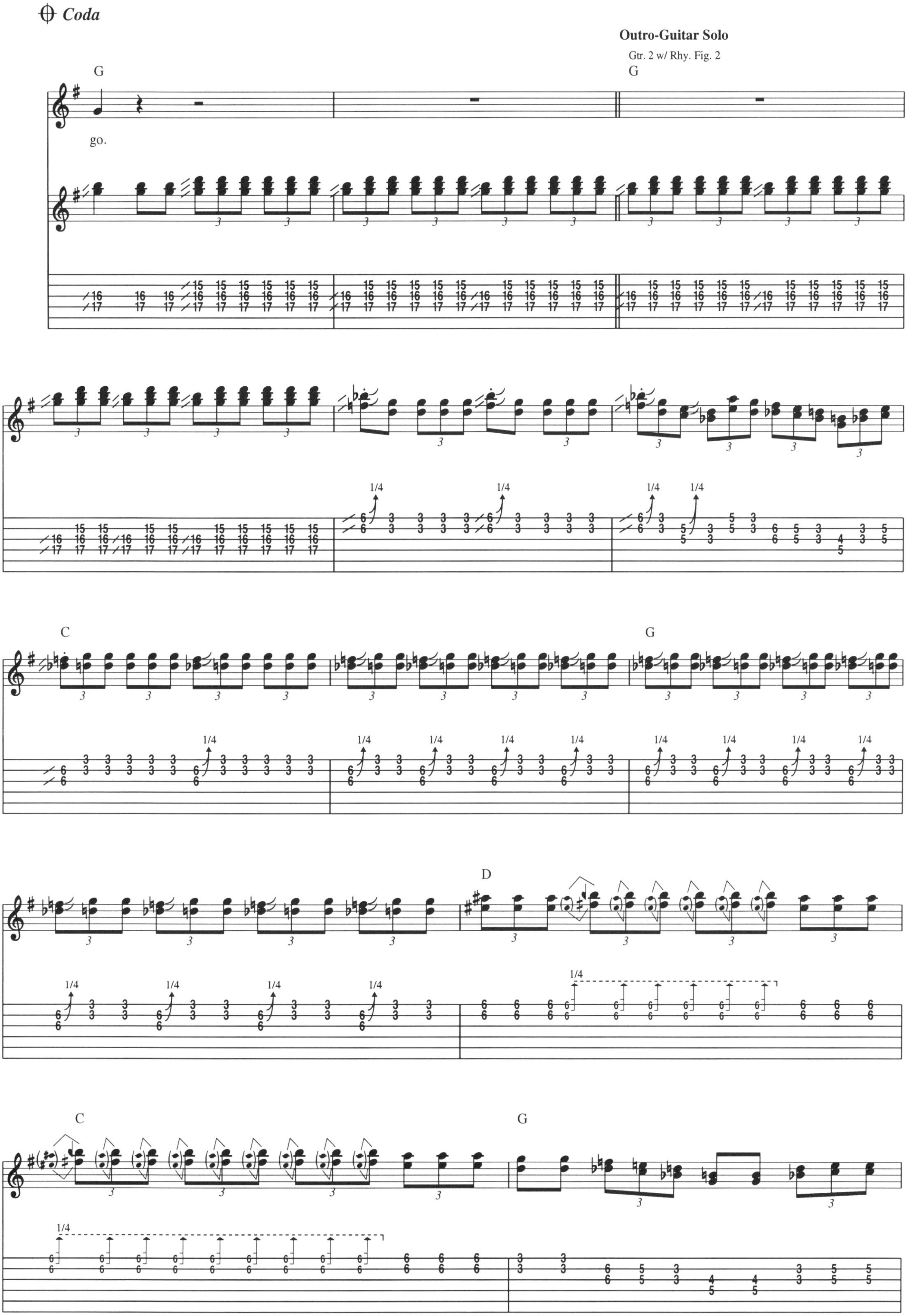
Coda
Outro-Guitar Solo
Gtr. 2 w/ Rhy. Fig. 2
G
G
go.
C
G
D
C
G

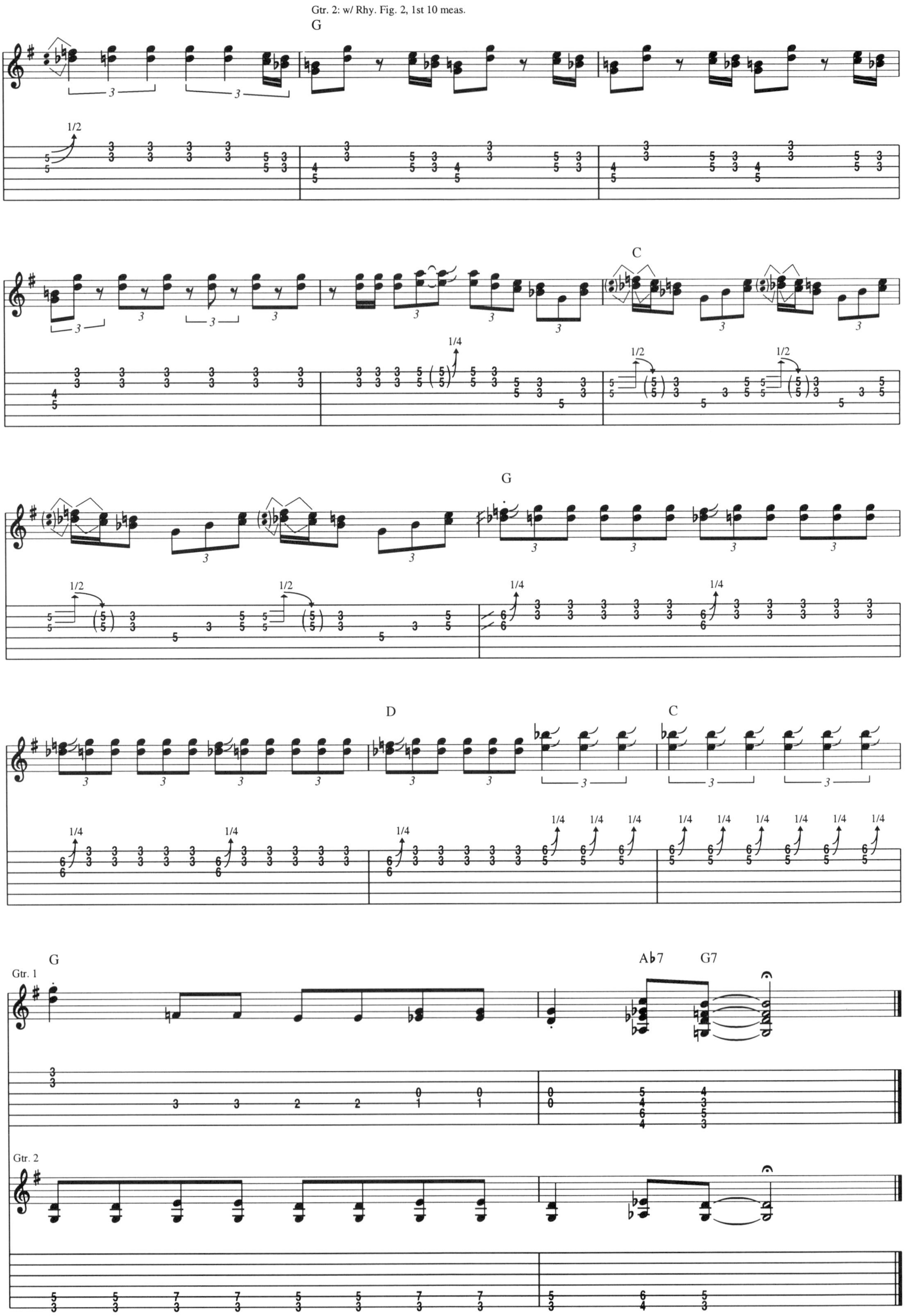
Gtr. 2: w/ Rhy. Fig. 2, 1st 10 meas.
G
C
G
D
C
G
Gtr. 1
A♭7
G7
Gtr. 2

Oh, Pretty Woman

Words and Music by Roy Orbison and Bill Dees

Tune Down 1/2 Step:
① = E♭   ④ = D♭
② = B♭   ⑤ = A♭
③ = G♭   ⑥ = E♭

Intro
Moderate Rock ♩ = 130

Gtr. 1 (dist.) *Asus2   F#m11   Asus2   F#m11

f w/ chorus
let ring throughout

* Chord symbols reflect implied tonality.

Copyright © 1964 (Renewed 1992) by Acuff-Rose Music, Inc., Barbara Orbison Music Company, Orbi-Lee Music and R-Key Darkus Music
All Rights Reserved   Used by Permission

111

Asus2
F♯m11
D
wom-an, the kind I'd like to meet. Pret-ty wom-an, I don't be-
P.M.
P.M.
P.M.
E9
lieve you. It must be true. No one could look as good as you.
End Rhy. Fig. 1
P.M.
Interlude
E7
Mer-cy.
2. Pret-ty
P.M.
P.M.
P.M.
P.M.
Verse
Gtr. 1: w/ Rhy. Fig. 1
Asus2
F♯m11
Asus2
F♯m11
wom-an, won't you par-don me? Pret-ty wom-an, I could-n't help but see. Pret-ty
D
E9
wom-an, oh, you look love-ly as you can be. Are you

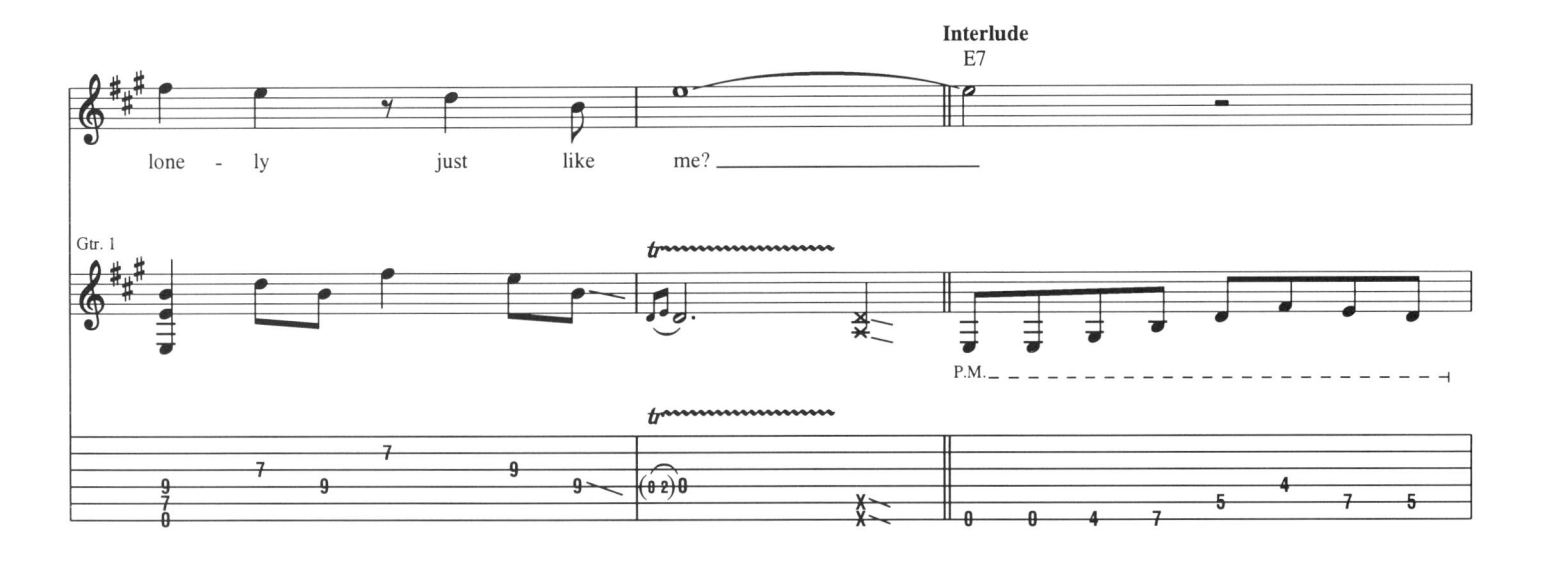

lone-ly just like me?

Interlude
E7

Bridge
Dm G5 Cadd9 G/B Asus2 Am Asus4

Pret-ty wom-an, stop a-while. Pret-ty wom-an, talk a-while.

let ring throughout

Dm
G5
Cadd9
C
Pret-ty wom - an, give your smile to me.
Dm
G5
C
G/B
Asus2
Asus4
Pret-ty wom - an, yeah, yeah, yeah.
Pret-ty wom - an, look my way.

Pret-ty wom - an, say you'll stay with me 'cause I need you, need you to-night.

Gtr. 2 tacet
3. Pret - ty
Gtr. 1
P.M.
Verse
Gtr. 1: w/ Rhy. Fig. 1
Asus2
F#m11
Asus2
F#m11
wom-an, don't walk on by. Pret - ty wom-an, don't make me cry. Pret - ty
D
E9
wom - an, don't walk a - way, hey.
O. K. If that's the way it must be, O.
Gtr. 1
K. I guess I'll go on home. It's late.

There'll be tomorrow night. But wait! What do I see?

She's walking back to me.

Outro

Whoa, whoa, pretty woman.

Ramblin' Man

Words and Music by Dickey Betts

*Tune Up 1/2 Step:
①= E# ④= D#
②= B# ⑤= A#
③= G# ⑥= E#

Intro
Fast Rock ♩ = 184

* or Capo 1

* Gtr. 1 to left of slash in TAB.

Chorus
Gtr. 2 tacet

Lord, I was born a ramblin' man.

Try'n to make a living, and doin' the best I can.

An' when it's time for

Copyright © 1973 by Unichappell Music Inc. and F.R. Betts Music Co.
All Rights Administered by Unichappell Music Inc.
International Copyright Secured   All Rights Reserved

G
Em
C
leav - in' ___ I hope you'll un - der - stand, ___
G
D6
G
that I was born ___ a ram - blin' man.
End Rhy. Fig. 1
Verse
G
C6
1. Well, my fath - er was ___ a gam - bler down in
2. on my way ___ to New ___ Or - leans this
mf
G
Geor - gia, ___ and he wound up on ___ the wrong
morn - in', ___ and leav - in' out ___ of
C6
D6
D
___ end of a gun. ___ And
Nash - ville, Ten - nes - see. ___ They're

120

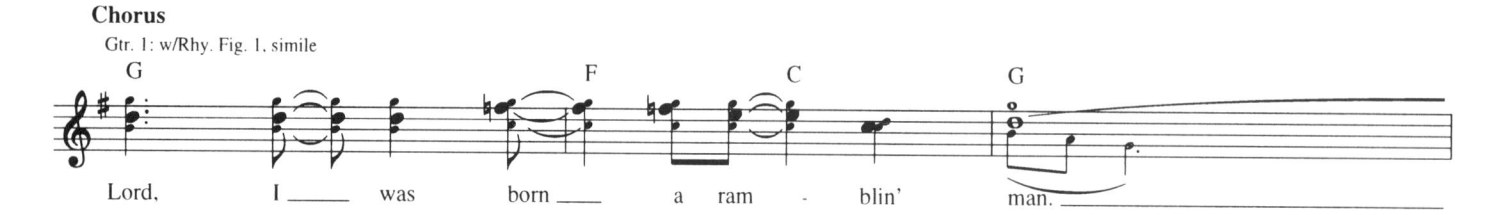

Interlude
Gtr. 2
D
N.C.
8va
loco
Piano
Gtr. 1
Gtr.1 divisi
Guitar Solo
Gtrs. 1 & 2 tacet
Gtr. 3
G
C
G
full
Al - right!
C
D
C
G
Em
C
1/2
D.S. al Coda
G
D
G
2. I'm

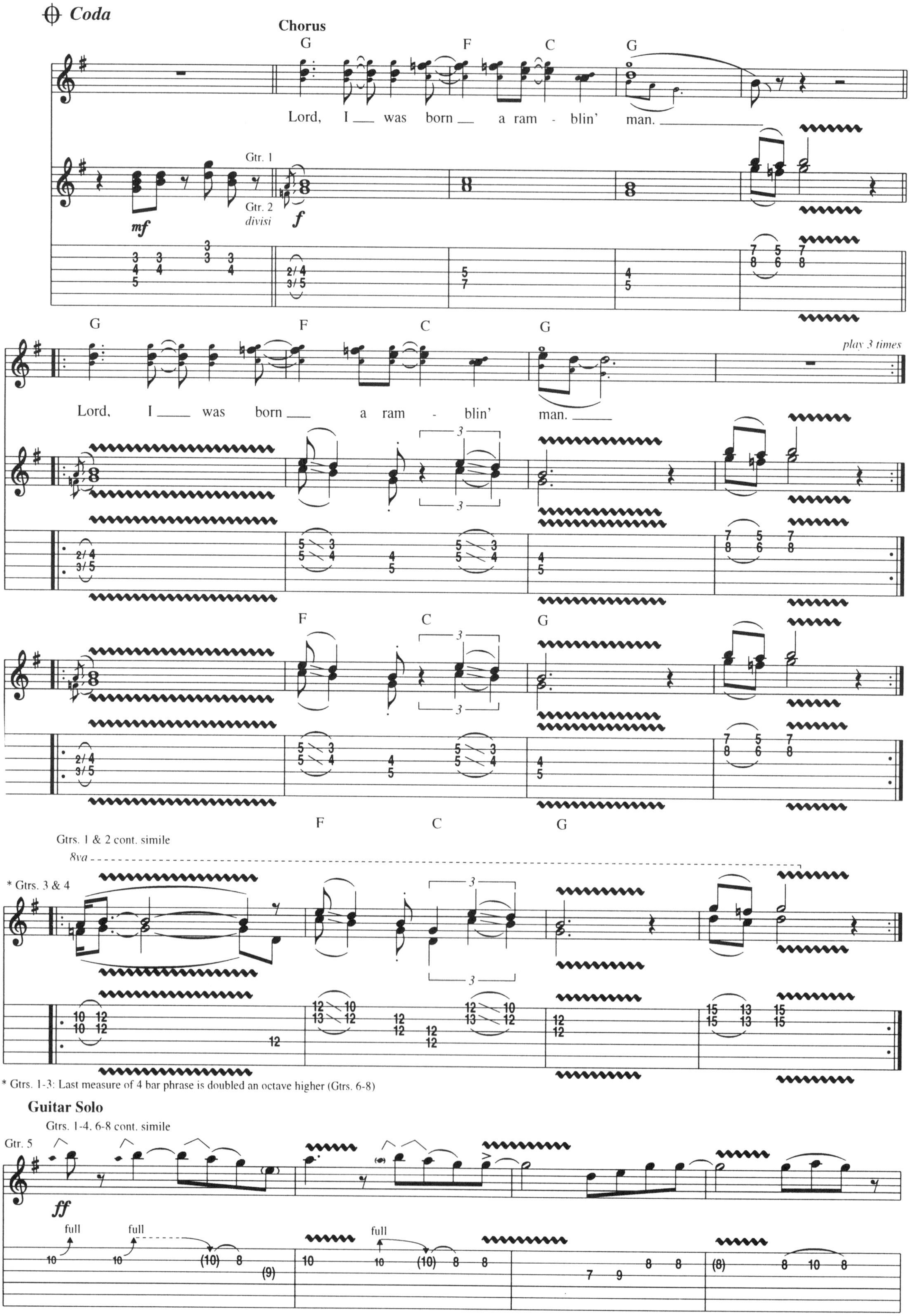
Coda
Chorus
G F C G
Lord, I was born a ram - blin' man.
Gtr. 1
Gtr. 2 divisi
mf
f
G F C G
play 3 times
Lord, I was born a ram - blin' man.
F C G
F C G
Gtrs. 1 & 2 cont. simile
8va
* Gtrs. 3 & 4
* Gtrs. 1-3: Last measure of 4 bar phrase is doubled an octave higher (Gtrs. 6-8)
Guitar Solo
Gtrs. 1-4, 6-8 cont. simile
Gtr. 5
ff
full
full
full

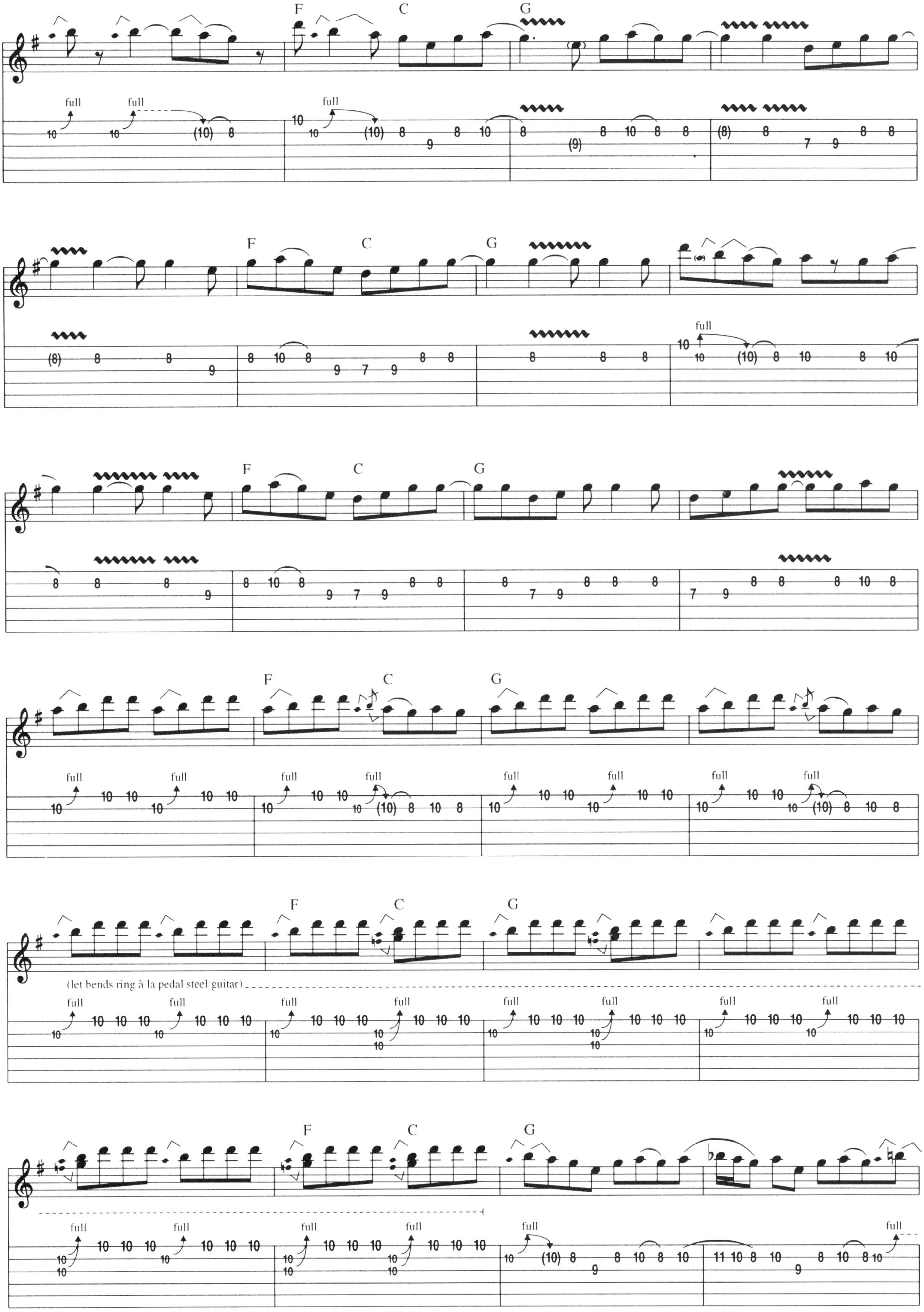
F
C
G
full
(let bends ring à la pedal steel guitar)

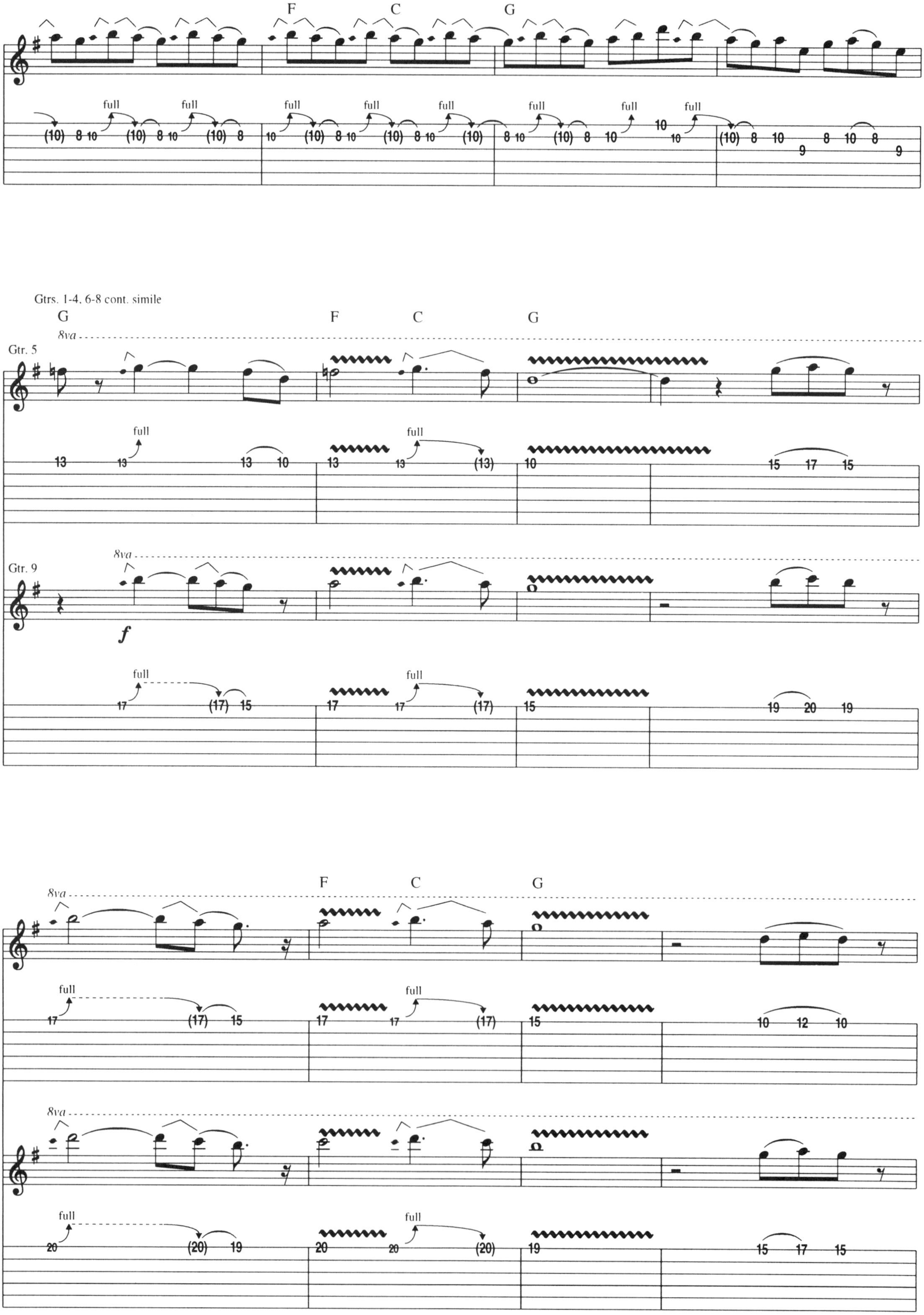
F C G
full
Gtrs. 1-4, 6-8 cont. simile
G F C G
8va
Gtr. 5
Gtr. 9
f
F C G
8va

125

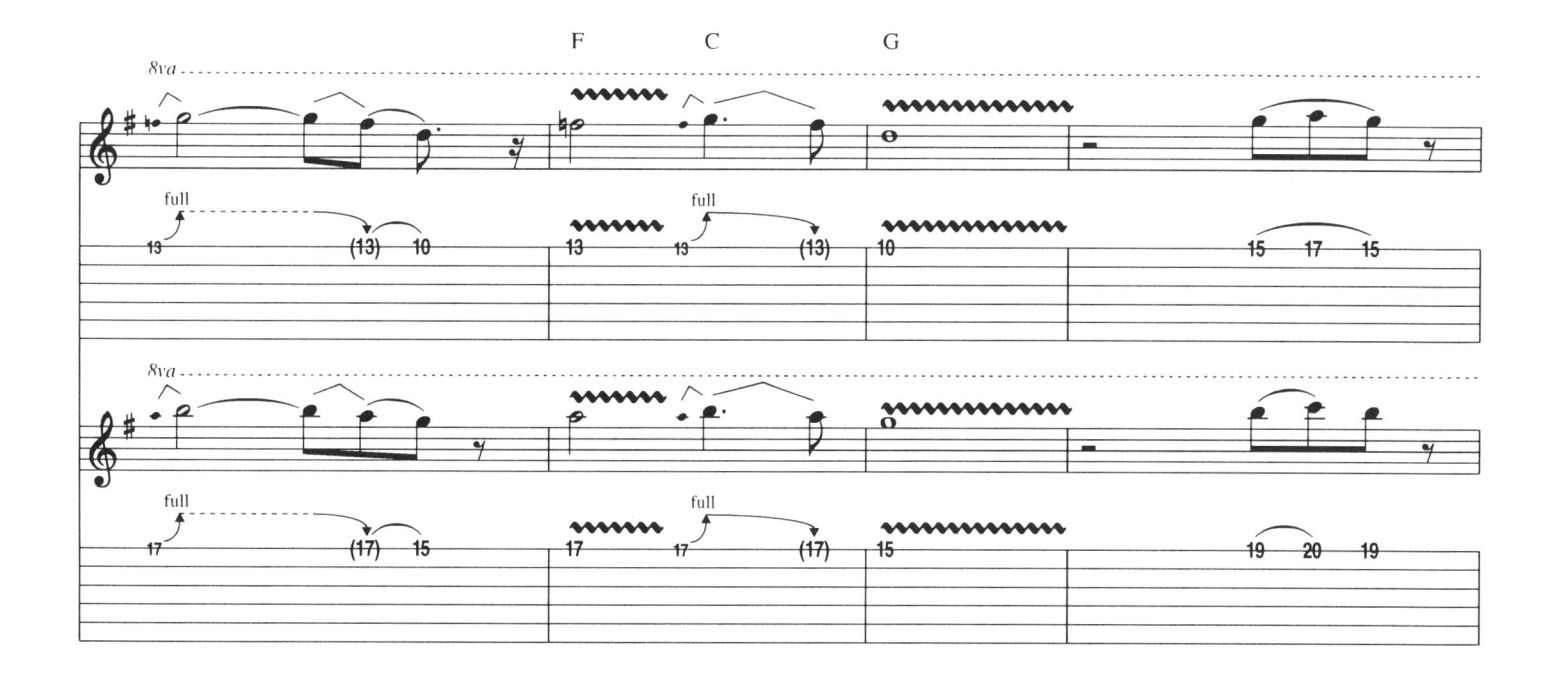

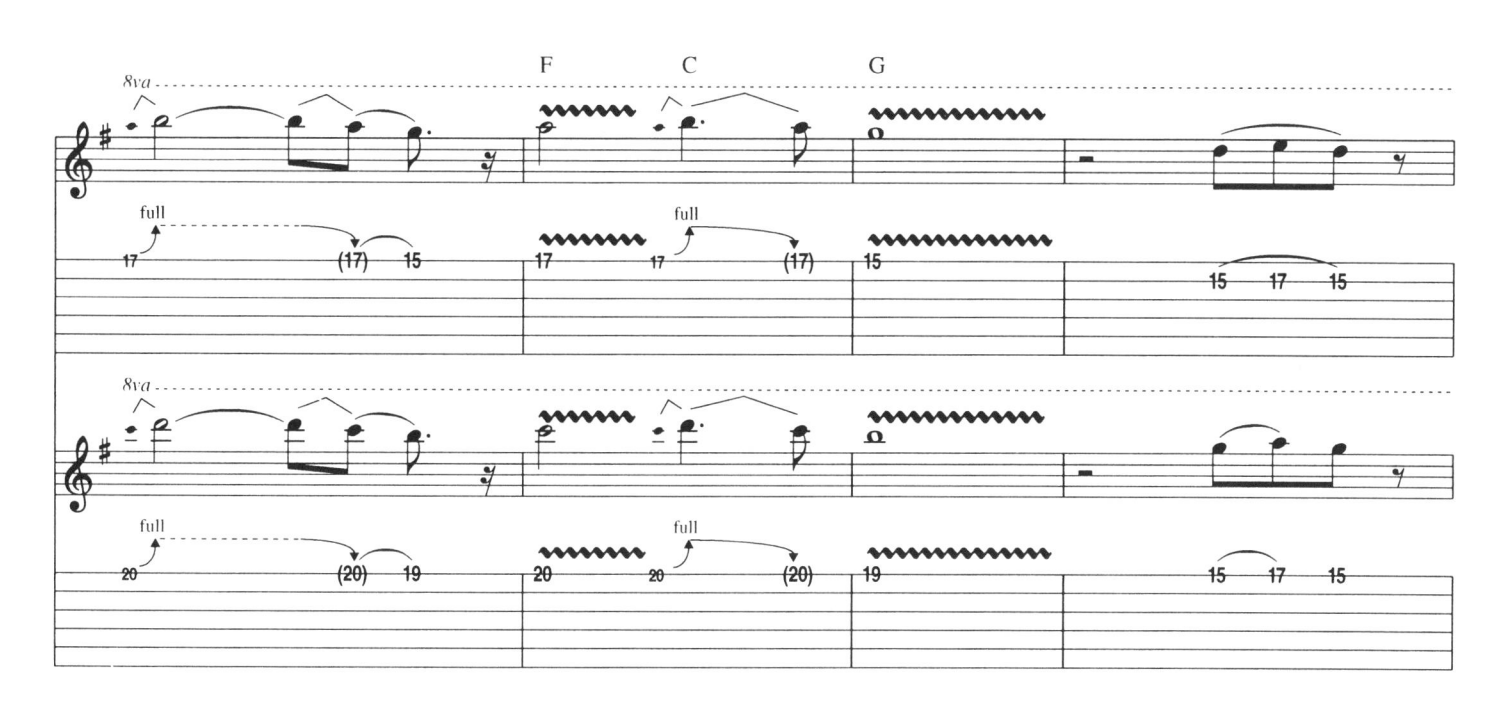

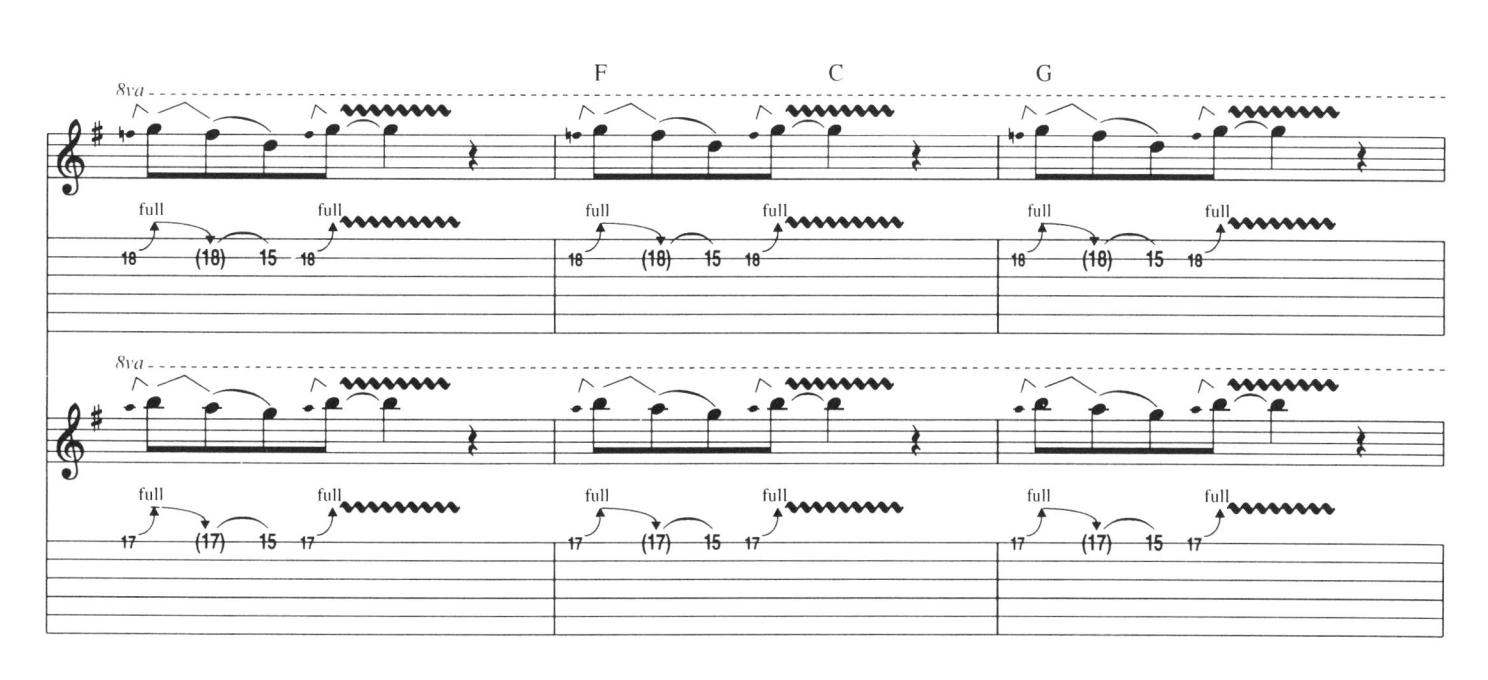

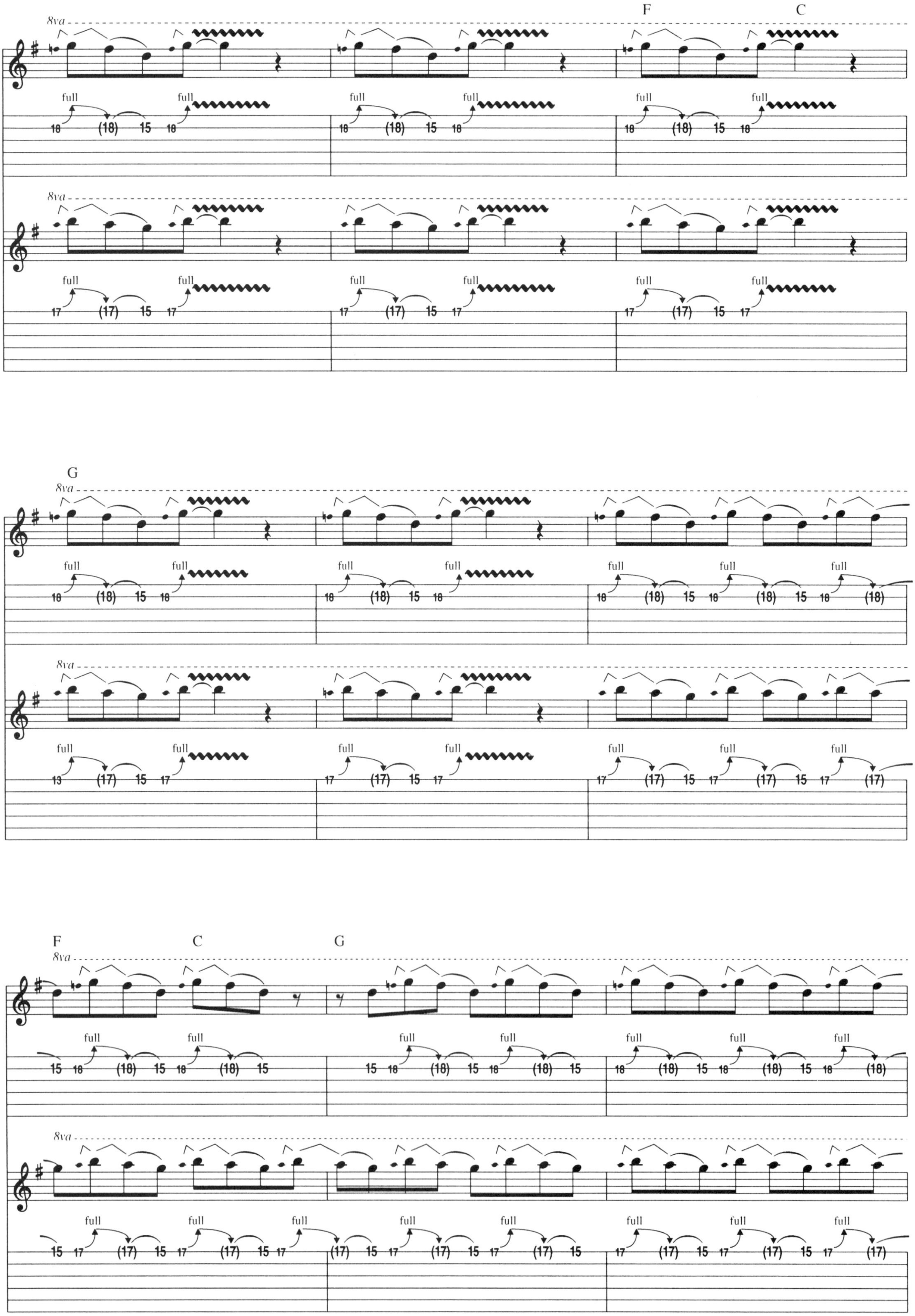
F
C
8va
full
G
8va
full
F
C
G
8va
full

F C G
8va
Gtr. 10
full
w/slide
Gtrs. 5 & 9 tacet
(Gtrs. 1-4, 6-8 cont. simile)
(w/slide)
Begin Fade
Fade Out

Ridin' the Storm Out

Words and Music by Gary Richrath

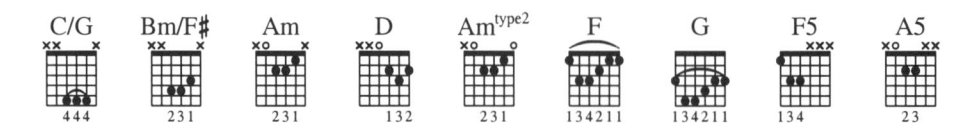

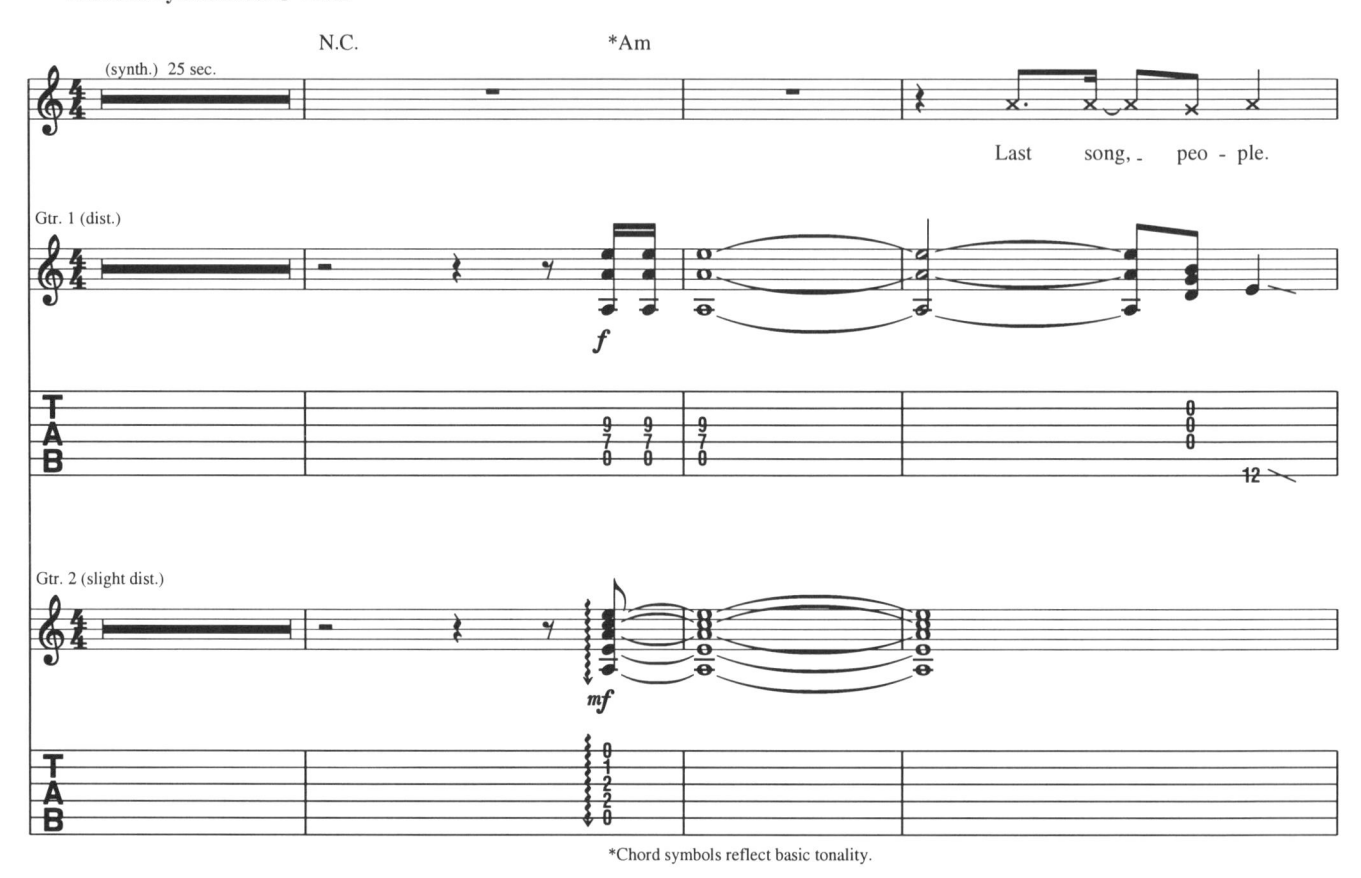

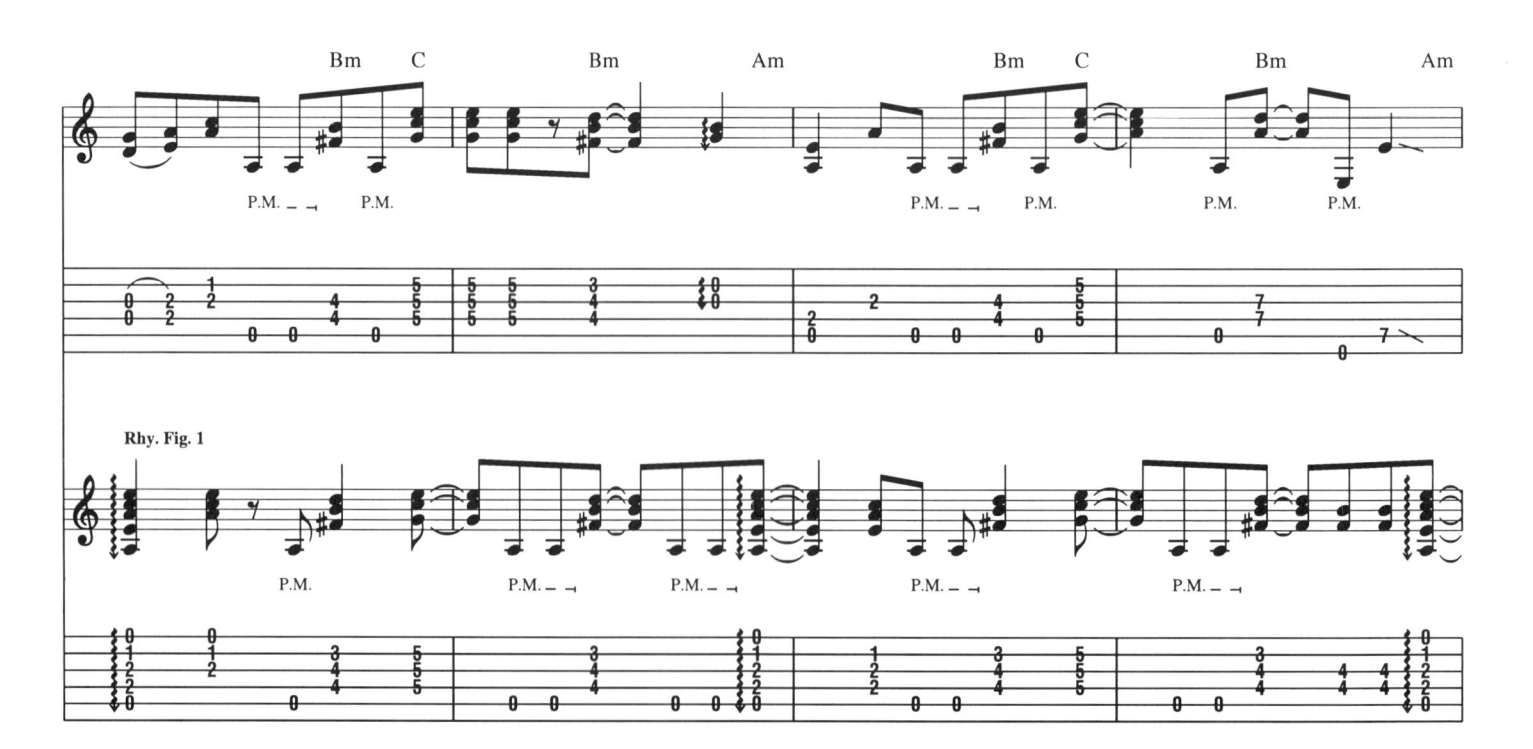

Bm C Bm Am Bm C Bm Am
P.M. P.M. P.M. P.M.
full
grad. release
End Rhy. Fig. 1
P.M. P.M.
Verse
Gtr. 2: w/ Rhy. Fig. 1, 1 5/8 times, simile
Bm C Bm Am Bm C Bm Am
1. Rid - in' the storm out, wait-in' for the thaw out on a full
Gtr. 1
Rhy. Fig. 2
End Rhy. Fig. 2
mf
let ring
Bm C Bm Am Bm C Bm Am
moon night in the Rock - y Moun - tain win - ter.
P.M. * P.M. P.M. P.M. f P.M.
* ghost note probably not intended
Bm C Bm Am Bm C Bm Am
Wine bot-tle's low watch - in' for the snow and
mf
P.M. P.M. P.M.

Bm C C/G Bm/F♯ Am
Rhy. Fig. 3
End Rhy. Fig. 3
Gtr. 2
think-in' a - bout what I've been mis-sin' in the cit - y.
And I'm
P.M. P.M. P.M. let ring P.M.
Pre-Chorus
D A D Am type 2 E G
open open 3fr
Rhy. Fig. 4
End Rhy. Fig. 4
(cont. in notation)
not mis-sin' a thing,
watch-ing the full moon cross - ing the range.
steady gliss.
Chorus
F G Am G5 F5
Rid - in' the storm out.
*Gtrs. 1 & 2
Rhy. Fig. 5
* composite arrangement
Gtr. 2: w/ Rhy. Fig. 1, last 4 meas., simile
Bm C
End Rhy. Fig. 5
Gtr. 1

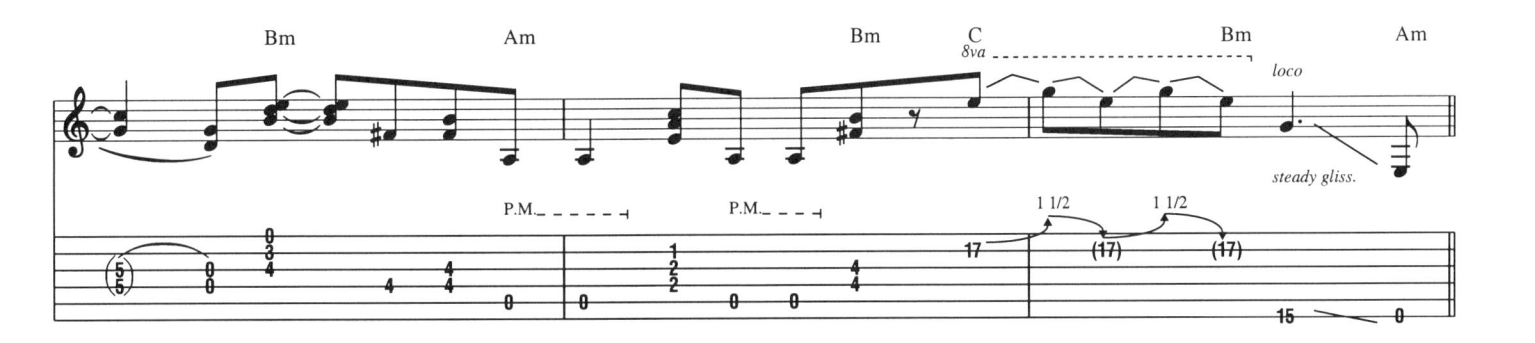

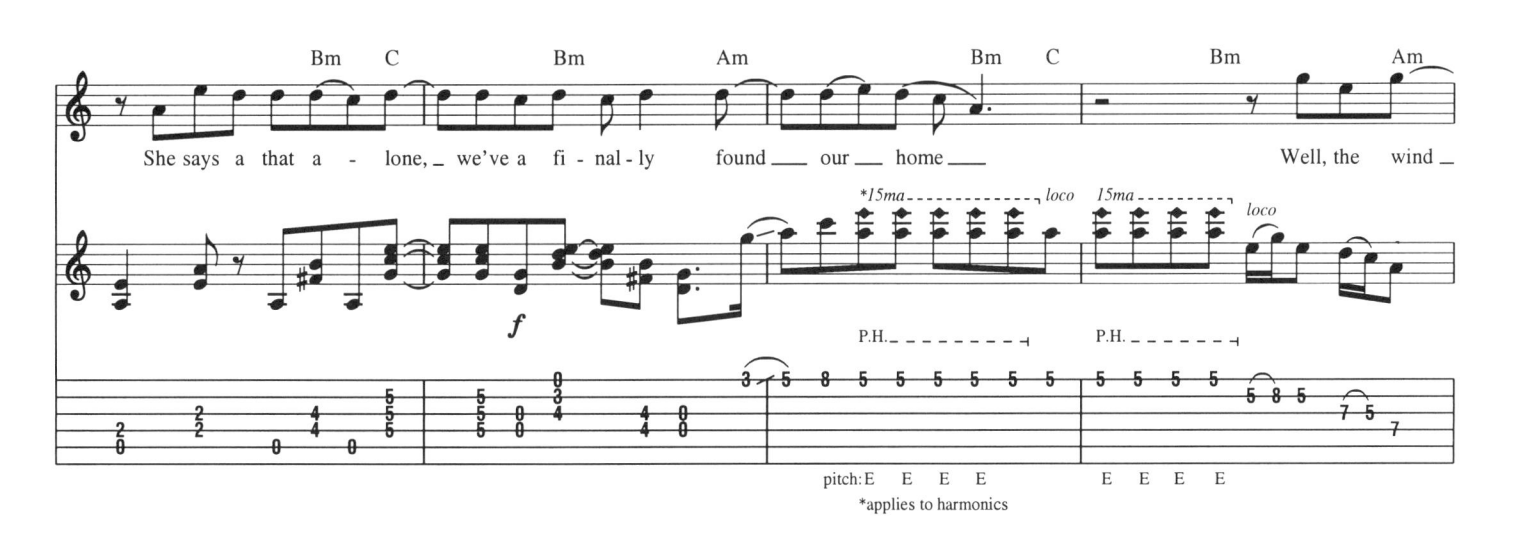

Verse

Gtr. 2: w/ Rhy. Fig. 1, 1 5/8 times, simile

2. La- dy be- side me, well, she's a there to guide me.

She says a that a- lone, we've a fi- nal- ly found our home. Well, the wind out- side is a fright- 'nin', but it's kind- er than a light- nin' life in the cit- y. A

131

Gtr. 2: w/ Rhy. Fig. 3, simile
Bm C C/G Bm/F♯ Am
hard life to live, but it gives back a what you give.
mf
Pre-Chorus
Gtr. 2: w/ Rhy. Fig. 4, simile
N.C. D N.C. D Am
And I'm not mis-sin' a thing, watch-ing the full moon cross-
Chorus
Gtr. 2: w/ Rhy. Fig. 5, simile
F G Am G5 F5 F G Am
- ing the range. Rid - in' the storm out. Rid - in' the storm
G5 F5 G Am G5 F5 Am
out. Rid - in' the storm out. Rid - in' the storm

133

3. Rid - in' the storm out. I'm a - wait - in' for the thaw out on a full moon night in the Rock - y Moun - tain kind a win-

Bm C Bm Am Bm C
- ter. Oh, yeah. Wine bot - tle's low.
8va
full
Bm Am Bm C Bm Am
I'm a watch - in' for the snow. I'm
8va loco 8va
1 1/2 full full full 2 full full
loco
Gtr. 2: w/ Rhy. Fig. 3, simile
Bm C C/G Bm/F♯ Am N.C.
think-in' a - bout what I've been a - mis - sin' in the cit - y. Oh, ho, ho, well, I'm
mf
P.M.
Pre-Chorus
Gtr. 2: w/ Rhy. Fig. 4, simile
D N.C. D Am
not mis-sin' a thing. I'm a watch - in' the full moon cross - in' the range.
8va loco
Harm.

Chorus
Gtr. 2: w/ Rhy. Fig. 5, 1st 6 meas., simile
F G Am G5 F5 F G Am G5 F5
Rid - in' the storm out. Rid - in' the storm out.
F G Am G5 F5
Half-Time Feel
F G E F5
6 open
Gtr. 2
Rid - in' the storm out. Rid - in',
let ring
F F5 G F5 F G
End Half-Time Feel
rid - in', rid - in' the storm

137

8va
Bm
C
loco
Am
full
1 1/2
steady gliss.
P.M.
let ring
Outro
Gtr. 1
F
G
Free Time
fdbk.
Gtr. 2
(cont. in slash)

139

Rock and Roll All Nite

Words and Music by Paul Stanley and Gene Simmons

Tune down 1/2 step:
(low to high) Eb-Ab-Db-Gb-Bb-Eb

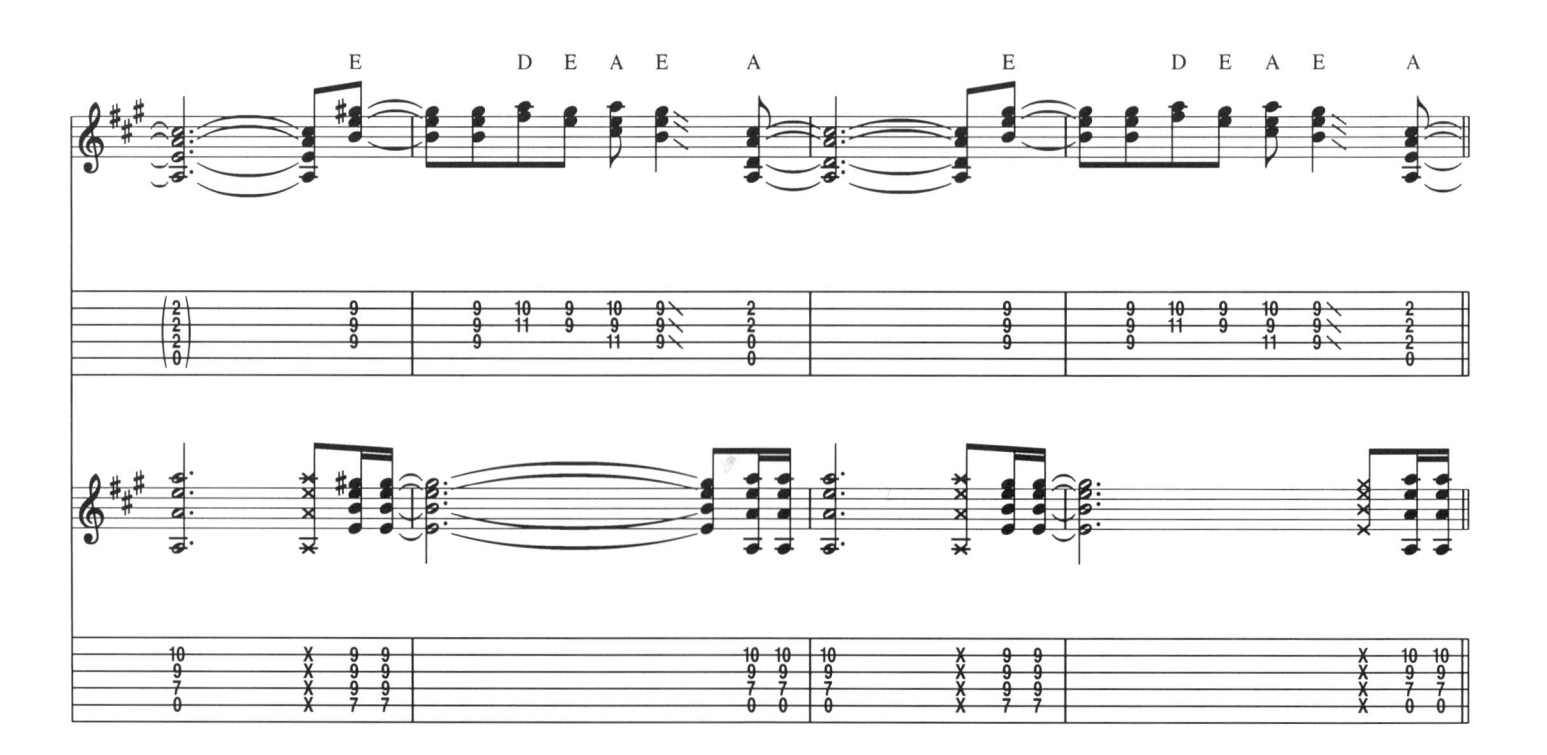

Intro
Moderately fast Rock ♩=142

*Chord symbols reflect combined harmony.

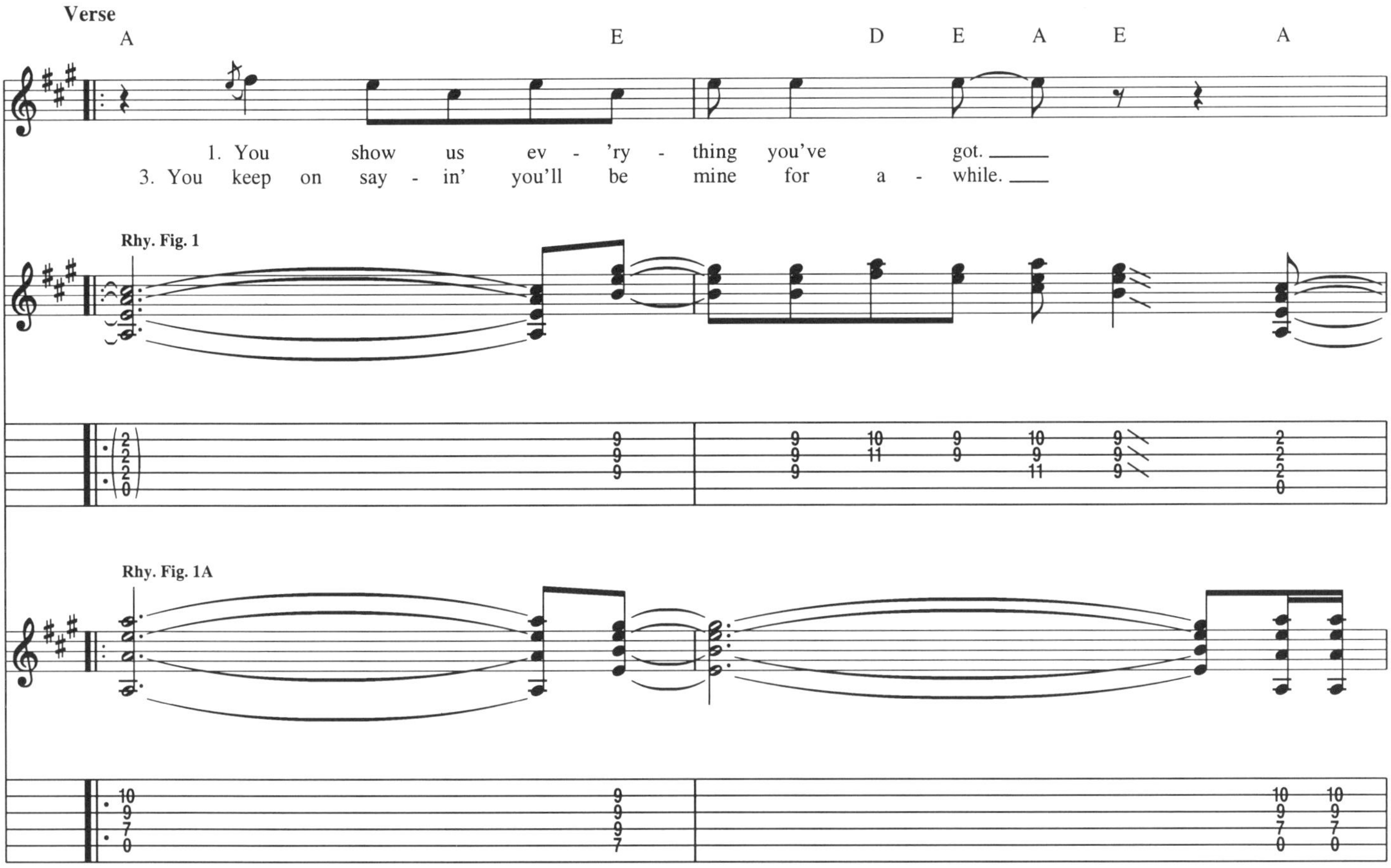
Verse
A E D E A E A
1. You show us ev - 'ry - thing you've got.
3. You keep on say - in' you'll be mine for a - while.
Rhy. Fig. 1
Rhy. Fig. 1A

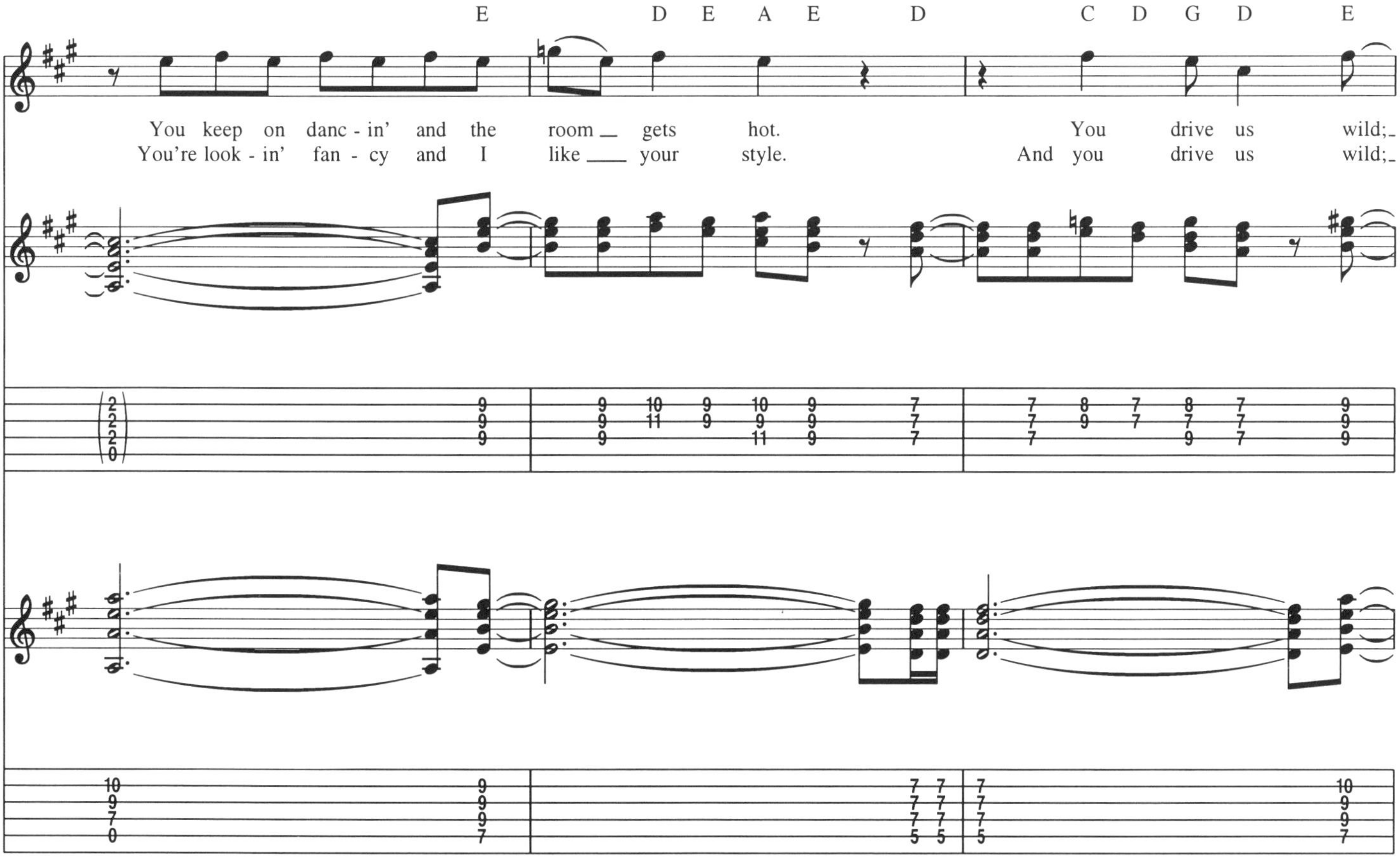
E D E A E D C D G D E
You keep on danc - in' and the room gets hot. You drive us wild;
You're look - in' fan - cy and I like your style. And you drive us wild;

D E A E
Gadd9
D Gadd9 D A
we'll drive you cra - zy.
we'll drive you cra - zy.
End Rhy. Fig. 1
End Rhy. Fig. 1A
Verse
Gtrs. 1 & 2: w/ Rhy. Figs. 1 & 1A
A E D E A E A E
2. And you say you wan - na go for a spin.
4. And you show us ev - 'ry - thing you've got.
The par - ty's just be - gun; we'll
Well, ba - by, ba - by, that's
D E A E D C D G D E D E A E
let you in. You drive us wild; we'll drive you cra -
quite a lot. And you drive us wild; we'll drive you cra -
Gadd9 D Gadd9 D F5
- zy.
- zy.
Rhy. Fill 1B
Gtr. 1
End Rhy. Fill 1B
Gtr. 2

Pre-Chorus
3rd time, Gtr. 2: w/ Fill 1
F5 F6 F5 F6 G5 G6 G5 G6 G5 N.C.
You keep on shout - in', you keep on shout - in',
Chorus
A5 D G D E
I wan-na rock and roll all nite
Fill 1
Gtr. 2
8va
w/ pick & fingers

144

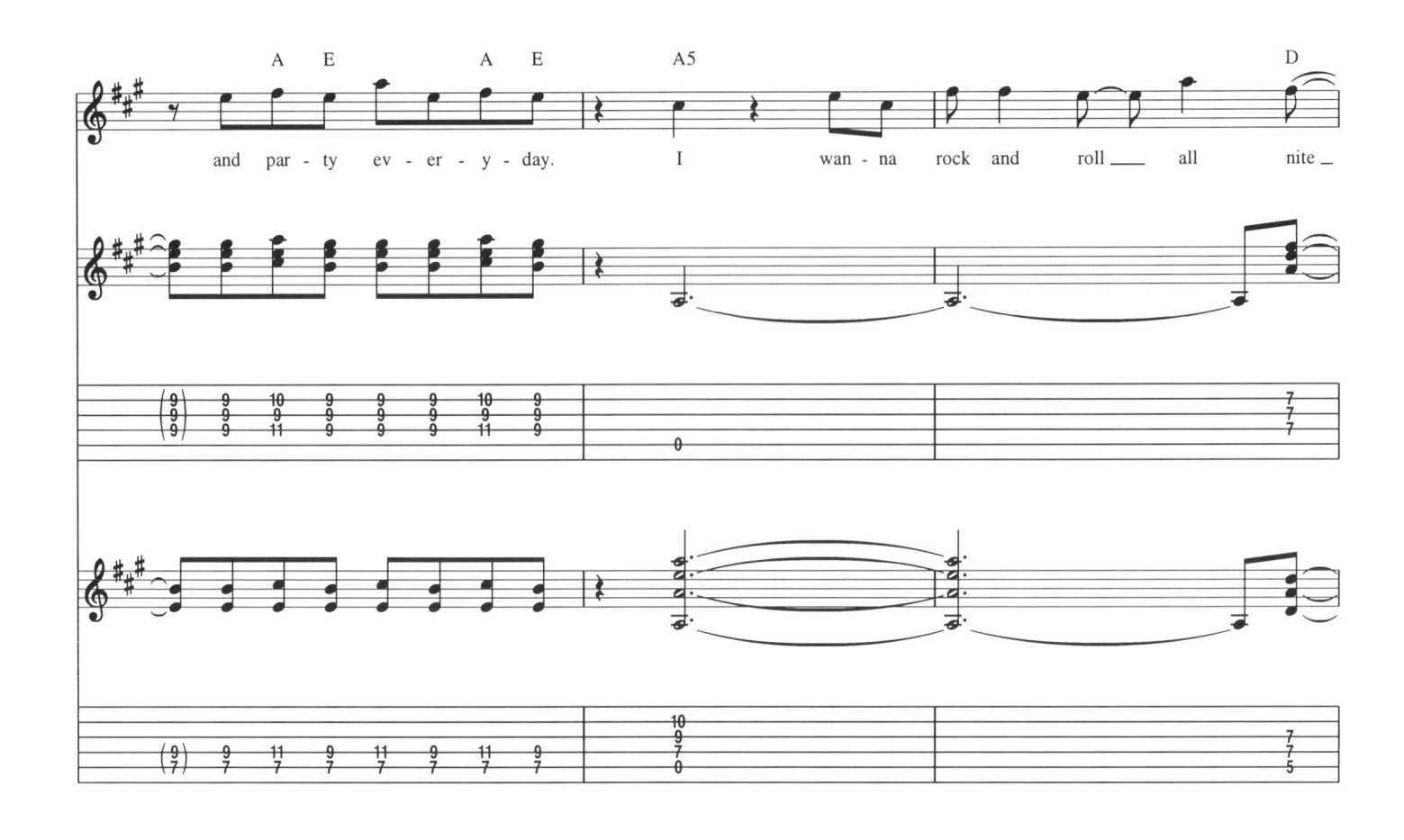

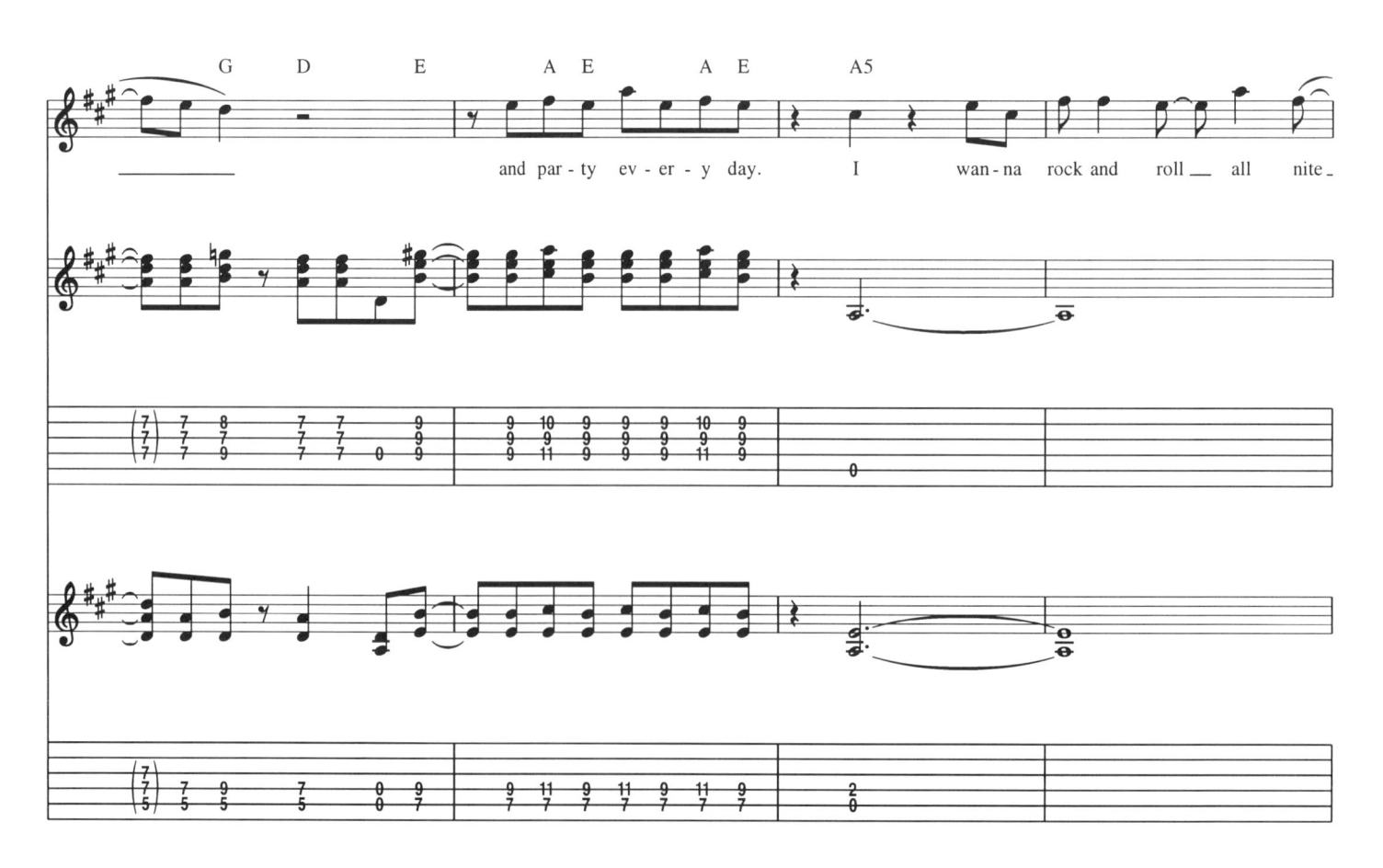

145

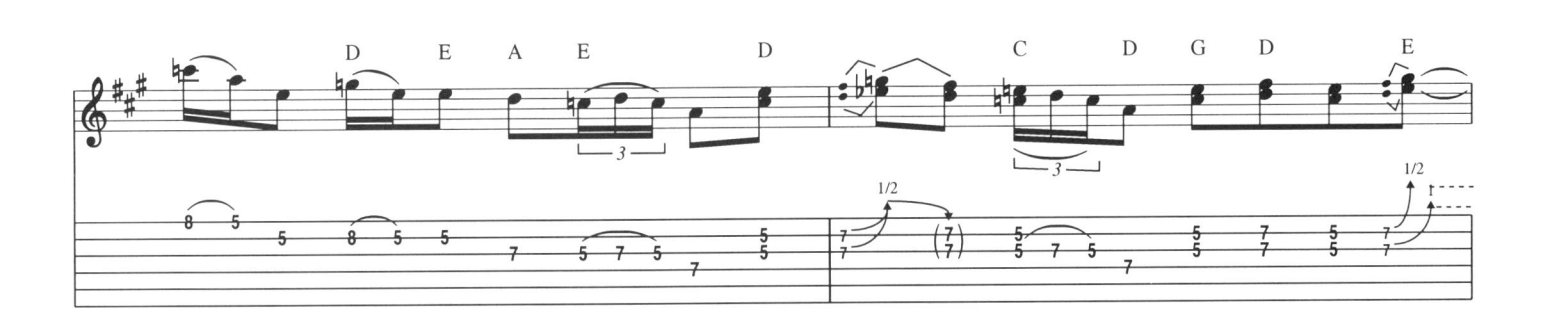

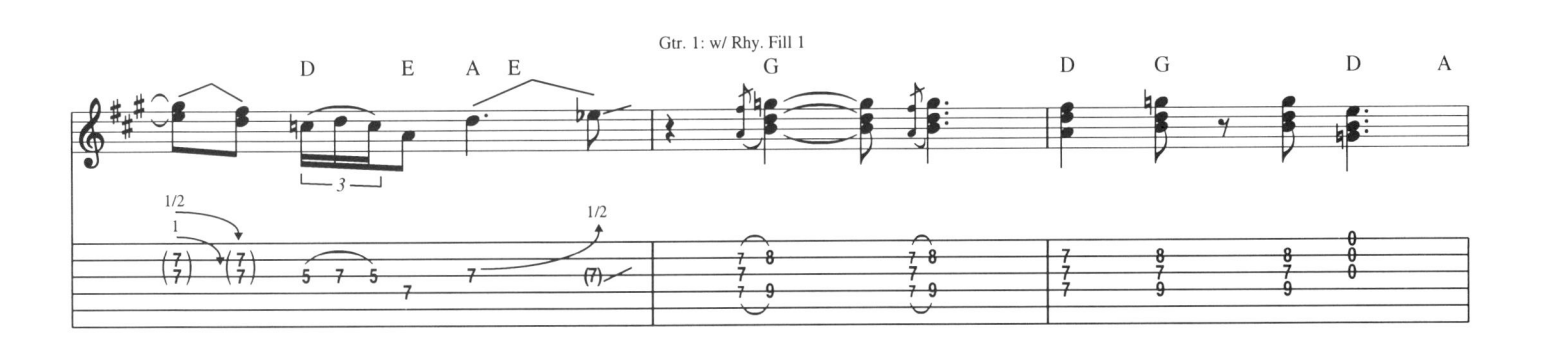

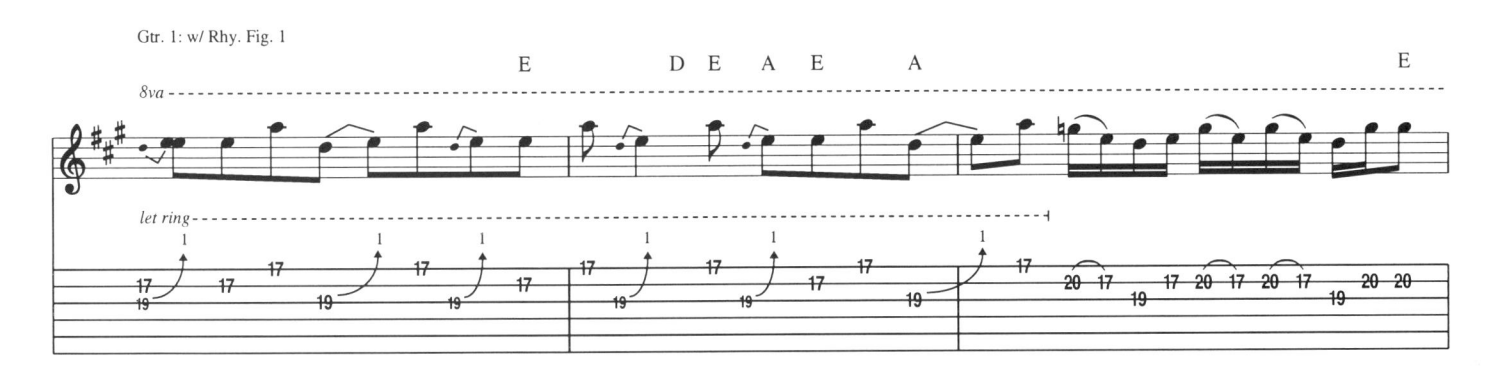

D E A E D C D G D E
8va
D.S. al Coda
Gtr. 1: w/ Rhy. Fill 1B
D E A E G D G D F5
8va
loco
Coda
Outro
Gadd9 D Gadd9 D F5 F6 F5 F6 G5
Gtr. 1
Gtr. 2
G6 G5 G6 N.C. A5
1/2

School's Out

Words and Music by Alice Cooper, Neal Smith, Michael Bruce, Glen Buxton and Dennis Dunaway

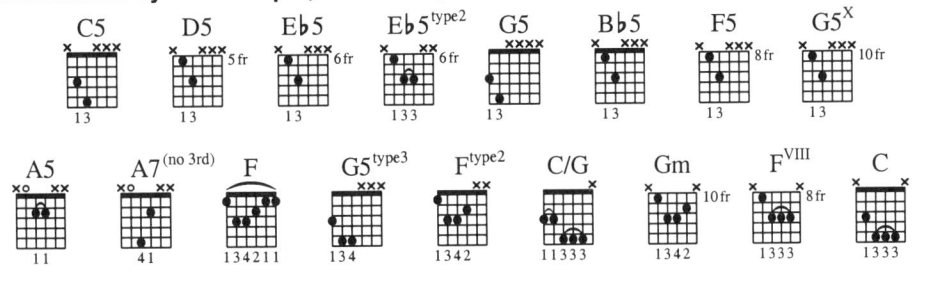

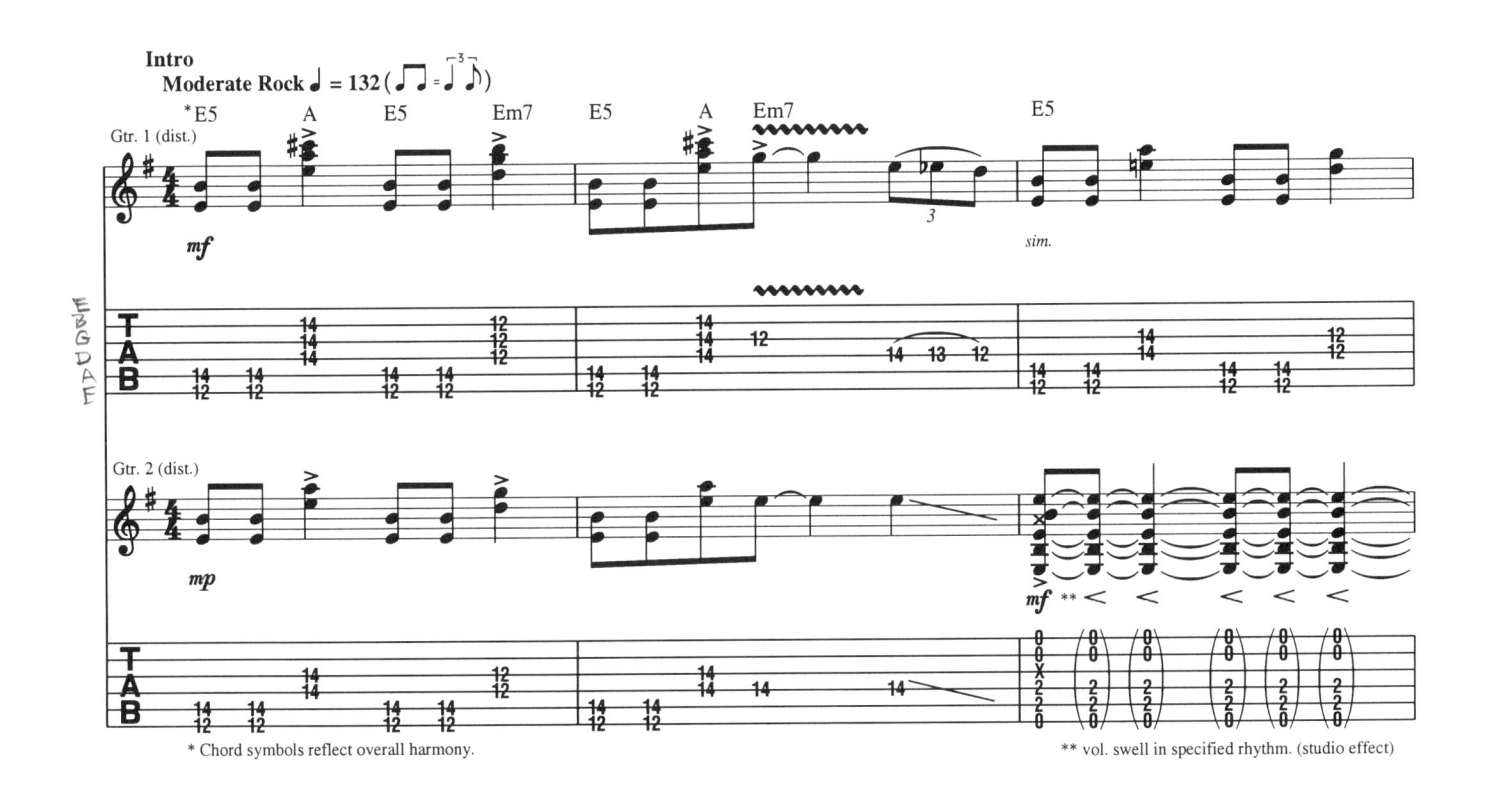

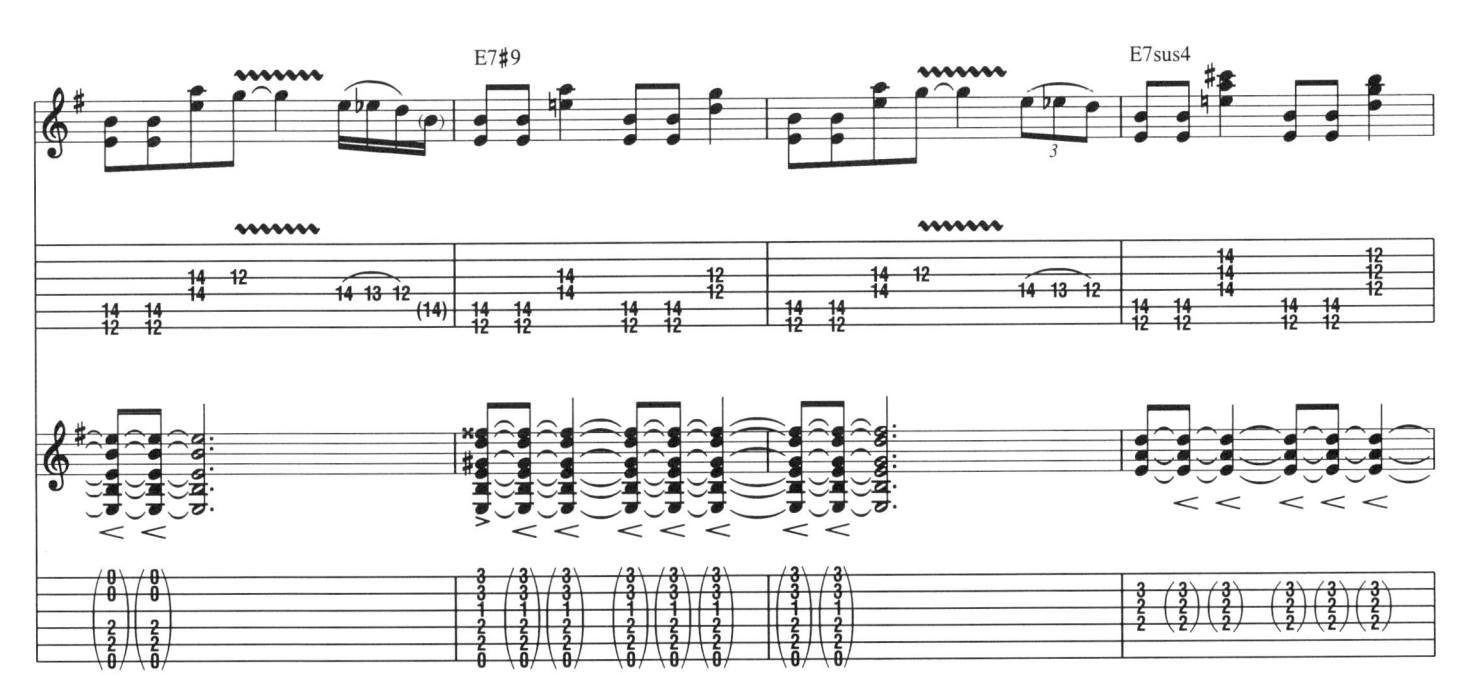

Intro
Moderate Rock ♩ = 132

* Chord symbols reflect overall harmony.
** vol. swell in specified rhythm. (studio effect)

Copyright © 1972 Bizarre Music, Sony/ATV Songs LLC and Ezra Music
Copyright Renewed
Administered by Bizarre Music
All Rights Reserved

E5 A/E E5 Em7 E5 A/E Em E5 A/E E5 Em7
Rhy. Fig. 1
End Rhy. Fig. 1
Rhy. Fig. 2
Verse
Gtr. 2: w/ Rhy. Fig. 2, 4 times
E5 A/E Em E5 A/E E5 Em7 E5 A/E Em
1. Well, we got no choice, all the girls
Rhy. Fig. 3
End Rhy. Fig. 3
End Rhy. Fig. 2
Gtr. 1: w/ Rhy. Fig. 3, 3 times
E5 A/E E5 Em7 E5 A/E Em E5 A/E E5 Em7
and boys mak - in' all their noise,
E5 A/E Em E5 A/E E5 Em7 E5 A/E Em
'cause they found new toys. Well, we

Pre-Chorus

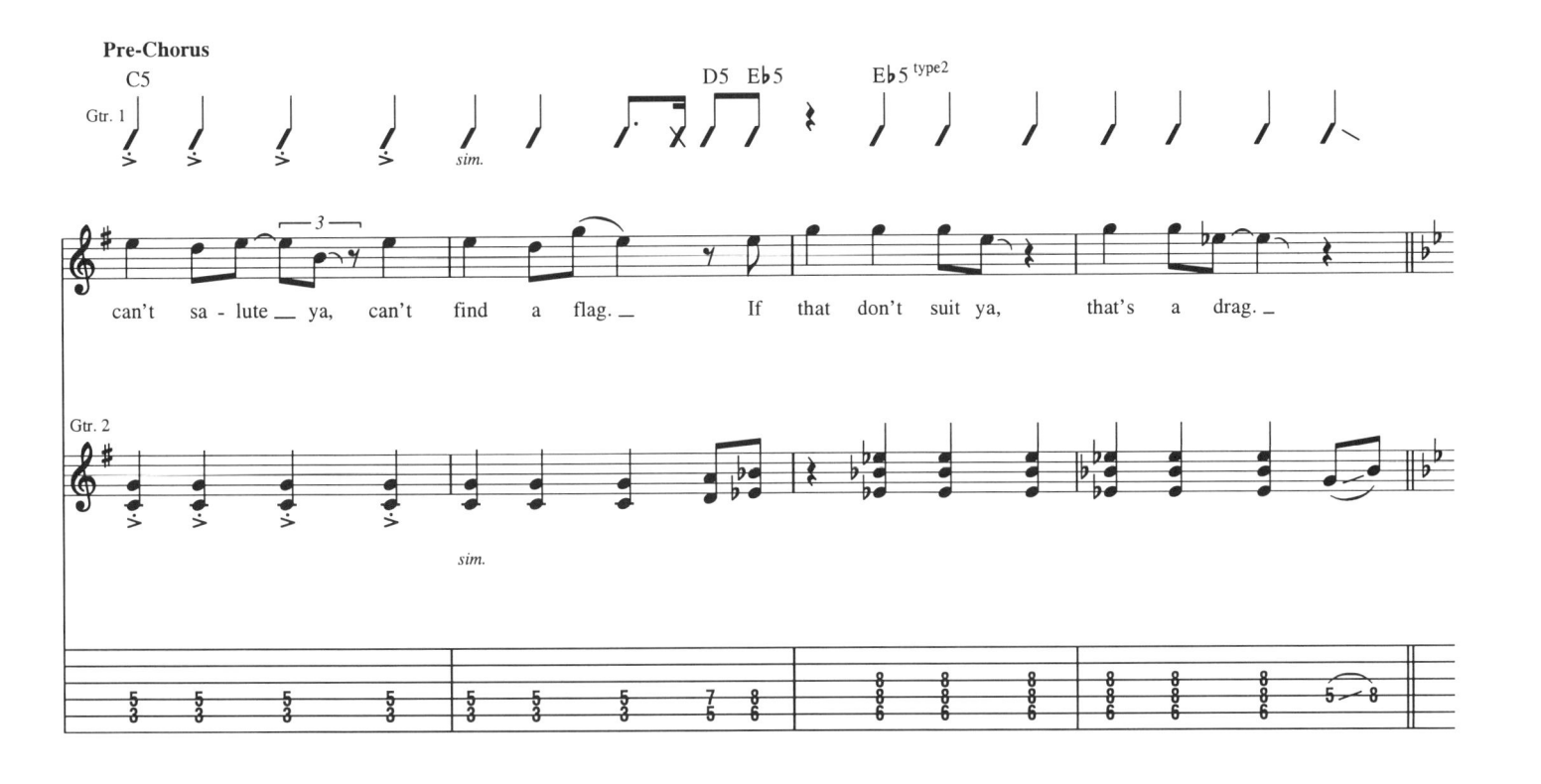

can't sa-lute ya, can't find a flag. If that don't suit ya, that's a drag.

Chorus

School's out for sum-mer!

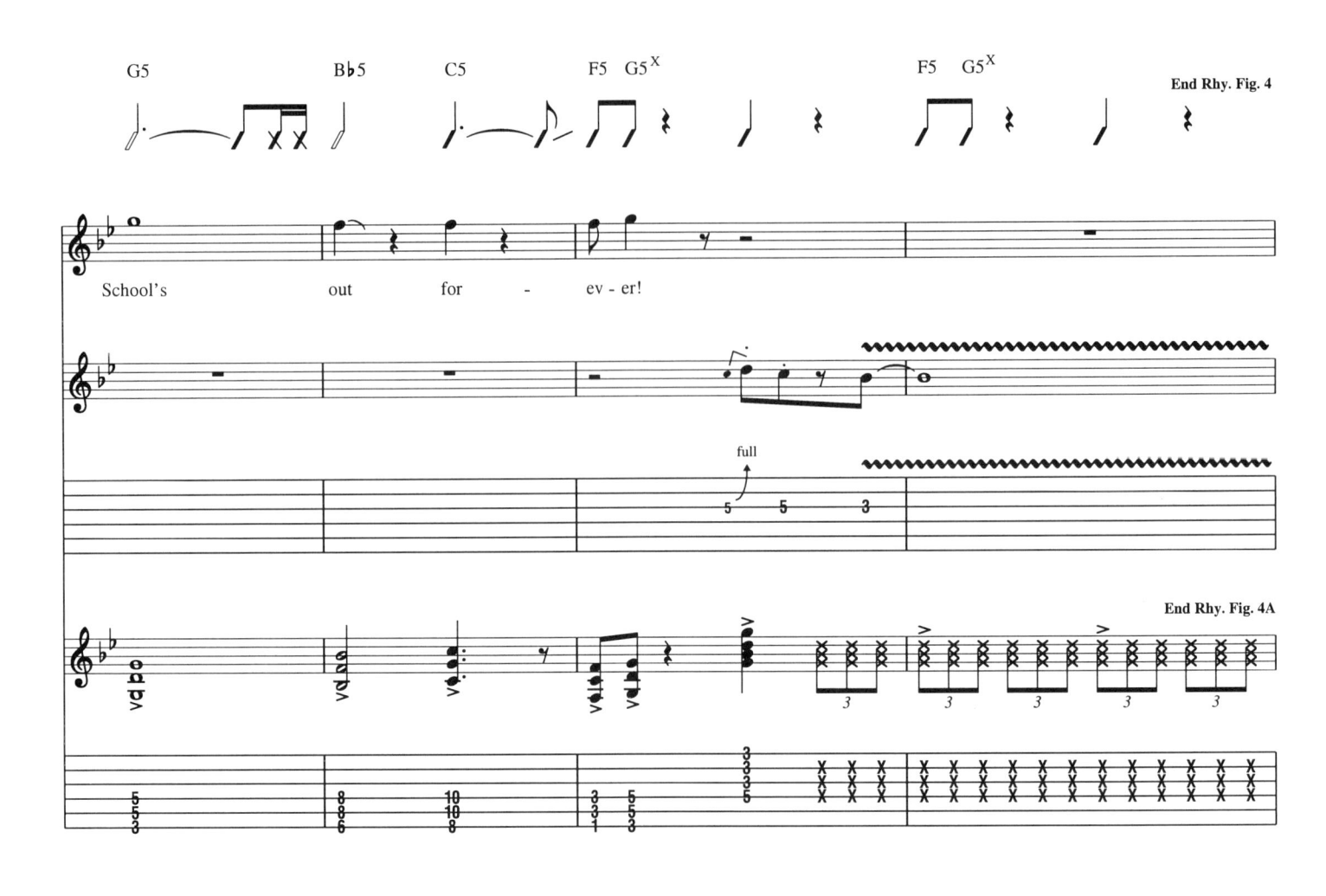

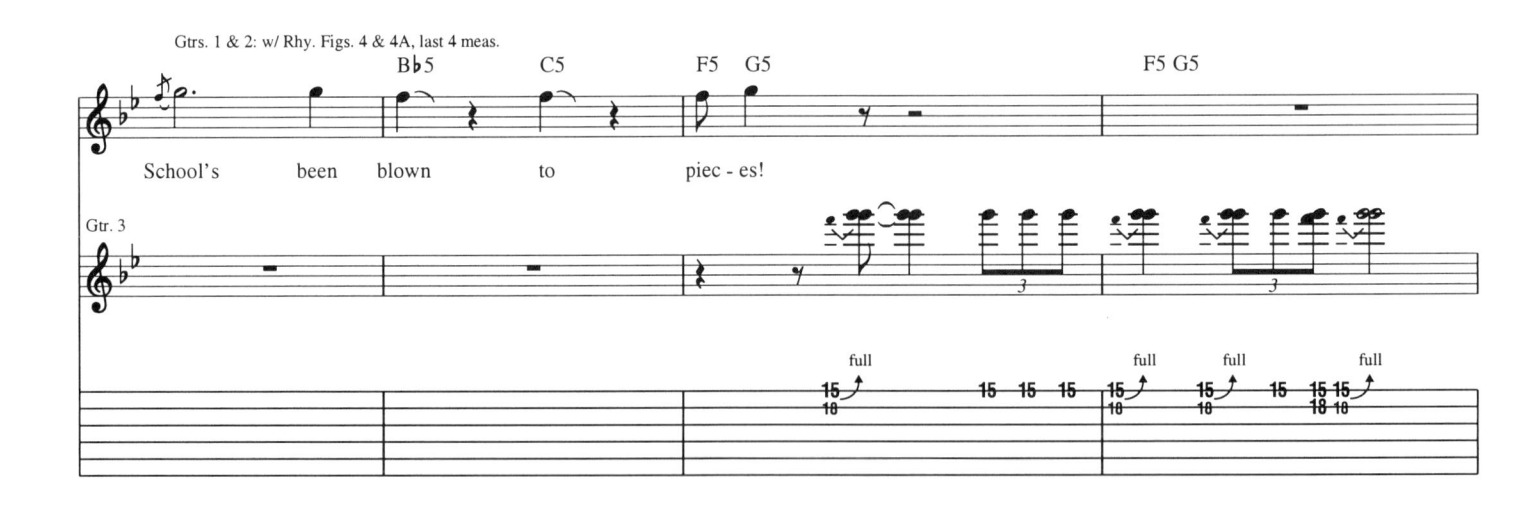

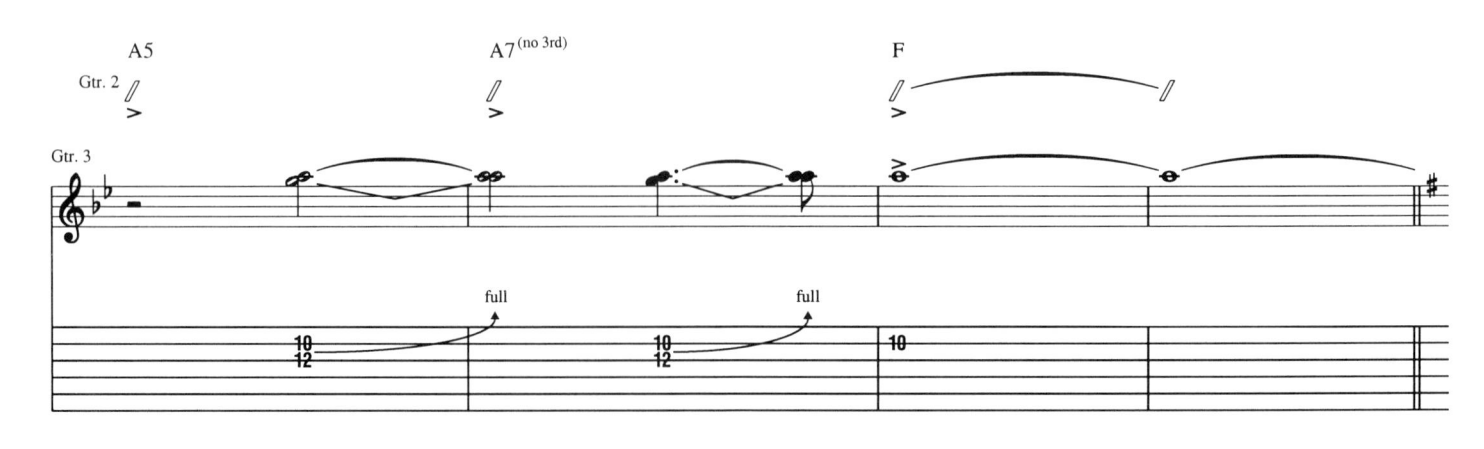

School's out for - ev - er!

School's been blown to piec - es!

Bridge

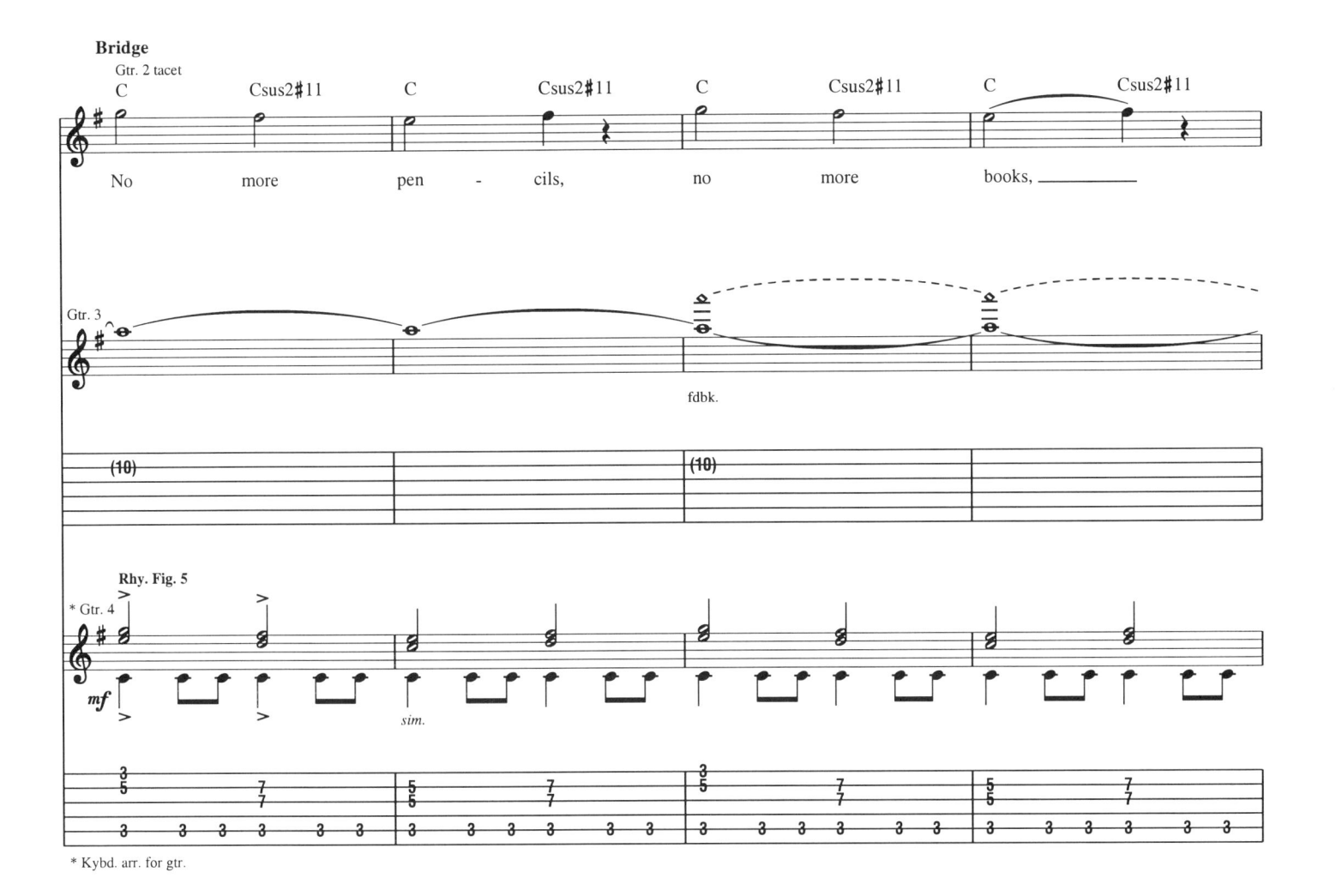

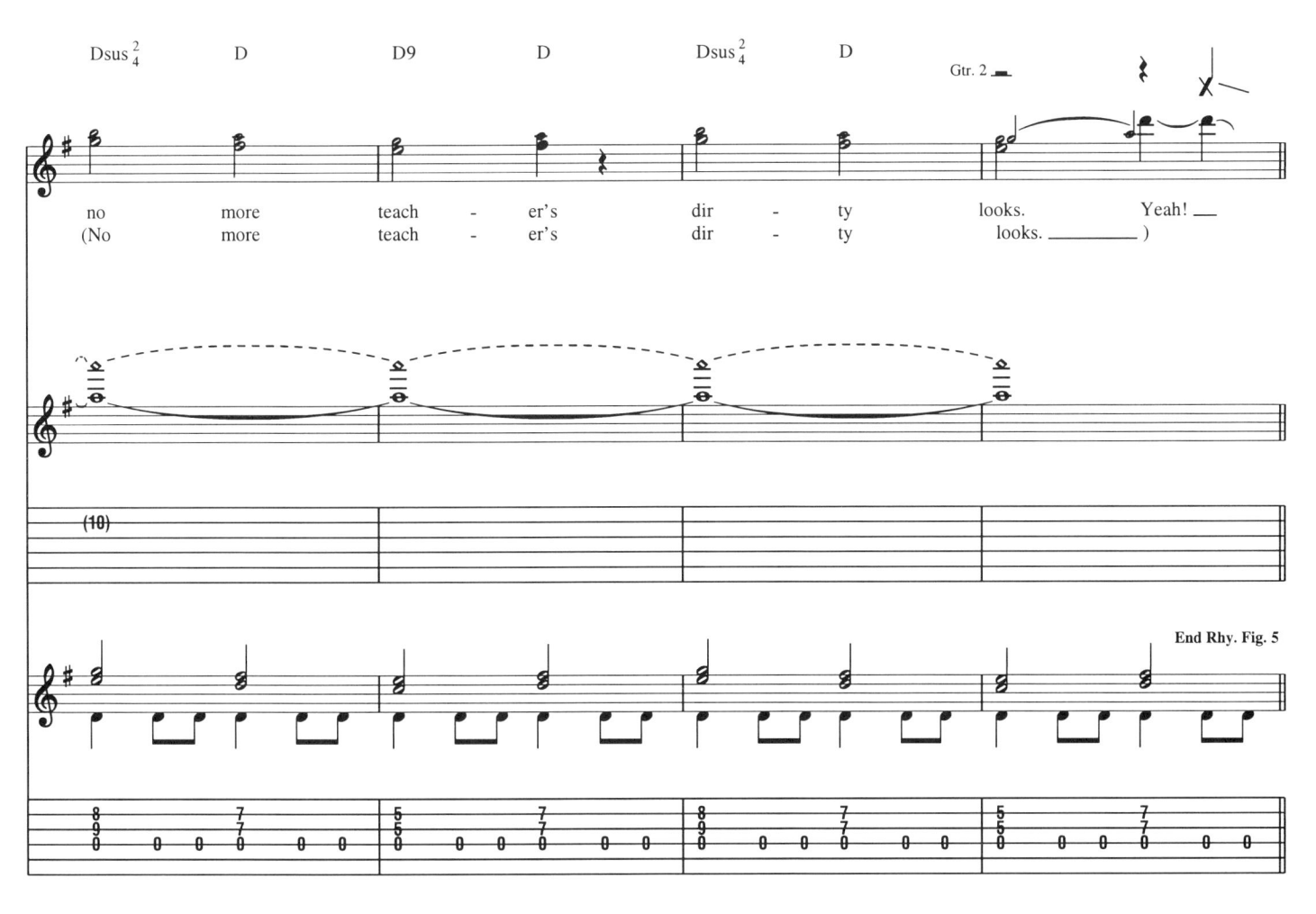

Lyrics: No more pen-cils, no more books, no more teach-er's dir-ty looks. Yeah!
(No more teach-er's dir-ty looks.)

Guitar Solo
Gtr. 4 tacet
Gtr. 2: w/ Rhy. Fig. 1, 2 times
Gtr. 1: w/ Rhy. Fig. 6, 3 times
E5 A/E E5 Em E5 A/E Em E5 A/E E5 Em E5 A/E Em
Gtr. 3
full
fdbk.
Rhy. Fig. 6
End Rhy. Fig. 6
Gtr. 1
w/ bar
E5 A/E E5 Em E5 A/E E5 Em E5 A/E Em
2. Well, we got
Gtr. 3
Gtr. 2
Verse
Gtr. 1: w/ Rhy. Fig. 3, 4 times
Gtr. 2: w/ Rhy. Fig. 2, 3 1/2 times
Gtr. 3 tacet
E5 A/E E5 Em7 E5 A/E Em E5 A/E E5 Em7
no class, and we got no prin - ci - ples,
E5 A/E Em E5 A/E E5 Em7 E5 A/E Em E5 A/E E5 Em7
and we got no in - no-cence. We can't e - ven think of a word that rhymes!

Chorus

Lyrics:
School's out for sum-mer!
School's out for-ev-er! My
school's been blown to piec-es!
No more pen-cils, no more books, no more teach-er's dirty looks.
Out for sum-mer, out till fall.

Chorus
Gtrs. 1 & 2: w/ Rhy. Figs. 4 & 4A, 1 1/2 times, simile
Dsus 2 4 D D9 D Dsus 2 4 D G5 B♭5 C5
We might not go back at all! School's out for
Gtr. 3
Gtr. 1
divisi
full
F5 G5 F5 G5 B♭5 C5
ev - er! School's out for
full
F5 G5 F5 G5 B♭5 C5 F5 G5
sum-mer! School's out with fe - ver!
8va
w/ bar
full
F5 G5 Gm F VIII C
w/ school bell
w/ children's cheers & tape effects
Gtr. 2
School's out com - plete - ly!
8va
loco
full 1/2
w/ bar
grad. bend
fdbk.

Surfin' U.S.A.

Words and Music by Chuck Berry

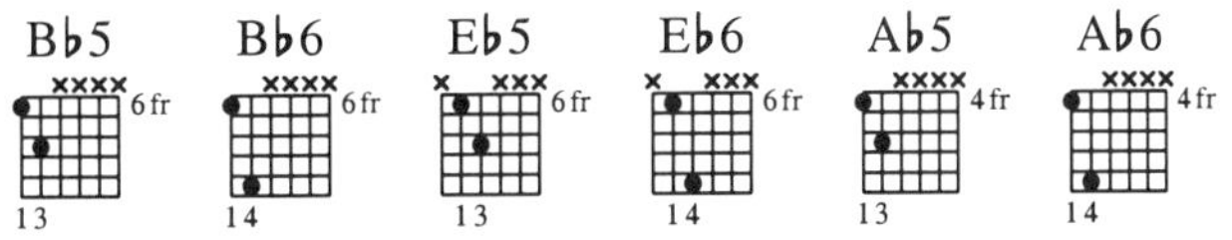

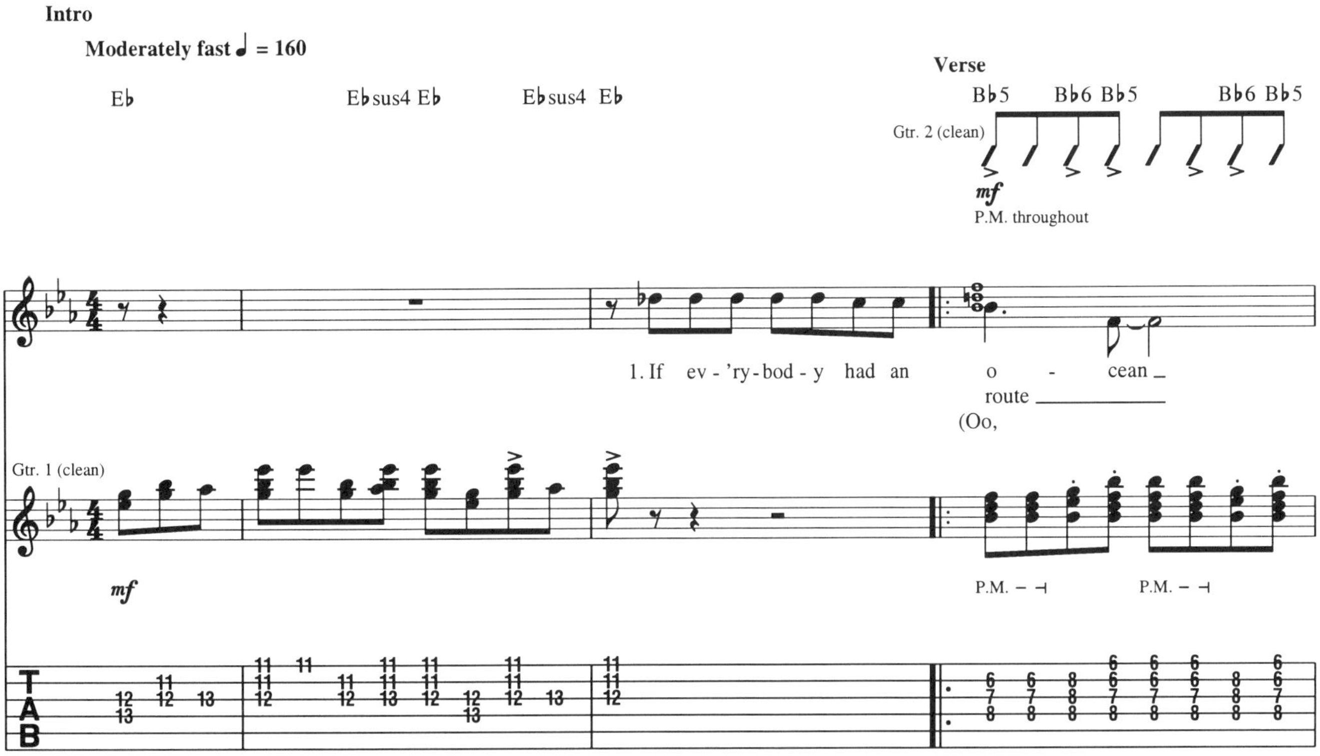

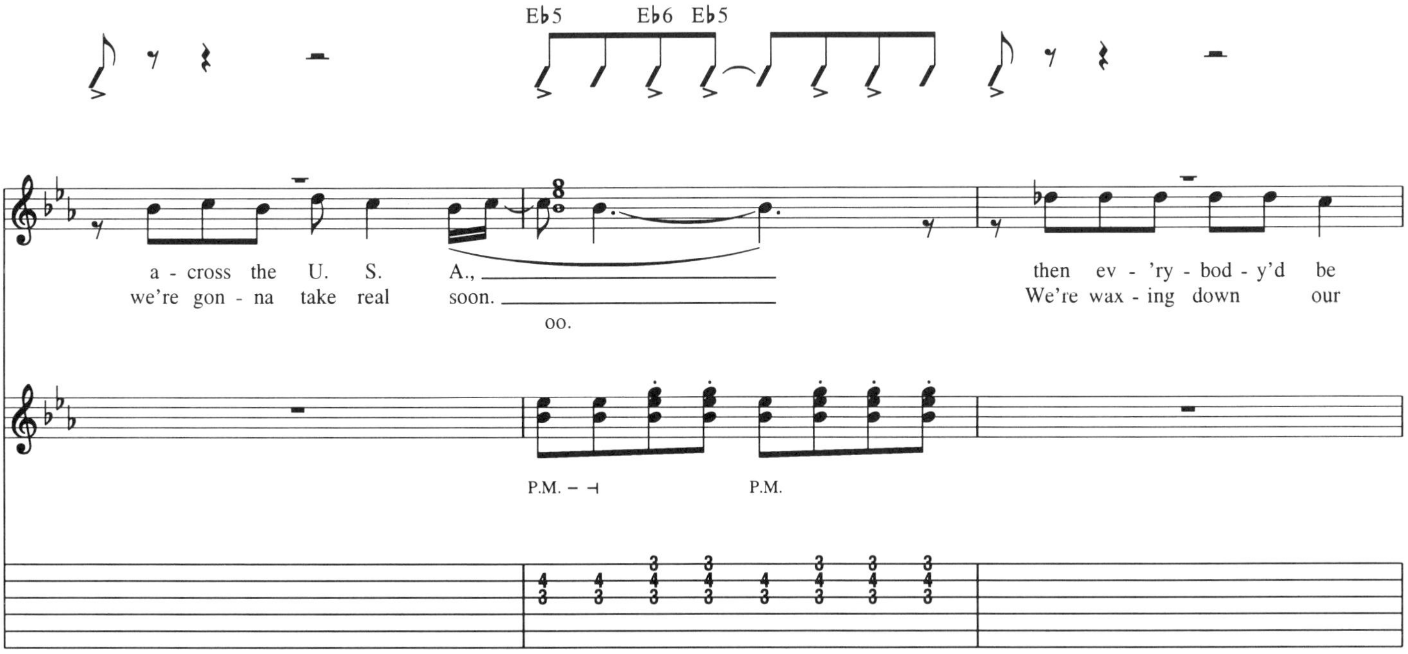

Bb5 Bb6 Bb5 Bb6 Bb5
sim.
surf - in' like Cal - i - forn - i - a.
surf - boards, we can't wait for June.
Oo, oo.
Eb5 Eb6 Eb5 Eb6 Eb5
P.M.
Ab5 Ab6 Ab5 Ab6 Ab5
You'd see 'em wear - ing their bag - gies, Hua - ra - chi sand - al's too.
We'll all be gone for the sum - mer, we're on surf - ari to stay.
Oo.
Eb5 Eb6 Eb5 Eb6 Eb5
Bb5 Bb6 Bb5 Bb6 Bb5
A bush - y, bush - y blonde hair - do,
Tell the teach - er we're surf - in',
oo. Oo,

Verse
Ab5
Eb5
Eb6 Eb5
Eb6 Eb5
Bb5
Bb6 Bb5
Bb6 Bb5
surf-in' U. S. A. ___
surf-in' U. S. A. ___
oo.) ___
2. You'll catch 'em surf-in' at Del Mar, _
4. And Hag-ger-ties and Swam - ies.
(In - side, out - side
P.M.
Bb6 Bb5
Bb6 Bb5
Eb5
Eb6 Eb5
Eb6 Eb5
Bb5
Ven-tu-ra Coun-ty line. ___
Pa-cif-ic Pal-i - sades. ___
San-ta Cruz and Trest - le, ___
San O-no-fre and Sun - set. ___
U. S. A. ___
In - side, out - side
U. S. A. ___
In - side, out - side
P.M.

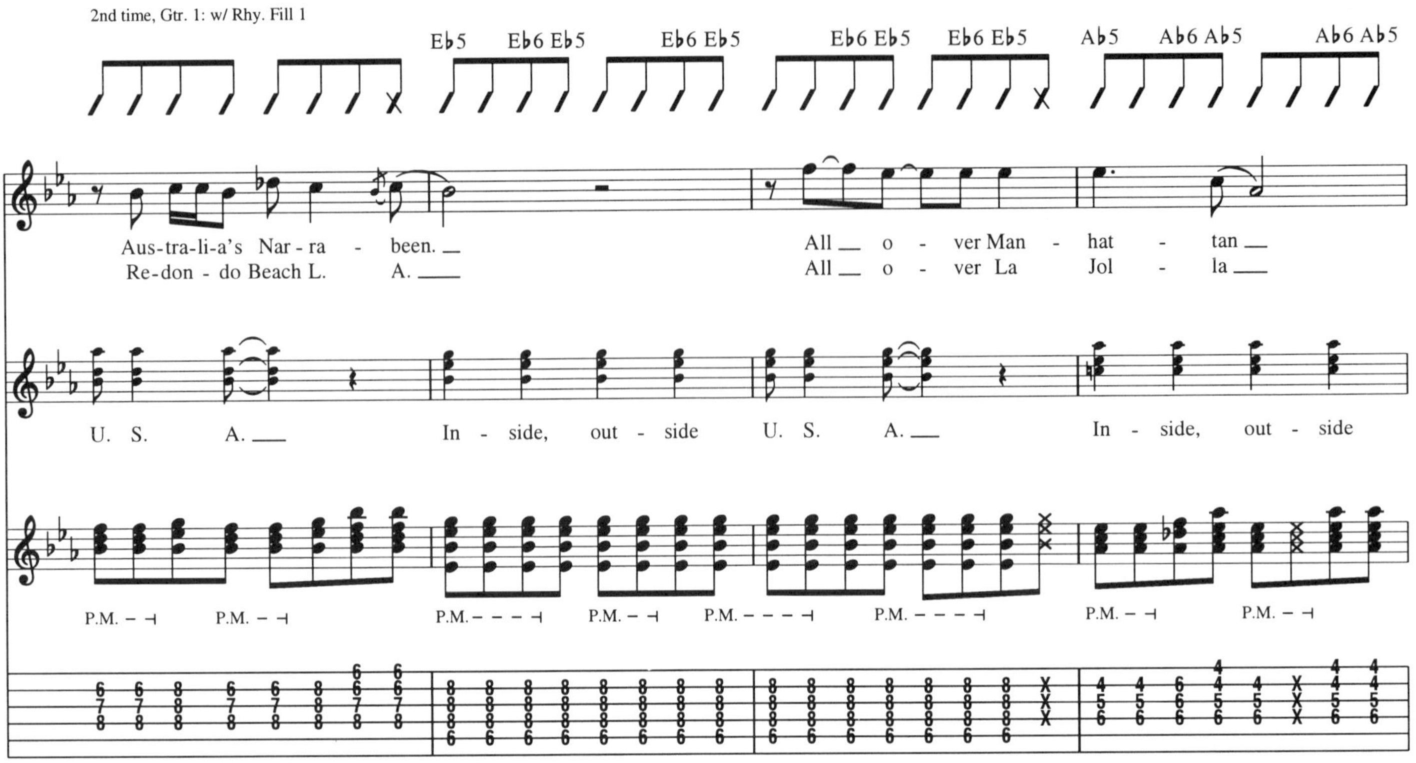
2nd time, Gtr. 1: w/ Rhy. Fill 1
Eb5 Eb6 Eb5 Eb6 Eb5 Eb6 Eb5 Eb6 Eb5 Ab5 Ab6 Ab5 Ab6 Ab5
Aus-tra-li-a's Nar-ra - been. All o - ver Man - hat - tan
Re-don - do Beach L. A. All o - ver La Jol - la
U. S. A. In - side, out - side U. S. A. In - side, out - side
P.M.

Eb5 Eb6 Eb5 Eb6 Eb5 Eb6 Eb5 Eb6 Bb5
and down Do-hen - y Way. Ev - 'ry-bod-y's gone surf - in',
at Wa - i - mi - a Bay.
U. S. A. In - side, out - side mm. Surf - in',
P.M.

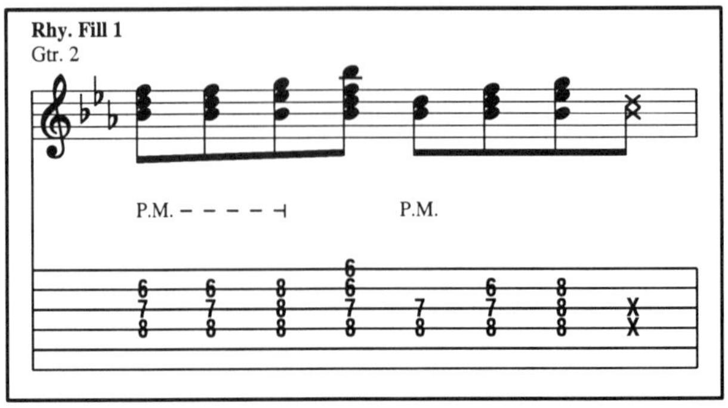
Rhy. Fill 1
Gtr. 2
P.M.

surf-in' U. S. A.

3. We'll all be plan-ning out a

Organ Solo

Guitar Solo
Ab5
Eb5
Ev - 'ry - bod - y's gone
(Mm.
let ring
let ring
1/2
1/2
P.M.
(cont. in slashes)
Outro-Chorus
Bb5
Bb6 Bb5 Ab5
Eb5
Eb6 Eb5
Eb6 Eb5
Eb
4
1fr
Gtr. 2 (clean)
P.M. throughout
surf - in',
surf - in',
surf-in' U. S. A.
Ev - 'ry-bod-y's gone
mm.
P.M.
P.M.
Repeat & fade
2nd time, Bkgd. Voc.: w/ Voc. Fill 1
Bb5
Ab5
Eb5
Eb6 Eb5
Eb6 Eb5
surf - in',
surf - in',
surf-in' U. S. A.
Ev - 'ry-bod-y's gone
Mm.)
P.M.
P.M.
P.M.
Voc. Fig. 1
Yeah.

Susie-Q

Words and Music by Dale Hawkins, Stan Lewis and Eleanor Broadwater

Gtr. 2: w/ Rhy. Fig. 1, 3 times
Em7
Rhy. Fig. 3
End Rhy. Fig. 3
Gtr. 2
baby, I love you, Susie Q.
and never leave me blue, Susie Q.
Like the way you walk.
Well, say that you'll be mine.
Gtr. 1
End Rhy. Fig. 2
Gtr. 1: w/ Rhy. Fig. 2
I like the way you talk.
Well, say that you'll be mine.
I like the way you walk,
Well, say that you'll be mine,
To Coda 2
To Coda 1
Gtr. 2: w/ Rhy. Fig. 3
Gtr. 2: w/ Rhy. Fig. 1
I like the way you talk, Susie Q.
baby, all the time, Susie Q.
Guitar Solo
Gtr. 2: w/ Rhy. Fig. 1, 2 times
w/ dist.
Gtr. 2: w/ Rhy. Fig. 3
Gtr. 2: w/ Rhy. Fig. 1, 3 times
15ma
loco
P.H.
pitches: A B♭ C♯ D

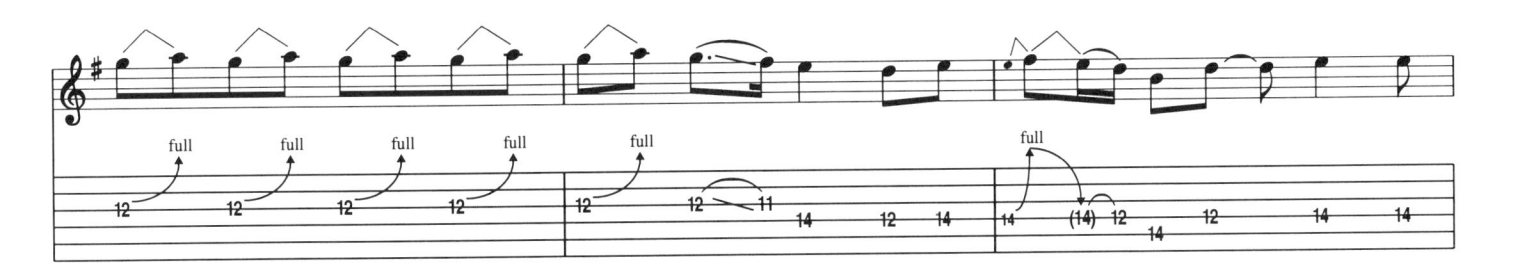

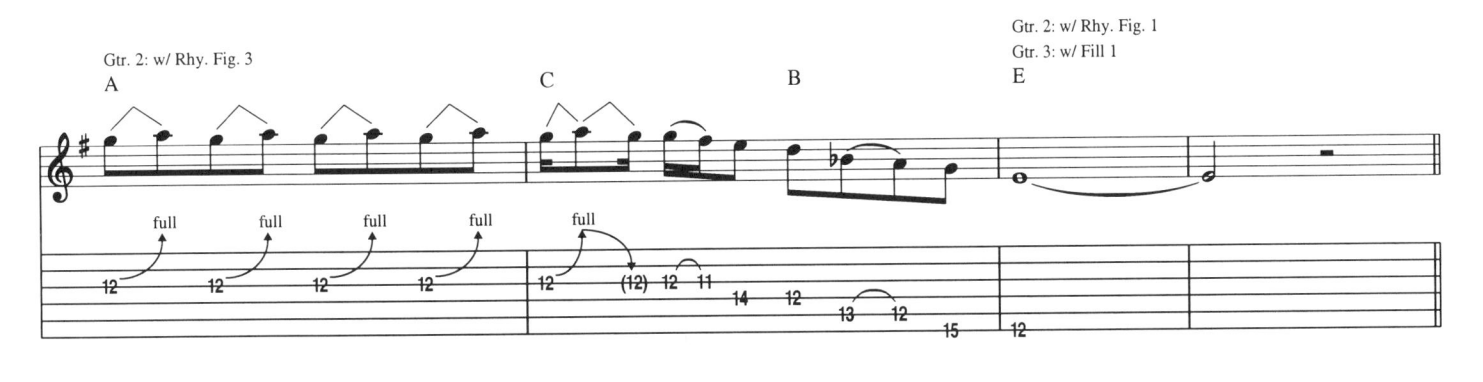

Interlude

Em7

2. Well, say that you'll be true.

⊕ Coda 1
Guitar Solo

Fill 1

Interlude

3. Oh, _____ Su - sie - Q.

D.S. al Coda 2

Coda 2
Gtr. 1: w/ Rhy. Fig. 2
Gtr. 2: w/ Rhy. Fig. 1, 2 times
Em7
Oh, Su - sie - Q.
Oh, Su - sie - Q.
Gtr. 2: w/ Rhy. Fig. 3
A
C
B
Gtr. 2: w/ Rhy. Fig. 1
Gtr. 3: w/ Fill 2
Em7
Oh, Su - sie - Q, ba - by, I love you, Su - sie - Q.
Outro-Solo
Gtr. 2: w/ Rhy. Fig. 1, till fade, simile
E
Gtr. 1
w/ dist.
Fill 2
Gtr. 3
w/ fast tremolo
mf
f
p
dim.
grad. bend
*fade in

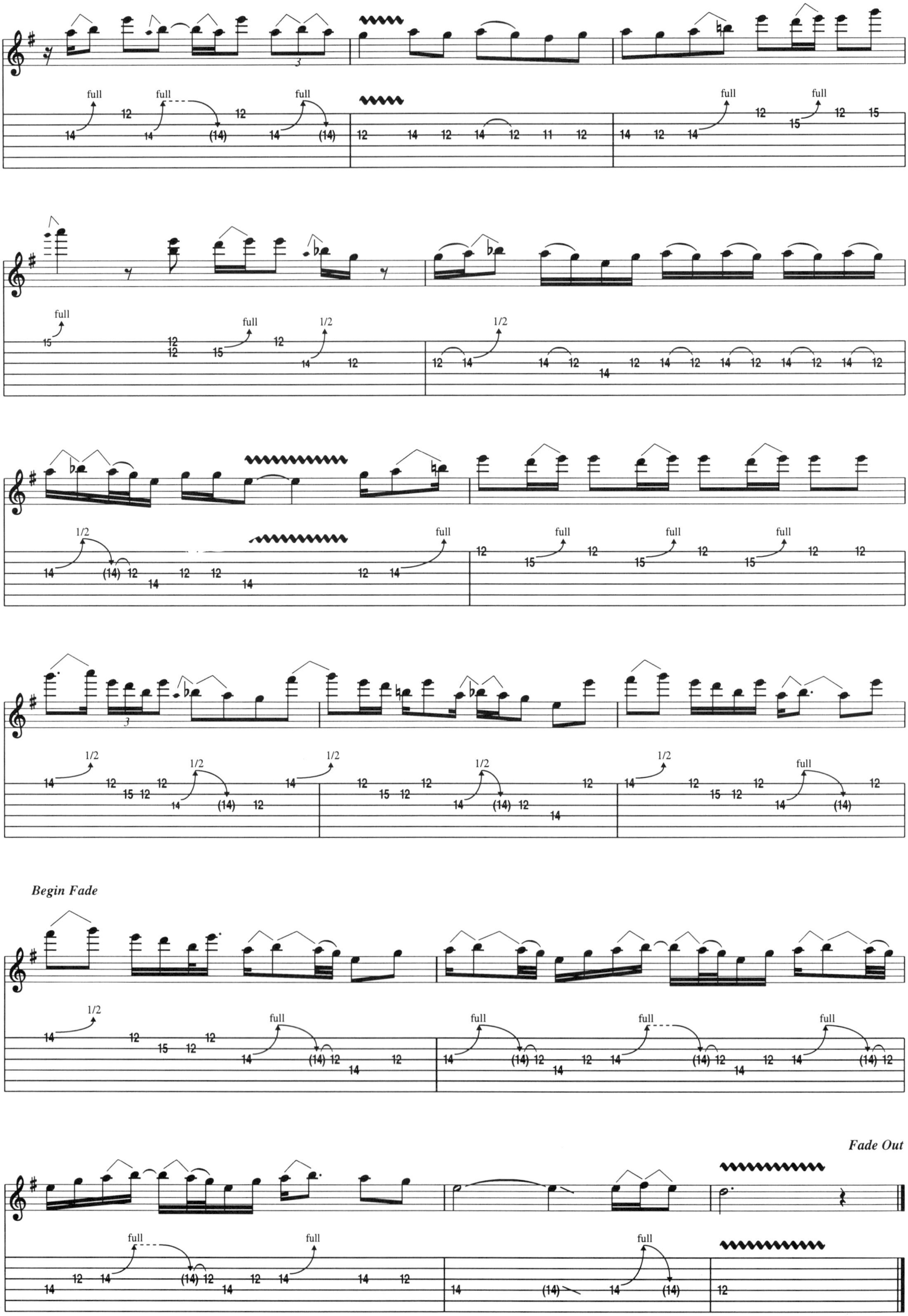
Begin Fade
Fade Out

Sweet Child O' Mine

Words and Music by W. Axl Rose, Slash, Izzy Stradlin', Duff McKagan and Steven Adler

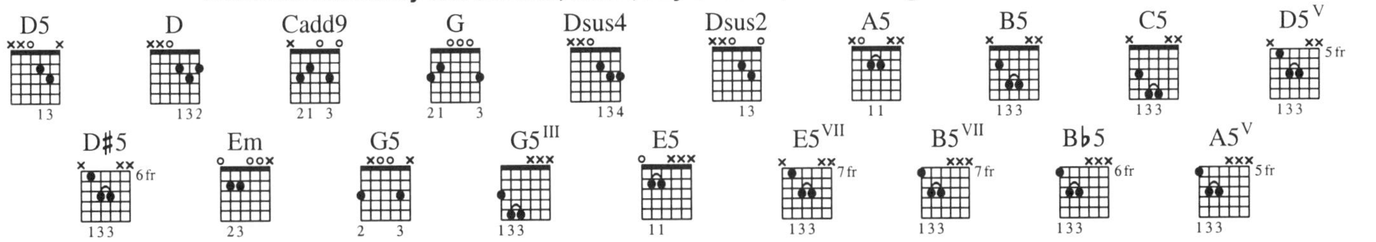

Tune Down 1/2 Step:

(1) = E♭ (4) = G♭
(2) = A♭ (5) = B♭
(3) = D♭ (6) = E♭

Intro

Medium Rock ♩ = 122

168

G
D
Dsus4 D Dsus2 D
Gtr. 2
stared too long, I'll prob-'ly break down and cry.
pray for the thun - der and the rain to qui - et - ly pass me by.
Chorus
A5
Rhy. Fig. 3
B5 C5
Gtr. 1: w/ Fill 2, 3rd time
D
Dsus4 D Dsus2 D
End Rhy. Fig. 3
Whoa, whoa, whoa, sweet child o' mine.
*Gtr. 1
*On D.S., double Gtr. 2
To Coda
A5
B5 C5
D
Whoa, oh, oh, oh, sweet love o' mine.
Fill 2
Gtr. 1
1/2
1/4
TAB

Gtr. 2: w/ Rhy. Fig. 1
Gtr. 3: w/ Rhy. Fig. 2
D
C
1.
G
full
full
full
full
D
2.
G
D
1/2
1/2
hold bend
Gtr. 2: w/ Rhy. Fig. 1, first 7 meas.
Gtr. 3: w/ Rhy. Fig. 2
C
1/2
1/2
G
Dsus4 D Dsus2 D
D.S. al Coda
Gtr. 2
8va
full
full
full
full
Coda
Gtrs. 1 & 2: w/ Rhy. Fig. 3, 1 1/2 times
Gtr.1: w/ Fill 2
D
A5
B5 C5
D
Gtrs. 1 & 2
Oh, oh, oh, oh, sweet child o' mine.
A5
B5 C5
D5
D#5
Gtrs. 1 & 2
Woo, yeah, yeah! Ooh, sweet love o' mine.

Guitar Solo

Em
C
B7
Am
8va
loco
Gtr. 1
full
Gtr. 4
Rhy. Fig. 4
End Rhy. Fig. 4
Gtr. 4: w/ Rhy. Fig. 4, 2 times
1/2
Gtr. 4: w/ Rhy. Fig. 4, first 3 meas.
Gtr. 5: w/ Fill 3
Fill 3
Gtr. 5
w/ wah - wah
T
A
B

Gtr. 4: w/ Rhy. Fill 1
A5
G
F♯
3fr
2fr
Em
Rhy. Fig. 5
E
F♯
open
2fr
G5
Gtr. 2
P.M.
8va
Gtr. 5
w/ wah-wah
full
A5
B5
C5
D5
G5
End Rhy. Fig. 5
Gtr. 2: w/ Rhy. Fig. 5, 3 times
Em
G5
loco
1/2
hold bend
E5
1/4
Rhy. Fill 1
Gtr. 4
T
A
B

173

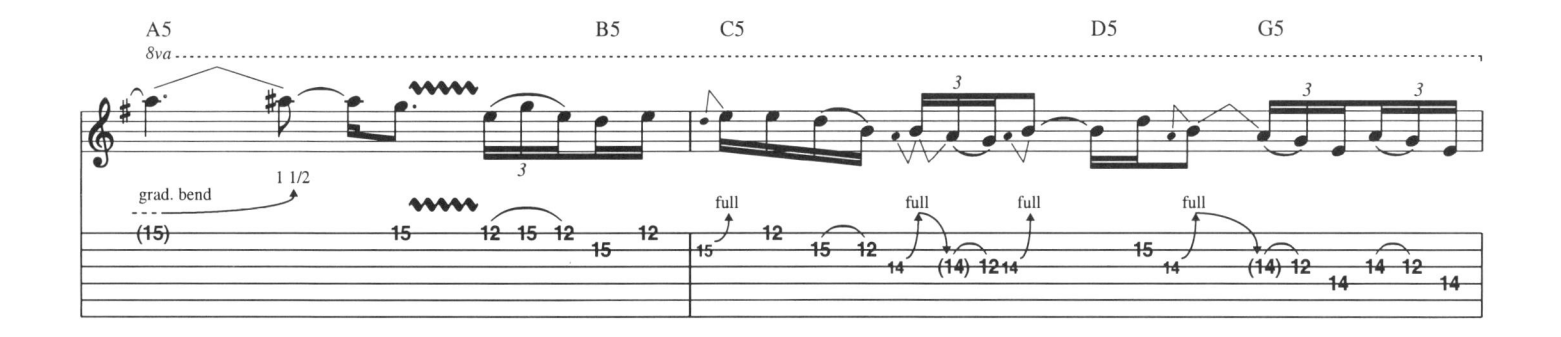

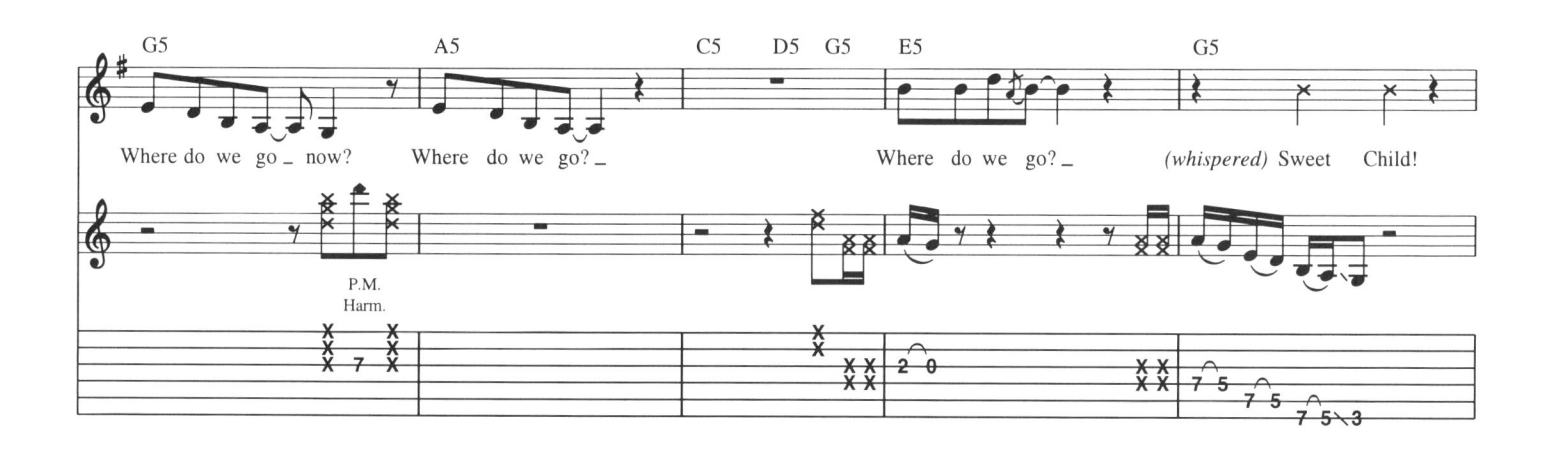

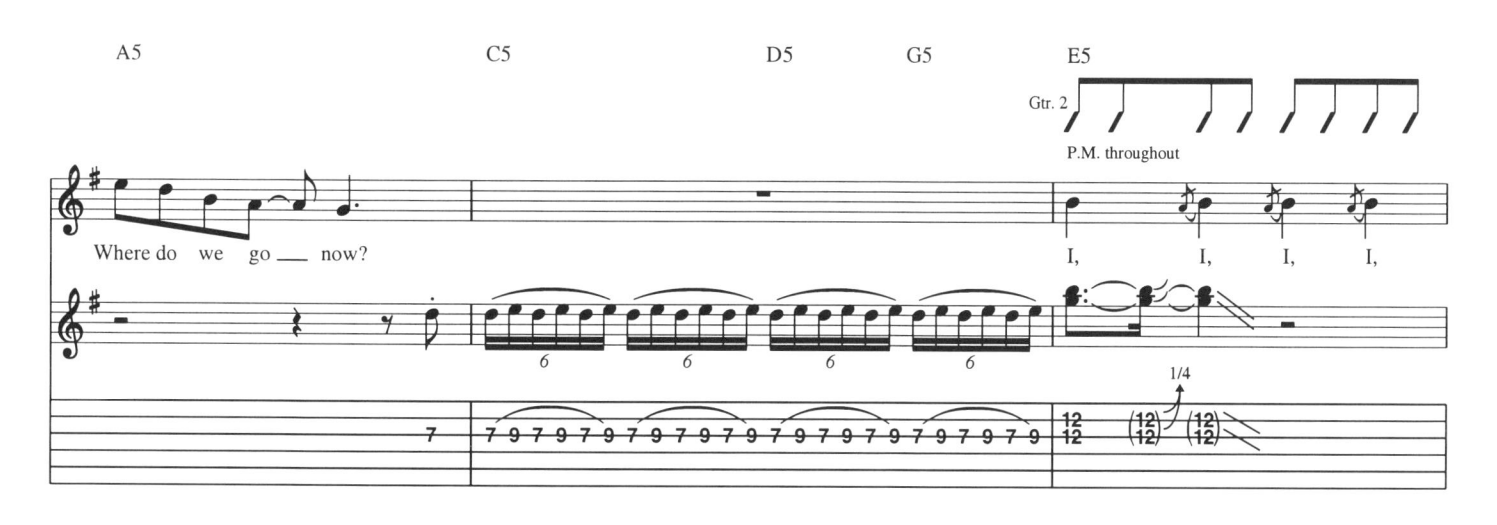

G5 A5 C5 D5V G5III
I, I, I, I, Where do we go now, now?
8va
full full
E5 E F# 6 open 6 2fr G5 A5 B5
Rhy. Fig. 7
Where do we go? Ah. Where do we go now?
8va
full full full full
C5 D5V G5III
End Rhy. Fig. 7
Gtr. 2: w/ Rhy. Fig. 7
E5 G5
8va
When do we go?
loco
full 1/2 full grad. bend full
A5 C5 D5 G5
8va
Where do we go now?
full full full full full

Gtr. 2: w/ Rhy. Fig. 7, first 3 meas.
E5
G5
A5
B5
E5 D5 B5 B♭5 A5 G
Gtr. 2
8va
Where do we go?
Where do we go now?
No, no, no, no, no, no,
grad. bend
full
1/2
Gtr. 2: w/ Rhy. Fig. 7, first 2 meas.
E5
A5
C5
D5
no. Sweet child, sweet child o'
E5
mine.
-1/2
Gtr. 4
Gtr. 1
divisi
*bend neck

Walk This Way

Words and Music by Steven Tyler and Joe Perry

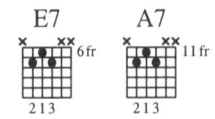

ain't seen noth-in' till you're down on a muf-fin and you're sure to be a-chang-in' your ways." I met a
three young la-dies in the school gym lock-er when I no-ticed they was look-in' at me. I was a

cheer - lead-er, was a real young bleed-er all the times I could rem - i - nisce, 'cause the
high school los - er, nev - er made it with a la - dy 'til the boys told me some-thin' I missed, then my

best things in lov-in' with a sis-ter and a cou-sin on-ly start-ed with a lit-tle kiss, a-like this!
next door neigh-bor with a daugh-ter had a fa-vor so I gave her just a lit-tle kiss a-like this!

Interlude
Gtr. 1: w/ Riff A, 2nd time
N.C.(E5)

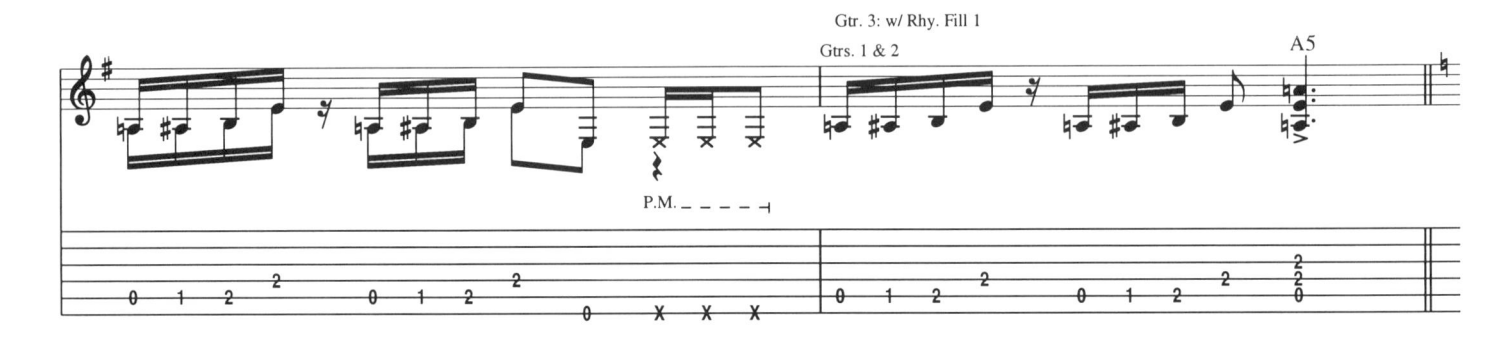

Gtr. 3: w/ Rhy. Fill 1
Gtrs. 1 & 2
A5

Verse
Gtrs. 1 & 2: w/ Rhy. Fig. 1, 3 times, simile
N.C.(C7)

2., 4. See-saw swingin' with the boys in the school and your feet flyin' up in the air,___ I sing,

"Hey did-dle did-dle" with your kit-ty in the mid-dle of the swing like you didn't care.___ So I

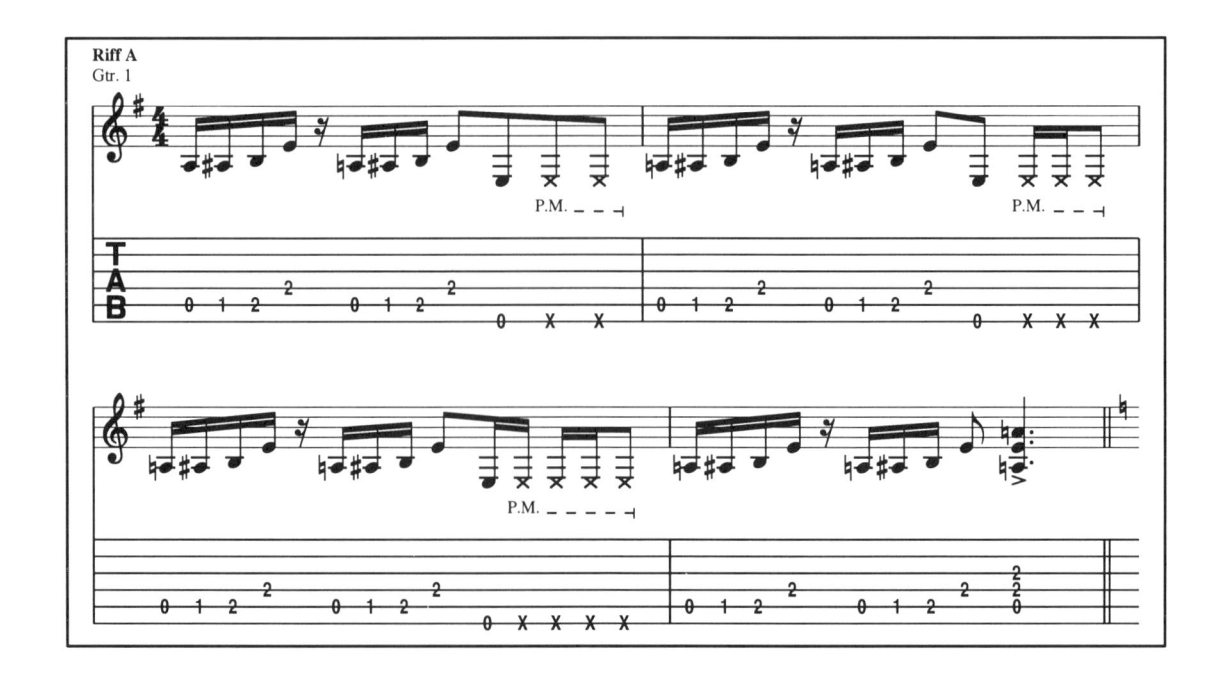

took a big chance at the high school dance with a miss-y who was read-y to play,___ was a

*Sing harmony 1st time only.

Riff A
Gtr. 1

178

me she was fool-in' 'cause she knew what she was do-in' and I know'd love was here to stay when she told me to...
when she told me how to walk this way. She told me to...

Chorus

(Walk this way, talk this way, walk this way,

walk this way.) Uh, just gim-me a kiss.

Guitar Solo

A5
A-like this!
full
1/2
full
Interlude
N.C.(E5)
Gtr. 1
Gtr. 2
divisi
Oo.
P.M.
Gtr. 3: w/ Rhy. Fill 1
D.S. al Coda
A5
Uh.
Gtrs. 1 & 2
P.M.
Coda
Chorus
C7
F7
(Walk this way, talk this way,
Gtr. 1
Gtr. 2

talk this way, walk this way, talk this way,

talk this way, walk this way, talk this way. Uh, just gim-me a kiss.

Guitar Solo

Gtrs. 1 & 2: w/ Rhy. Fig. 2

Guitar Solo

Gtrs. 1 & 2: w/ Riff B, till fade

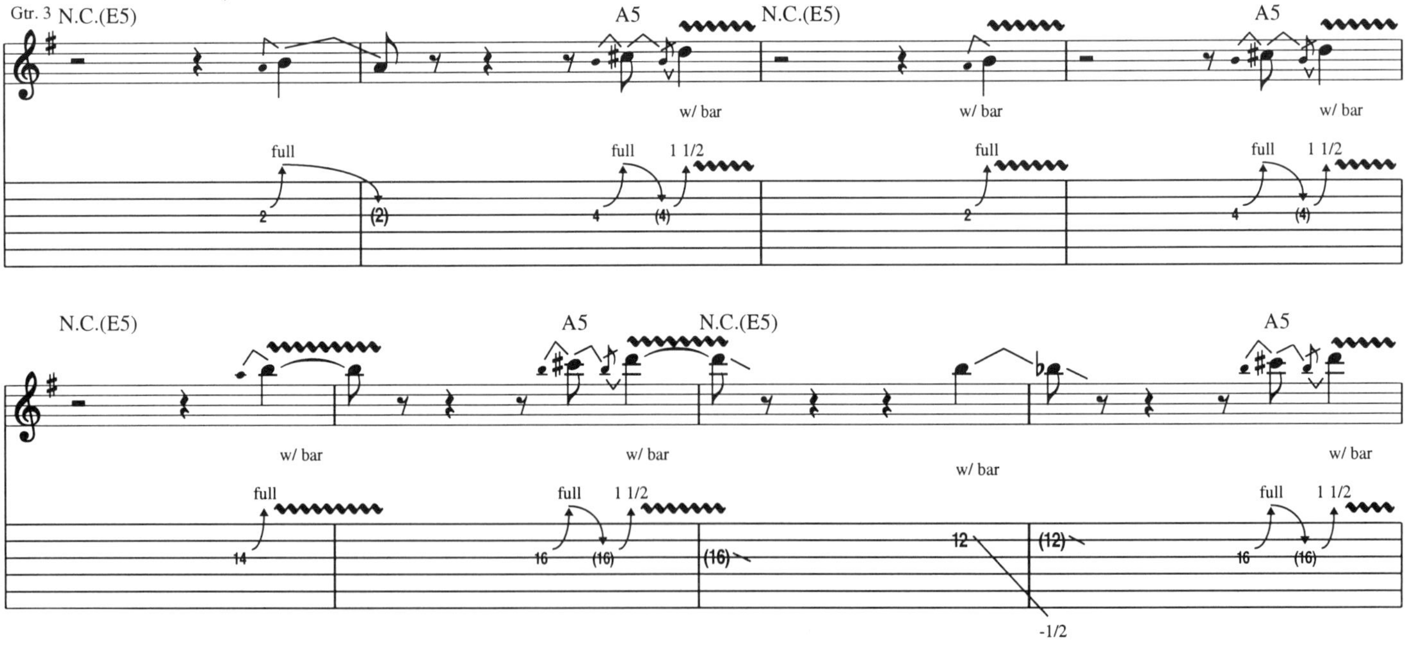

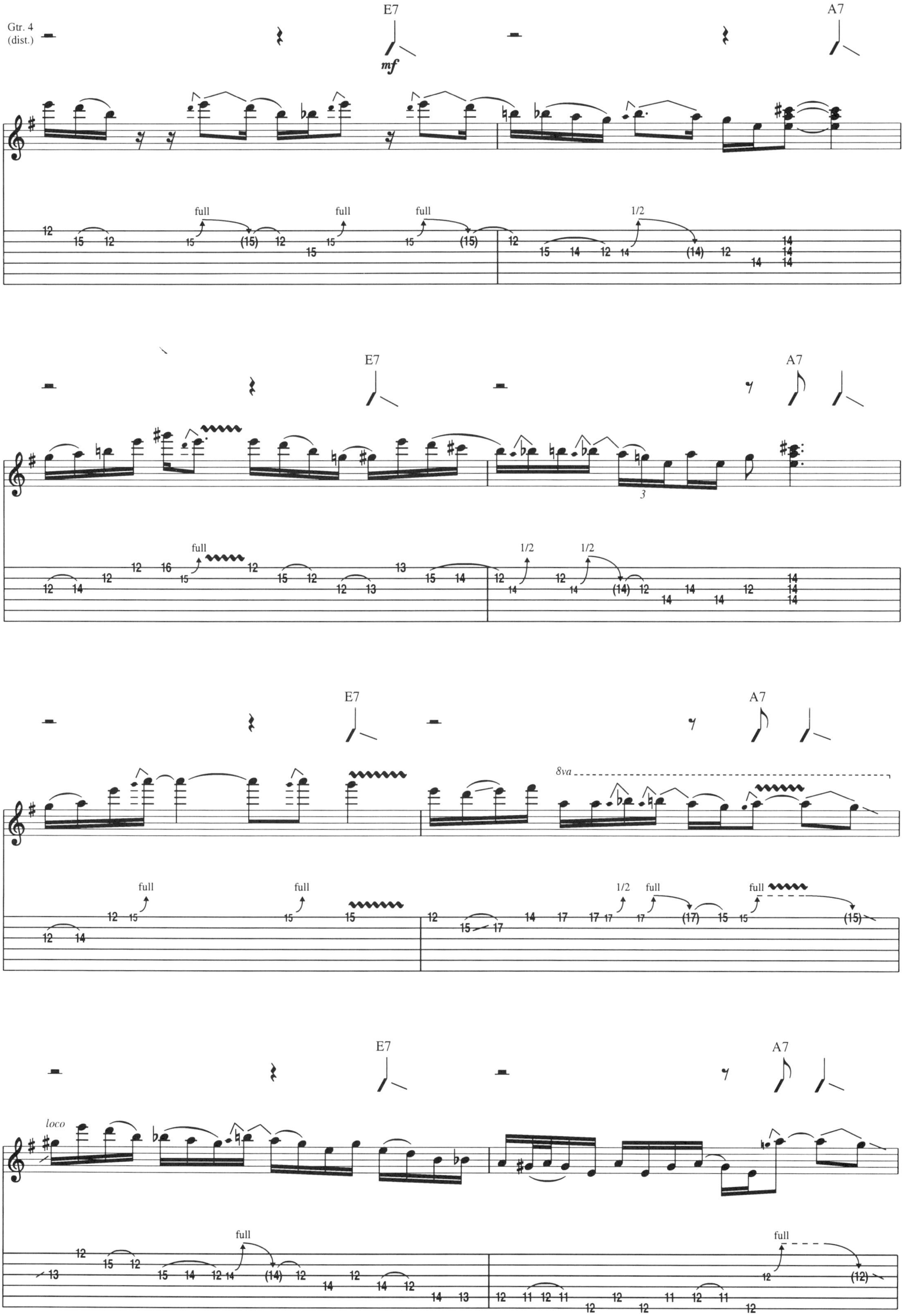
Gtr. 4
(dist.)
E7
A7
mf
full
1/2
8va
loco
3

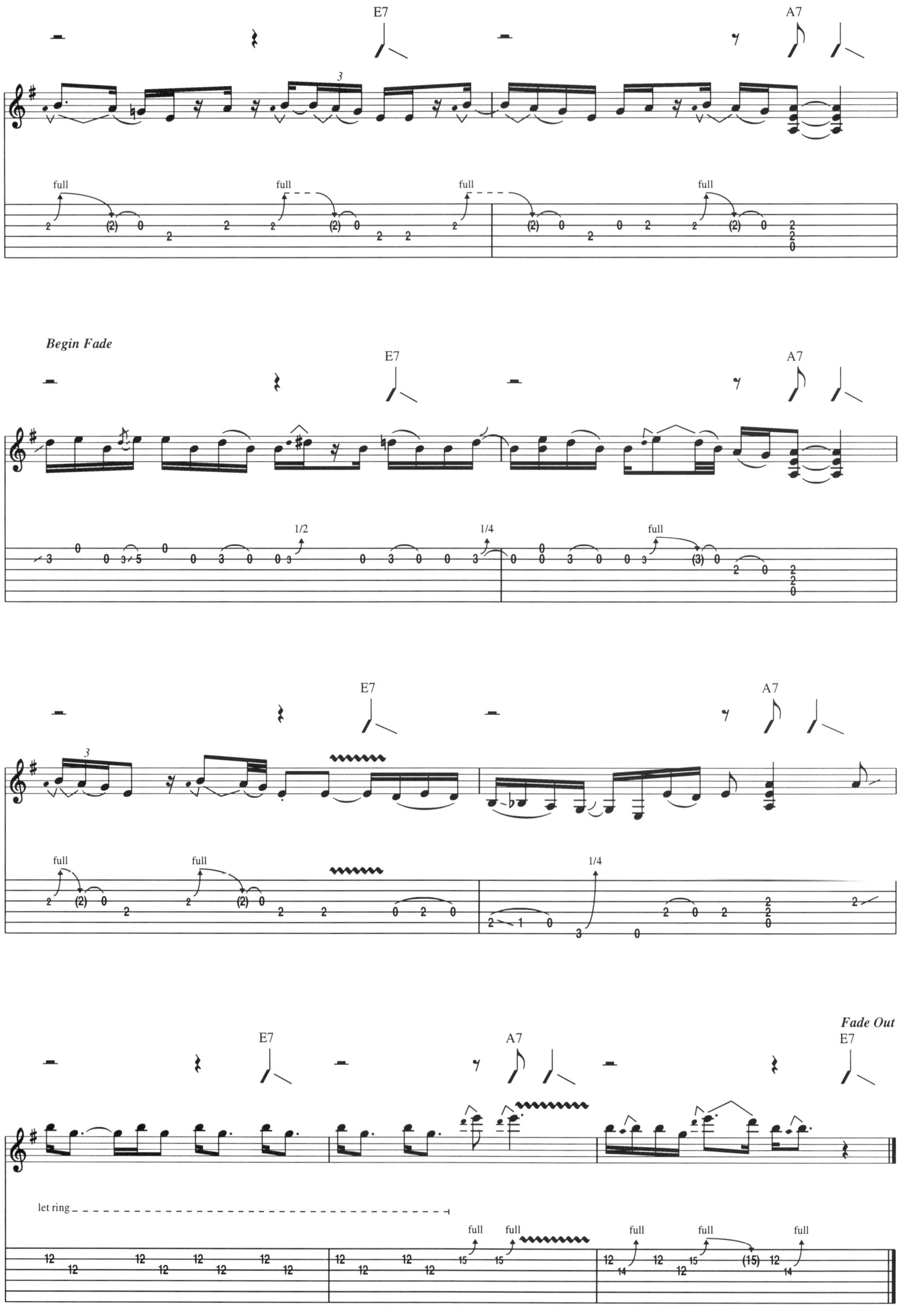
E7
A7
full
Begin Fade
1/2
1/4
Fade Out
let ring

We're Ready

Words and Music by Tom Scholz

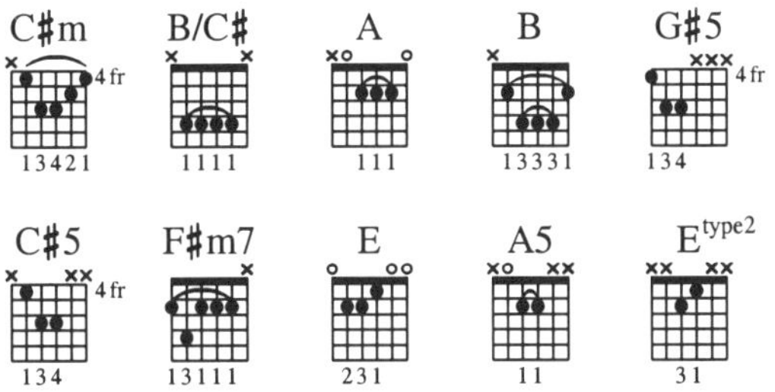

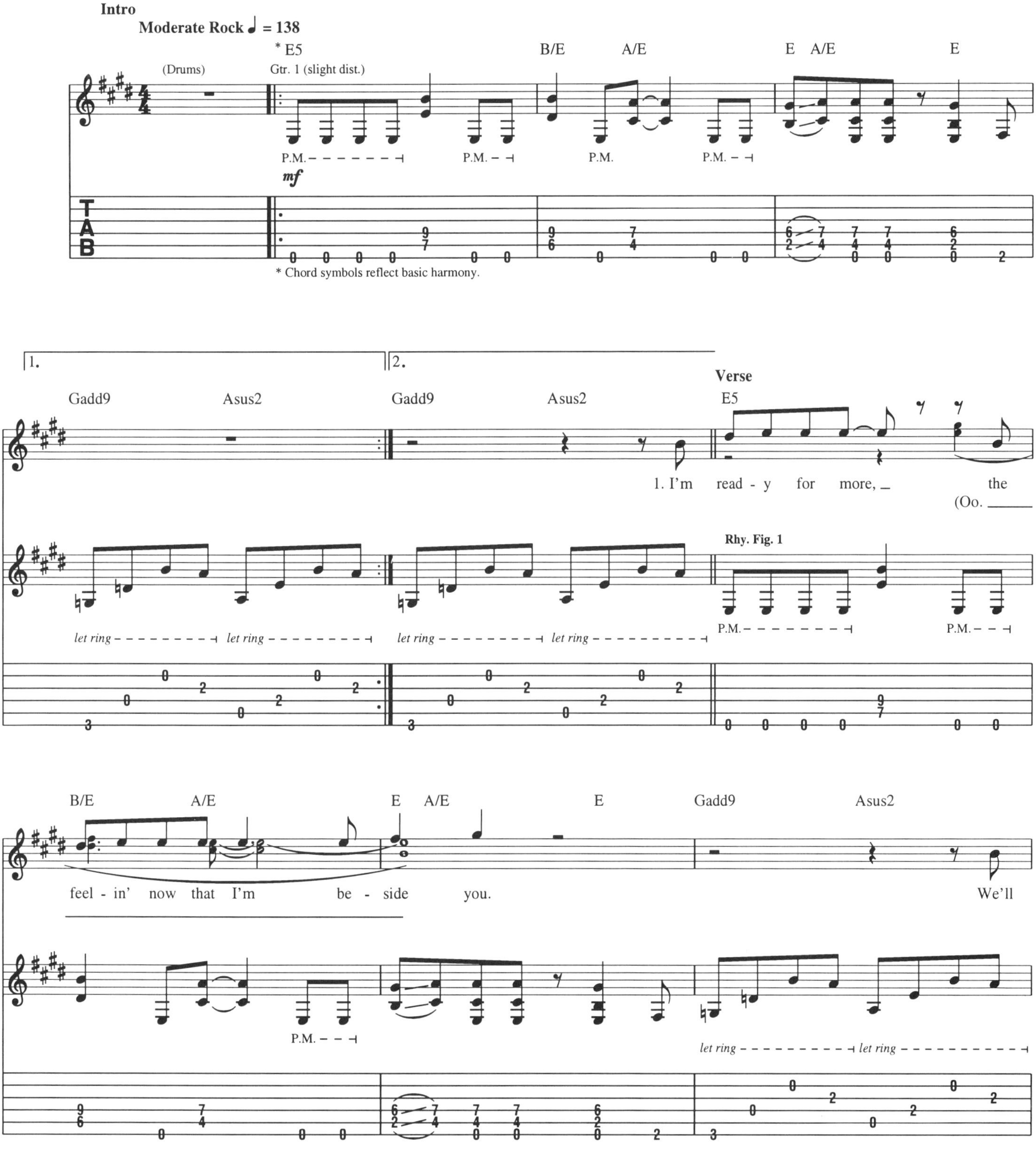

E5 B/E A/E E A/E E
o - pen the door, do an - y - thing that we de - cide to. And I
Oo.)
Gtr. 1
End Rhy. Fig. 1
P.M.
Gtr. 2 (dist.)
divisi
Rhy. Fill 1
End Rhy. Fill 1
Gtr. 1 tacet
G D5 A
know that there's some - thing that's just out of sight. And I
feel that it's time we were off on our way. We can
Gtr. 2
Rhy. Fig. 2
let ring
Cadd9 D5 G5 Em Em7
feel like I'm fi - nal - ly see - ing the light. Hold - in' on, girl, I
go so much far - ther than we've come to - day. Hold - in' on, girl, and
let ring
Chorus
Am D5 Dsus4 D E5 A5
know it's right, I know it's right. We're read - y!
come what may, come what may, we're read - y!
End Rhy. Fig. 2
let ring
P.M.

To Coda
Verse
Gtr. 1: w/ Rhy. Fig. 1
E5 B5 A5 E A5 E5 B5 E5
Hey! Yeah!
2. You and I,
(Oo.
P.M.
Gtr. 2 tacet
B/E A/E E A/E E Gadd9 Asus2
oo, will find a rea - son to
D.S. al Coda
Gtr. 2: w/ Rhy. Fill 1
E5 B/E A/E E A/E E
sim - pli - fy a change of sea - son. And I
sim - pli - fy a change of sea - son.)
Coda
E5 B5 A5 Esus4 E A5 E5 B5 A5
We're read - y. We're
Gtr. 2
E A5 E5 B5/E
Guitar Solo
C♯m
Rhy. Fig. 3
read - y. We're read - y. Come on!
Yeah!
Gtr. 3 (dist.)
Gtr. 2 divisi
(Gtr. 2 cont. in slashes)
Gtr. 3
f
1/2

B/C♯ C♯m
A
G♯ ⑥ 4fr
A
B
Come on!
Come
* Gtr. 4
Gtr. 3 divisi
* Three gtrs. arr. for one.
Gtr. 5: w/ Fill 1
G♯5
B/C♯
C♯5
B ③ 4fr
F♯m7
on!
Yeah!
8va
Gtr. 4
Rhy. Fig. 4
Fill 1
Gtr. 5 (dist.)
8va

E
B
F♯
6
2fr
A
B
We can
8va
Gr. 5
Gtr. 3
divisi
1
1/2
Gtr. 4
End Rhy. Fig. 4
Gtrs. 3, 4 & 5 tacet
A5
Gtr. 2 tacet
Asus2
End Rhy. Fig. 3
find a way.
Gtr. 6 (clean)
let ring throughout
(cont. in slashes)
Etype2
Gtr. 6
Gtr. 6 tacet
B/E
A/E
E
A/E
E
A5
A/B
3. We're
Gtr. 1
P.M.
let ring

Verse
Gtr. 1: w/ Rhy. Fig. 1
E5 B/E A/E E A/E E Gadd9 Asus2
read - y now, catch - in' a wave __ to ride on.
(Oo. ____
E5 B/E A/E
Gtr. 2: w/ Rhy. Fill 1
E A/E E
Gtr. 2: w/ Rhy. Fig. 2
G D
Stead - y now, head - in' where we __ de - cide on. __ And I know that there's some - thing that's
Oo.) ____
A Cadd9 D G
just out of sight. And I feel like we're try - in' to do some - thing right.
Em Em7 Am D5 Dsus4 D
Come on, make it if we hold on tight, __ hold on tight. __ We're
Chorus
E5 A5 E5 B5 A5 E A5 E5 B5
read - y! Yeah, ____ yeah! __ We're
Gtr. 2
P.M.
E5 A5 E5 B5 A5 E A5 E5 B5 D
read - y! Yeah, _ yeah! __ We're read - y! Hoo, ____ hoo. _ We're

E A5 E5 B5 A5 E A5
read - y.
We're read - y, yeah, yeah.
P.M.
E B5 E A5 E5 B5 A5
Gtr. 3: w/ Fill 2
We're read - y, hey, yeah! We're
P.M.
Guitar Solo
Gtr. 2: w/ Rhy. Fig. 3
E A5 E5 B5 C♯m
read - y!
One! Two! Three! Four!
Come on!
Gtr. 3
Gtr. 2
divisi
P.M.
1/2
Fill 2
Gtr. 3
fdbk.

We can find a way.

A5 A/B E5 B/E A/E E A/E E
We're read - y now, oo, we're read - y now.
let ring let ring P.M. P.M. P.M. P.M.
Free time
Gtr. 1 tacet
Gadd9 Asus4 E5 B/E A/E Aadd9
rit.
We're read - y now, oo.
Gtr. 1 Gtr. 6
let ring let ring P.M. rit. P.M. Gtr. 6 divisi
Begin fade
Fade out

You Give Love a Bad Name

Words and Music by Desmond Child, Jon Bon Jovi and Richie Sambora

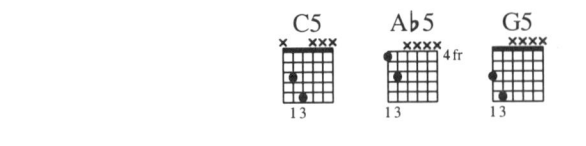

Intro
Moderate Rock ♩ = 123
band tacet
N.C.

Shot through the heart, and you're to blame, dar-lin', you give love a bad name.

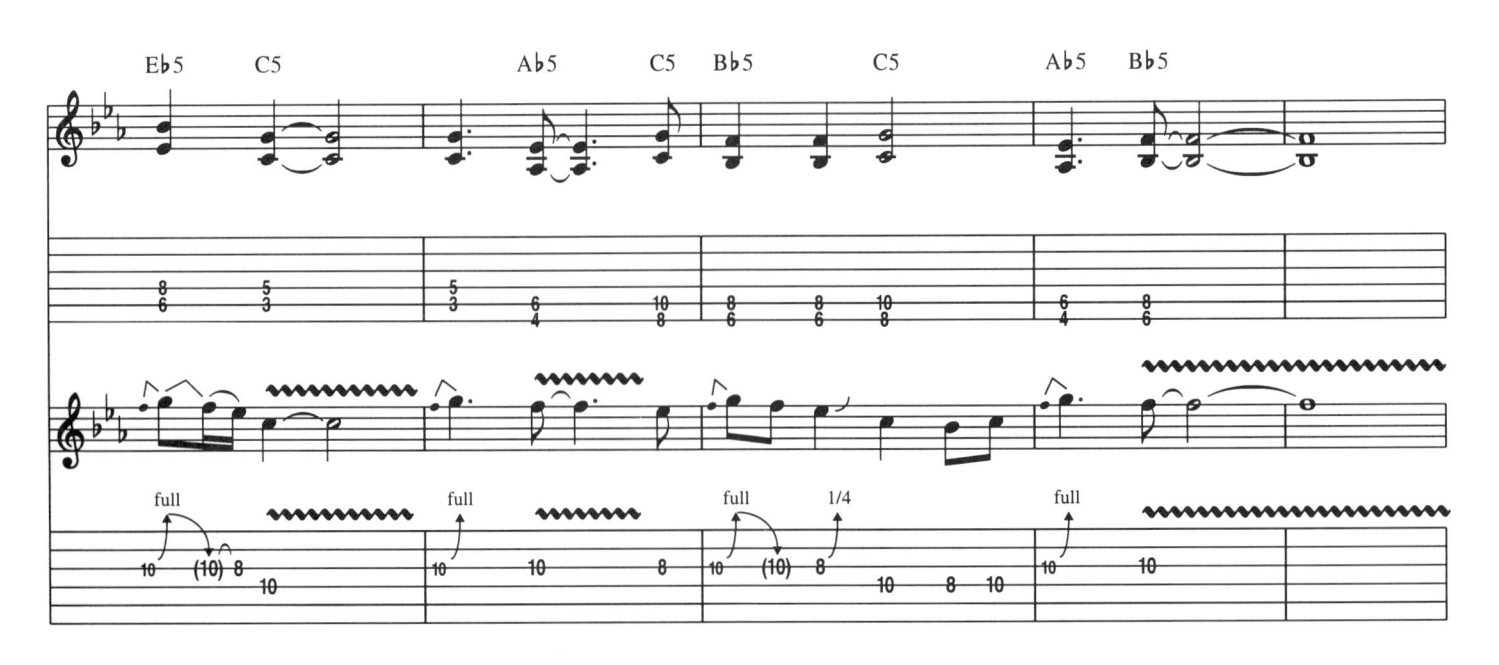

195

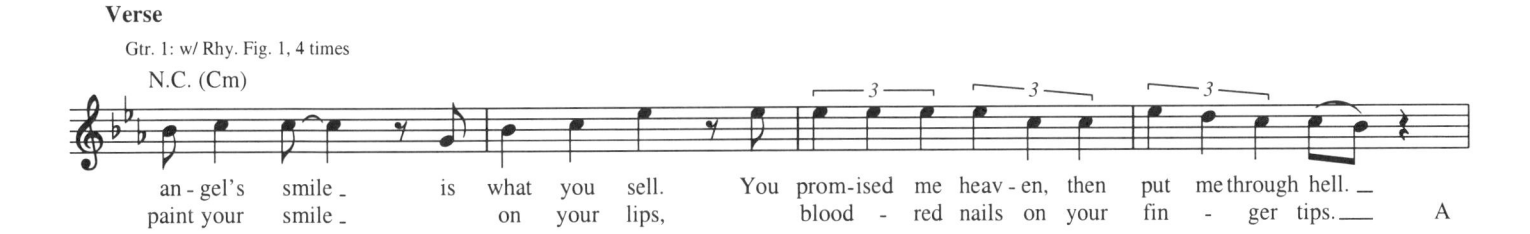

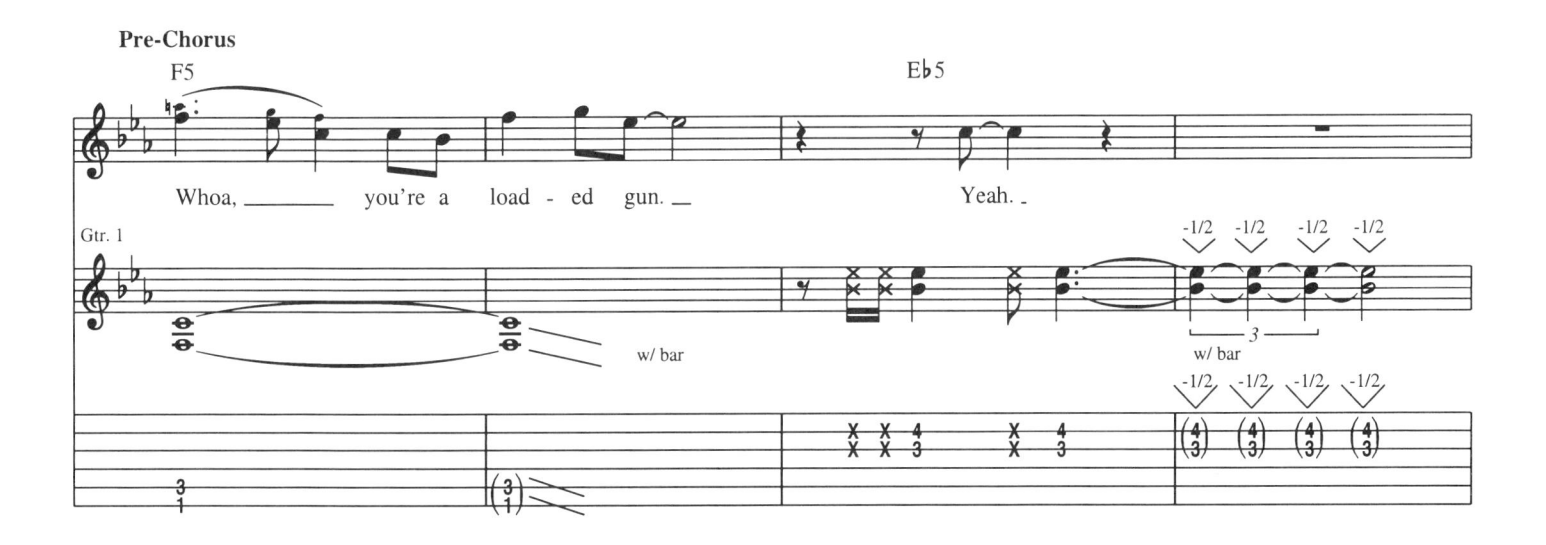

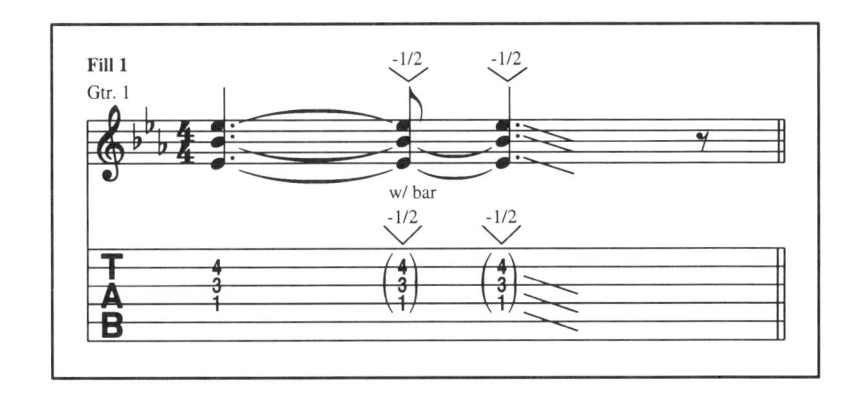

Bb5
N.C.(Bb)
Oh, there's no-where to run. No one can save me, the dam-age is done.
8va
loco
P.H.
w/ bar
pitch: D
Chorus
C5 Ab5 C5 Bb5 C5 Ab5 Bb5 Eb5 C5
Shot through the heart, and you're to blame. You give love a bad name, bad name. I
Rhy. Fig. 2
End Rhy. Fig. 2
play my part, and you play your game. You give love a bad name, bad name. And
you give love a bad name.
* Gtr. 2
Harm.
* w/ harmonizer

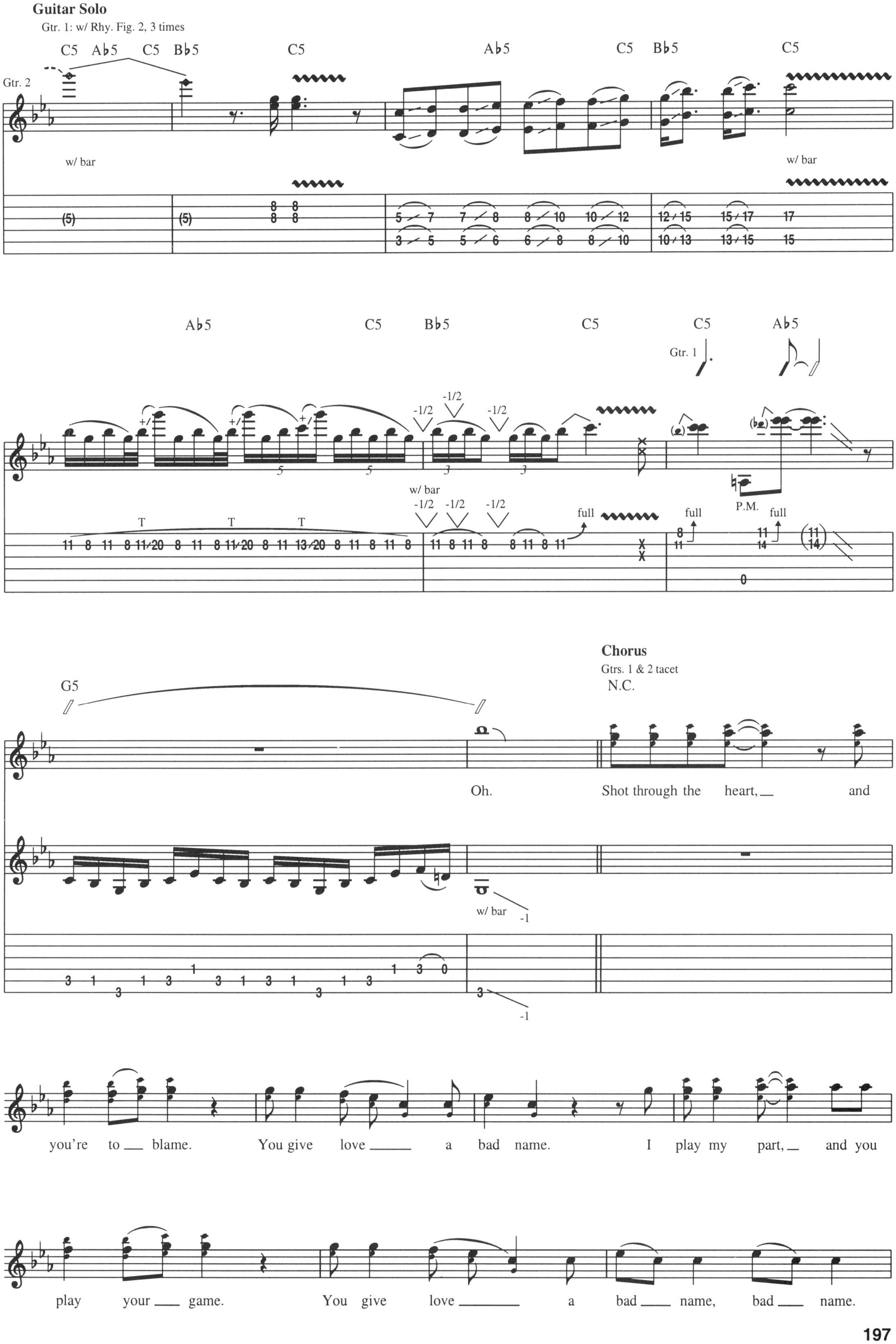
Guitar Solo
Gtr. 1: w/ Rhy. Fig. 2, 3 times
C5 Ab5 C5 Bb5 C5 Ab5 C5 Bb5 C5
Gtr. 2
w/ bar
Ab5 C5 Bb5 C5 C5 Ab5
Gtr. 1
w/ bar
-1/2
full
P.M.
G5
Chorus
Gtrs. 1 & 2 tacet
N.C.
Oh.
Shot through the heart, and
w/ bar
you're to blame. You give love a bad name. I play my part, and you
play your game. You give love a bad name, bad name.

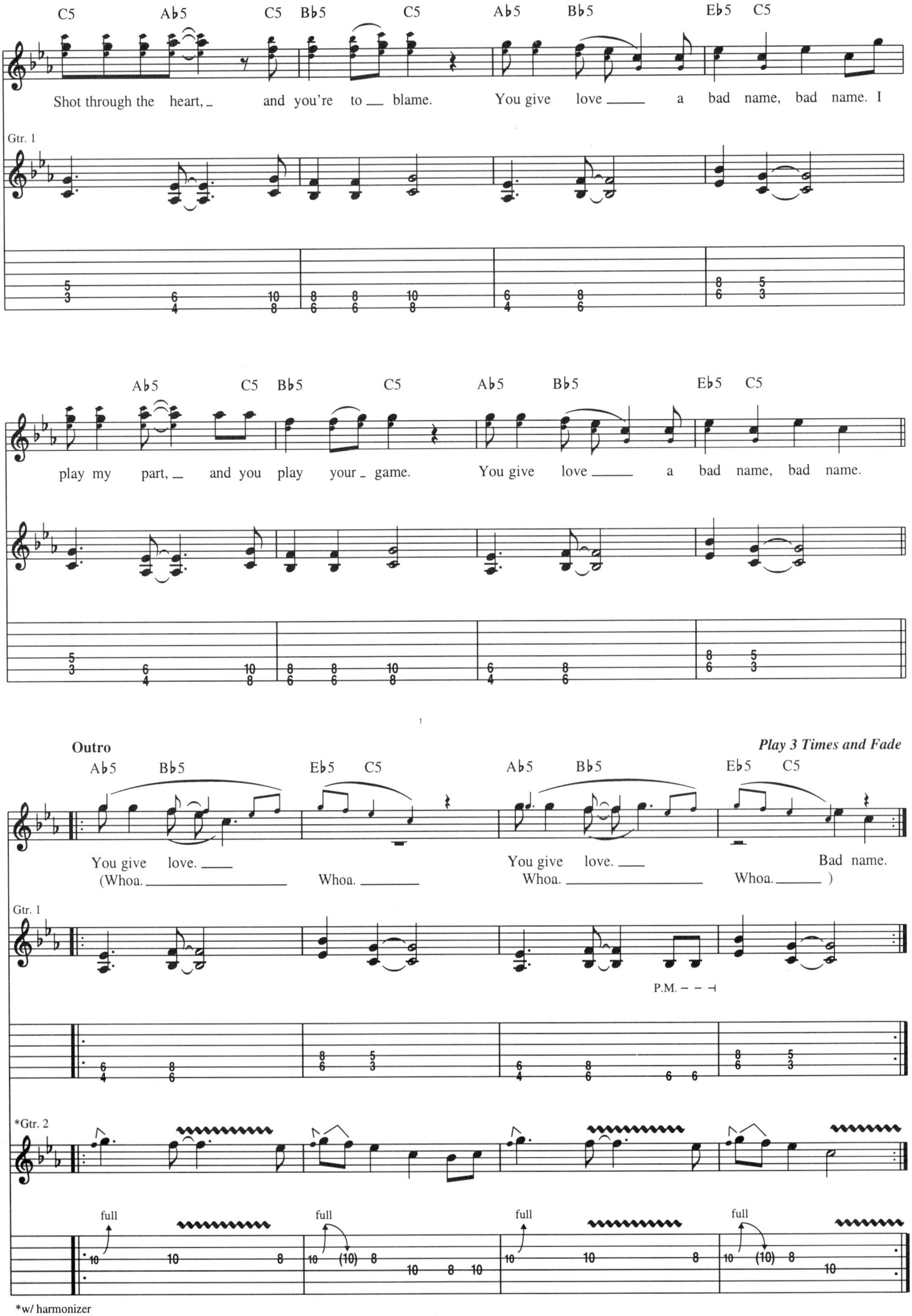

*w/ harmonizer

Guitar Notation Legend

Guitar Music can be notated three different ways: on a *musical staff*, in *tablature*, and in *rhythm slashes*.

RHYTHM SLASHES are written above the staff. Strum chords in the rhythm indicated. Use the chord diagrams found at the top of the first page of the transcription for the appropriate chord voicings. Round noteheads indicate single notes.

THE MUSICAL STAFF shows pitches and rhythms and is divided by bar lines into measures. Pitches are named after the first seven letters of the alphabet.

TABLATURE graphically represents the guitar fingerboard. Each horizontal line represents a string, and each number represents a fret.

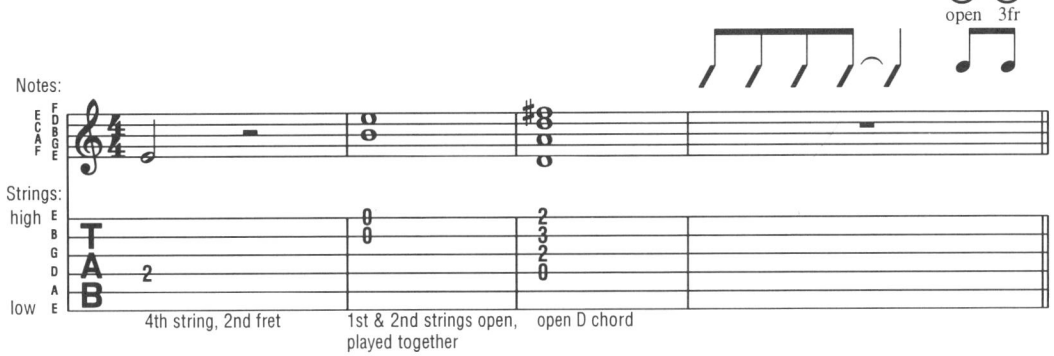

HALF-STEP BEND: Strike the note and bend up 1/2 step.

WHOLE-STEP BEND: Strike the note and bend up one step.

GRACE NOTE BEND: Strike the note and immediately bend up as indicated.

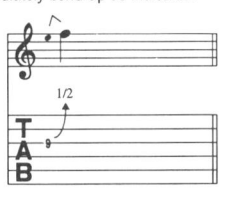

SLIGHT (MICROTONE) BEND: Strike the note and bend up 1/4 step.

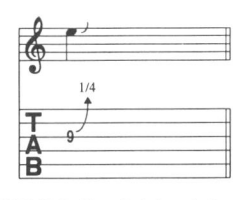

BEND AND RELEASE: Strike the note and bend up as indicated, then release back to the original note. Only the first note is struck.

PRE-BEND: Bend the note as indicated, then strike it.

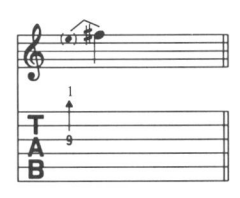

VIBRATO: The string is vibrated by rapidly bending and releasing the note with the fretting hand.

WIDE VIBRATO: The pitch is varied to a greater degree by vibrating with the fretting hand.

HAMMER-ON: Strike the first (lower) note with one finger, then sound the higher note (on the same string) with another finger by fretting it without picking.

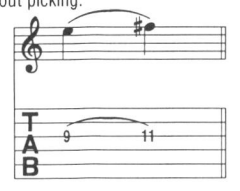

PULL-OFF: Place both fingers on the notes to be sounded. Strike the first note and without picking, pull the finger off to sound the second (lower) note.

LEGATO SLIDE: Strike the first note and then slide the same fret-hand finger up or down to the second note. The second note is not struck.

SHIFT SLIDE: Same as legato slide, except the second note is struck.

TRILL: Very rapidly alternate between the notes indicated by continuously hammering on and pulling off.

TAPPING: Hammer ("tap") the fret indicated with the pick-hand index or middle finger and pull off to the note fretted by the fret hand.

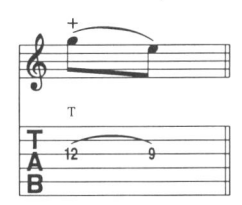

NATURAL HARMONIC: Strike the note while the fret-hand lightly touches the string directly over the fret indicated.

PINCH HARMONIC: The note is fretted normally and a harmonic is produced by adding the edge of the thumb or the tip of the index finger of the pick hand to the normal pick attack.

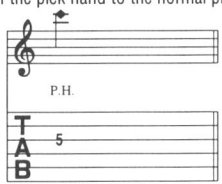

PICK SCRAPE: The edge of the pick is rubbed down (or up) the string, producing a scratchy sound.

MUFFLED STRINGS: A percussive sound is produced by laying the fret hand across the string(s) without depressing, and striking them with the pick hand.

PALM MUTING: The note is partially muted by the pick hand lightly touching the string(s) just before the bridge.

RAKE: Drag the pick across the strings indicated with a single motion.

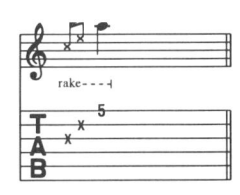

TREMOLO PICKING: The note is picked as rapidly and continuously as possible.

VIBRATO BAR DIVE AND RETURN: The pitch of the note or chord is dropped a specified number of steps (in rhythm) then returned to the original pitch.

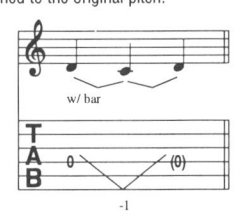

VIBRATO BAR SCOOP: Depress the bar just before striking the note, then quickly release the bar.

VIBRATO BAR DIP: Strike the note and then immediately drop a specified number of steps, then release back to the original pitch.

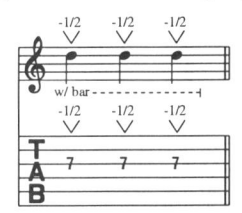

199

RECORDED VERSIONS
The Best Note-For-Note Transcriptions Available

ALL BOOKS INCLUDE TABLATURE

00690016	Will Ackerman Collection	$19.95
00690146	Aerosmith – Toys in the Attic	$19.95
00694865	Alice In Chains – Dirt	$19.95
00694932	Allman Brothers Band – Volume 1	$24.95
00694933	Allman Brothers Band – Volume 2	$24.95
00694934	Allman Brothers Band – Volume 3	$24.95
00694877	Chet Atkins – Guitars For All Seasons	$19.95
00690418	Best of Audio Adrenaline	$17.95
00694918	Randy Bachman Collection	$22.95
00690366	Bad Company Original Anthology - Bk 1	$19.95
00690367	Bad Company Original Anthology - Bk 2	$19.95
00694880	Beatles – Abbey Road	$19.95
00694863	Beatles – Sgt. Pepper's Lonely Hearts Club Band	$19.95
00690383	Beatles – Yellow Submarine	$19.95
00690174	Beck – Mellow Gold	$17.95
00690346	Beck – Mutations	$19.95
00690175	Beck – Odelay	$17.95
00694884	The Best of George Benson	$19.95
00692385	Chuck Berry	$19.95
00692200	Black Sabbath – We Sold Our Soul For Rock 'N' Roll	$19.95
00690115	Blind Melon – Soup	$19.95
00690305	Blink 182 – Dude Ranch	$19.95
00690028	Blue Oyster Cult – Cult Classics	$19.95
00690219	Blur	$19.95
00690168	Roy Buchanan Collection	$19.95
00690364	Cake – Songbook	$19.95
00690337	Jerry Cantrell – Boggy Depot	$19.95
00690293	Best of Steven Curtis Chapman	$19.95
00690043	Cheap Trick – Best Of	$19.95
00690171	Chicago – Definitive Guitar Collection	$22.95
00690415	Clapton Chronicles – Best of Eric Clapton	$17.95
00690393	Eric Clapton – Selections from Blues	$19.95
00660139	Eric Clapton – Journeyman	$19.95
00694869	Eric Clapton – Live Acoustic	$19.95
00694896	John Mayall/Eric Clapton – Bluesbreakers	$19.95
00690162	Best of the Clash	$19.95
00690166	Albert Collins – The Alligator Years	$16.95
00694940	Counting Crows – August & Everything After	$19.95
00690197	Counting Crows – Recovering the Satellites	$19.95
00694840	Cream – Disraeli Gears	$19.95
00690401	Creed – Human Clay	$19.95
00690352	Creed – My Own Prison	$19.95
00690184	dc Talk – Jesus Freak	$19.95
00690333	dc Talk – Supernatural	$19.95
00660186	Alex De Grassi Guitar Collection	$19.95
00690289	Best of Deep Purple	$17.95
00694831	Derek And The Dominos – Layla & Other Assorted Love Songs	$19.95
00690322	Ani Di Franco – Little Plastic Castle	$19.95
00690187	Dire Straits – Brothers In Arms	$19.95
00690191	Dire Straits – Money For Nothing	$24.95
00695382	The Very Best of Dire Straits – Sultans of Swing	$19.95
00660178	Willie Dixon – Master Blues Composer	$24.95
00690250	Best of Duane Eddy	$16.95
00690349	Eve 6	$19.95
00313164	Eve 6 – Horrorscope	$19.95
00690323	Fastball – All the Pain Money Can Buy	$19.95
00690089	Foo Fighters	$19.95
00690235	Foo Fighters – The Colour and the Shape	$19.95
00690394	Foo Fighters – There Is Nothing Left to Lose	$19.95
00690222	G3 Live – Satriani, Vai, Johnson	$22.95
00694807	Danny Gatton – 88 Elmira St	$19.95
00690438	Genesis Guitar Anthology	$19.95
00690127	Goo Goo Dolls – A Boy Named Goo	$19.95
00690338	Goo Goo Dolls – Dizzy Up the Girl	$19.95
00690117	John Gorka Collection	$19.95
00690114	Buddy Guy Collection Vol. A-J	$22.95
00690193	Buddy Guy Collection Vol. L-Y	$22.95
00694798	George Harrison Anthology	$19.95
00690068	Return Of The Hellecasters	$19.95
00692930	Jimi Hendrix – Are You Experienced?	$24.95
00692931	Jimi Hendrix – Axis: Bold As Love	$22.95
00692932	Jimi Hendrix – Electric Ladyland	$24.95
00690218	Jimi Hendrix – First Rays of the New Rising Sun	$27.95
00690038	Gary Hoey – Best Of	$19.95
00660029	Buddy Holly	$19.95
00660169	John Lee Hooker – A Blues Legend	$19.95
00690054	Hootie & The Blowfish – Cracked Rear View	$19.95
00694905	Howlin' Wolf	$19.95
00690136	Indigo Girls – 1200 Curfews	$22.95
00694938	Elmore James – Master Electric Slide Guitar	$19.95
00690167	Skip James Blues Guitar Collection	$16.95
00694833	Billy Joel For Guitar	$19.95
00694912	Eric Johnson – Ah Via Musicom	$19.95
00690169	Eric Johnson – Venus Isle	$22.95
00694799	Robert Johnson – At The Crossroads	$19.95
00693185	Judas Priest – Vintage Hits	$19.95
00690277	Best of Kansas	$19.95
00690073	B. B. King – 1950-1957	$24.95
00690098	B. B. King – 1958-1967	$24.95
00690444	B.B. King and Eric Clapton – Riding with the King	$19.95
00690134	Freddie King Collection	$17.95
00690157	Kiss – Alive	$19.95
00690163	Mark Knopfler/Chet Atkins – Neck and Neck	$19.95
00690296	Patty Larkin Songbook	$17.95
00690018	Living Colour – Best Of	$19.95
00694845	Yngwie Malmsteen – Fire And Ice	$19.95
00694956	Bob Marley – Legend	$19.95
00690283	Best of Sarah McLachlan	$19.95
00690382	Sarah McLachlan – Mirrorball	$19.95
00690354	Sarah McLachlan – Surfacing	$19.95
00690442	Matchbox 20 – Mad Season	$19.95
00690239	Matchbox 20 – Yourself or Someone Like You	$19.95
00690244	Megadeath – Cryptic Writings	$19.95
00690236	Mighty Mighty Bosstones – Let's Face It	$19.95
00690040	Steve Miller Band Greatest Hits	$19.95
00694802	Gary Moore – Still Got The Blues	$19.95
00694958	Mountain, Best Of	$19.95
00690448	MxPx – The Ever Passing Moment	$19.95
00694913	Nirvana – In Utero	$19.95
00694883	Nirvana – Nevermind	$19.95
00690026	Nirvana – Acoustic In New York	$19.95
00690121	Oasis – (What's The Story) Morning Glory	$19.95
00690204	Offspring, The – Ixnay on the Hombre	$17.95
00690203	Offspring, The – Smash	$17.95
00694830	Ozzy Osbourne – No More Tears	$19.95
00694855	Pearl Jam – Ten	$19.95
00690053	Liz Phair – Whip Smart	$19.95
00690176	Phish – Billy Breathes	$22.95
00690424	Phish – Farmhouse	$19.95
00690331	Phish – The Story of Ghost	$19.95
00690428	Pink Floyd – Dark Side of the Moon	$19.95
00693800	Pink Floyd – Early Classics	$19.95
00690456	P.O.D. – The Fundamental Elements of Southtown	$19.95
00694967	Police – Message In A Box Boxed Set	$70.00
00694974	Queen – A Night At The Opera	$19.95
00690395	Rage Against The Machine – The Battle of Los Angeles	$19.95
00690145	Rage Against The Machine – Evil Empire	$19.95
00690179	Rancid – And Out Come the Wolves	$22.95
00690055	Red Hot Chili Peppers – Bloodsugarsexmagik	$19.95
00690379	Red Hot Chili Peppers – Californication	$19.95
00690090	Red Hot Chili Peppers – One Hot Minute	$22.95
00694937	Jimmy Reed – Master Bluesman	$19.95
00694899	R.E.M. – Automatic For The People	$19.95
00690260	Jimmie Rodgers Guitar Collection	$19.95
00690014	Rolling Stones – Exile On Main Street	$24.95
00690186	Rolling Stones – Rock & Roll Circus	$19.95
00690135	Otis Rush Collection	$19.95
00690031	Santana's Greatest Hits	$19.95
00690150	Son Seals – Bad Axe Blues	$17.95
00690128	Seven Mary Three – American Standards	$19.95
00120105	Kenny Wayne Shepherd – Ledbetter Heights	$19.95
00120123	Kenny Wayne Shepherd – Trouble Is	$19.95
00690196	Silverchair – Freak Show	$19.95
00690130	Silverchair – Frogstomp	$19.95
00690041	Smithereens – Best Of	$19.95
00690385	Sonicflood	$19.95
00694885	Spin Doctors – Pocket Full Of Kryptonite	$19.95
00694921	Steppenwolf, The Best Of	$22.95
00694957	Rod Stewart – Acoustic Live	$22.95
00690021	Sting – Fields Of Gold	$19.95
00690242	Suede – Coming Up	$19.95
00694824	Best Of James Taylor	$16.95
00690238	Third Eye Blind	$19.95
00690403	Third Eye Blind – Blue	$19.95
00690267	311	$19.95
00690030	Toad The Wet Sprocket	$19.95
00690228	Tonic – Lemon Parade	$19.95
00690295	Tool – Aenima	$19.95
00690039	Steve Vai – Alien Love Secrets	$24.95
00690172	Steve Vai – Fire Garden	$24.95
00690023	Jimmie Vaughan – Strange Pleasures	$19.95
00690370	Stevie Ray Vaughan and Double Trouble – The Real Deal: Greatest Hits Volume 2	$22.95
00690455	Stevie Ray Vaughan – Blues at Sunrise	$19.95
00660136	Stevie Ray Vaughan – In Step	$19.95
00690417	Stevie Ray Vaughan – Live at Carnegie Hall	$19.95
00694835	Stevie Ray Vaughan – The Sky Is Crying	$19.95
00694776	Vaughan Brothers – Family Style	$19.95
00120026	Joe Walsh – Look What I Did...	$24.95
00694789	Muddy Waters – Deep Blues	$24.95
00690071	Weezer	$19.95
00690286	Weezer – Pinkerton	$19.95
00690447	Who, The – Best of	$24.95
00694970	Who, The – Definitive Collection A-E	$24.95
00694971	Who, The – Definitive Collection F-Li	$24.95
00694972	Who, The – Definitive Collection Lo-R	$24.95
00694973	Who, The – Definitive Collection S-Y	$24.95
00690319	Stevie Wonder Hits	$17.95

Prices and availability subject to change without notice.
Some products may not be available outside the U.S.A.

FOR A COMPLETE LIST OF GUITAR RECORDED VERSIONS TITLES, SEE YOUR LOCAL MUSIC DEALER, OR WRITE TO:

HAL•LEONARD CORPORATION
7777 W. BLUEMOUND RD. P.O. BOX 13819 MILWAUKEE, WI 53213

Visit Hal Leonard online at www.halleonard.com